DOCTRINES OF GREAT EDUCATORS

ds as Ends 92
AND RUSSELL *(1872-1970)*

ogy of the Oppressed 98
O FREIRE *(1921-1997)*

ooling Society 110
N ILLICH *(1926-2002)*

PART II: Indian Philosophers

Spirtual Absolutism 131
SAMKARA

9. Vidya is Endless 138
GURU NANAK *(1469-1539)*

20. Temporal and Spiritual Knowledge 145
Swami Dayananda (1824-1883)

21. Education in Natural Environment 150
RABINDRA NATH TAGORE *(1861-1941)*

22. Man-Making Education 156
SWAMI VIVEKANANDA *(1863-1902)*

23. Education Is Indivisible 166
MAHATMA GANDHI *(1869-1948)*

24. Integral Education 176
AUROBINDO GHOSE *(1872-1950)*

25. Education for Exaltation of Ego 184
MOHAMMAD IQBAL *(1873-1938)*

26. Education by Example and Precept 190
BHAGAT PHOOL SINGH *(1888-1942)*

27. Learning: Varities of Experience 195
SARVEPALLI RADHAKRISHNAN *(1888-1975)*

28. How To Live Education 208
SRI PARAMAHANSA YOGANANDA *(1893-1952)*

29. Education for Creating New Values 215
JIDDU KRISHNAMURTI *(1895-1986)*

0. Not Education But Educare 229
SATYA SAI BABA *(1926-2011)*

1. Views and Visions on Education: A Bird's Eye View 235

lect Bibliography 242

DOCTRINES OF GREAT EDUCATORS

A.S. Thakur
Former Dean of Education
University of Maiduguri, Nigeria

SHIPRA

Rs.1250; US$ 44.75

ISBN: 978-81-7541-868-4

First Published in India in 2016

Doctrines of Great Educators

Published by:

SHIPRA PUBLICATIONS
LG 18-19, Pankaj Central Market,
I.P. Ext., Patparganj, Delhi 110092
Ph.: +91-11- 47322068
info@shiprapublication.com
www.shiprapublication.com

Conte

Preface

PART I: Western Philos

1. Greek Philosophers: Liberal Education
2. Education: A Life-Long Process
   Plato (428-347 B.C.)
3. Education for Human Excellence
   Aristotle (382-322 B.C.)
4. Eloquence and Character: Roman Education Trai for Practical Life
   Quintilian (35-95 A.D.)
5. Christianity: Education for Here and the Hereafter
   St. Augustine and St. Thomas Aquinas
6. Teaching: Mediation between God and Man
   Saint Thomas Aquinas (1225-1274)
7. Education for Creativity and Individuality
   D. Erasmus (1467-1536)
8. Perfection of Reason: The Tutorial Conception of Education
   John Locke (1632-1704)
9. Follow Order of Nature
   J.J. Rousseau (1712-1778)
10. Psychology in Education—Anschauung: Form, Number and Name as Developmental Processes
   Johann Pestalozzi (1746-1827)
11. Methods of Step by Step Instruction
   J.F. Herbart (1776-1841)
12. The Pedagogies of Kindergarten: Education of the Total Individual and Society
   Fredrich Froebel (1782-1852)
13. Education in Freedom
   Maria Montessori (1870-1952)
14. Eclectic Tendencies: Instrumentalism and Experimentalism
   John Dewey (1859-1952)

Preface

The book entitled: *Doctrines of Great Educators:* contains some of the important philosophical positions, taken by the philosophers from ancient times to the present day. The wide spectrum representing thirty philosophers provides coverage to the educational wisdom, considered important to study for students, preparing for B.Ed, M.Ed., and M.Phil. degrees in the colleges of education and universities in India.

The book is divided into two parts—Part I deals with philosophers of the Western and countries in Latin America and Part II contains the philosophical positions of Indian philosophers.

As knowledge in the Western world was generated by the ancient Greeks, it is considered appropriate to mention *Socrates* first in the field of education, who said that knowledge was virtue and who established 'discussion' as a method to seek knowledge. His disciple, Plato presented the 'world of ideas' for education to explore it. For Aristole, education was to lead to self realization and happiness. The Greeks presented a system of liberal education. The impact of such an education was felt by the western world and gradually by almost the entire world.

The Roman education was education for practical life—soldiering, engineering, eloquence of speech etc. However, the Greek influence also permeated the Roman education. The outstanding educationist was *Quintilian* who wanted to produce through education an eloquent speaker, but such a speaker was to be a man of high moral character.

After the beginning of the Christian era, the Christan view points on education were provided by *St. Augustine* and *St. Aquinas.* The curriculum of the Christian scholar was broad and deep, but it was a prelude to the study of the Christian doctrines. For *St. Augustine,* teaching was the activity of causing pupils to learn, and for *St. Aquinas* to teach was to mediate between God and man.

The renaissance period represented a re-awakening of learning from the restrictions of the medieval period. *Erasmus,* a humanist, believed that man was the centre of the universe, and that teachers were to make students who wanted to learn. He outlined four principal functions of education, which were:

1. piety,
2. love and knowledge of biberal studies,
3. knowlege of the duties of life, and
4. habit of courteous manners.

The seventeenth century was an age of realism which tedency had resulted from the new discoveries. *Locke* introduced the tutorial conception of education. For him, learner's mind was the *tabula rasa* (a clean state) and it was the experience that filled in the clean state. His aim of education was to ensure vigour of the body and soul and knowledge or mental acquirements.

The eighteenth century made a break with the authority-centred traditions of the middle ages, which had managed to survive. *Rousseau's, The Emile,* presented the idea that all the essential liberty of natural man was to be safeguarded by education. For *Rousseau,* God made all things good, man meddled with them and they became evil. *Emile* was to be guided rather than taught by a teacher. *Rousseau's* ideas influenced *Pestalozzi, Froebel* and *Montessori.*

Pestalozzi introduced an educationally sound technique of instruction, based on three principles—form (drawing lines, angles, curves etc.), number (presenting concrete objects) and name (list of names of the most important objects in nature).

Herbart advocated four stages of instruction—clearness (learner to see the issue clearly in order to assimilate new subject), association (connection of the new ideas to the notions, already in the pupil's mind) and method (capability of the learner to add new aspects to the issue in view and apply the newly acquired knowledge to future problems). His disciples extended his steps to five, which were:

1. preparation,
2. presentation,
3. association,
4. generalization,
5. application.

Froebel's pedagogies of the kindergarten were based on the doctrine that the past could no longer be allowed to determine the future: it could only influence the trend of human development because the future was evolving, perhaps, much faster than man could understand or predict. For Froebel, education required the reconciliation of contrasts; it was to encourage creativity; and it was to be based on the needs of the children.

Montessori, a medical doctor, developed the exercises of practical life, the sensor-exercises and the didactic exercises. She stood for freedom to the learner and influenced education all over the world.

Dewey, an American educational philosopher, highlighted the concepts of 'instrumentalism' and 'experimentalism' in educational thought and practice—instrumentalism meant that ideas were instruments that function as guide to action and their validity was measured by the success of the action and experimentalism meant that knowledge was derived only from experience.

For *Russell* "educands were ends". This implied that education was to produce individuals who were creative, intelligent, sensitive, open-minded, patient and industrious by exposing them to a variety of subjects.

The study of the philosophers of the western world shows that there are messages which are of universal value, but philosophers are also influenced by factors, that are time-related, and thus some of their ideas were more relevant to those times. It is also worth appreciating that India has continued with the educational system, introduced by the colonial powers. Thus, it is in order to recognise the philosophical inputs of the western world—their strengths as well as their limitations, and their relevance as well as their futility. In any case, history is a great teacher and no one should discount its importance as a guide to action.

Paulo Freire of Brazil in his "*Pedagogy of the Oppressed*", championed that education was to allow the oppressed to regain their sense of humanity. He criticized the prevailing system of education as "banking"—in which the students were the deposits and the teacher was the depositor.

Ivan Illich worked in Maxico and Brazil. In his "*Deschooling Society*", he criticized education in the schools and stood for skill-learning in the open "market." According to him, these was a need to de-school not only educational institutions, but also the ethos of the society.

In so far as the Indian and other educational thinkers are concerned, a start has been made with *Samkara,* an eight century A.D. philosopher. For him, the ultimate aim of education was to a attain *moksha* (freedom).

Guru Nanak highlighted three aims of education—salvation (*mukti*), art of life (*jugti*) and the bliss of life (*bhagti*). The ultimate aim of education was self-realization.

Swami Dayananda wanted education to eliminate ignorance and prepare for happiness by increasing knowledge, developing culture, character, morality, good conduct and spirituality—ultimately to prepare people for salvation.

Tagore's name has become famous for putting his educational ideas into practice at *Vishwa Bharti.* He stood for a complete development of an individual with international outlook. For him, consciousness of the universe was an essential condition in realization of the self in the intellectually gratifying and spiritually elevating environment as was at *Vishwa Bharti* at *Shanti Niketan.*

Swami Vivekanada's 'Man Making Education' is *"life building, man-*

making, character making assimilation of ideas." Education, for him, was to be the *"manifestation of divine perfection, already existing in man."* It was a comprehensive education which developed an individual's character, mind and intellect, enabling one to stand on one's own feet.

Gandhiji could be considered as one of the Indian educational thinkers whose philosophy was complete in that his basic education was based on the metaphysical assumption that God is real and *"life, truth, light*". His epistemological position was that knowledge was drawn out of the learners by a competent teacher by motivating them through experiments and activities. The value system was to form character to ensure self-realization for the individual and society.

Aurobindo Ghose and 'The Mother' produced the concept of integral education which comprised physical, mental, psychic and spiritual and vital education. In fact, vital education was the integration of all other aspects of development.

Mohammad Iqbal was a poet, but his poetry was not only sublime, but also profound. The aim of education, for him, was to develop individuality (*Khudi*), but social, intellectual, cultural and moral aspects of development were also considered.

Bhagat Phool Singh followed the vedic traditions of education. The sacrifices, he made for the cause of humanity made him an ideal person, deserving of emulation. His Gurukul for girls at Khanpur Kalan in Sonepat, Haryana has developed in to a women's university of high standard.

Paramahansa Yogananda's 'How to Live Education' was learner-centred as well as teacher-centred; it was imparted formally as well as informally; it was purposive; and it was both art and science. The learners mastered the art and science of concentration (*pranayam*) to become *kriya yogis,* they benefited from formal schooling and correspondence lessons. They learnt the science of directing their manual energies upward and downward around the six spiritual centres and practised ten rules of happiness. They ultimately achieved victory over death.

Jiddu Krishnamurty advocated education for creating new values like learning how to look, how to listen to what the books are saying, whether they are saying something true or false. His KFI schools existed for flowering of teachers and students.

Satya Sai Baba emphasised *educare* over education. In *educare,* mind was shared by divine source within and the internal force generated by *sathya, dhama* and *prema* determined the actions. *Educare* was a divine philosophy (love and serve all), and render selfless service. The aims of *educare* were realized in schools, institutes, colleges and universities.

By and large what emerges from the philosophical positions of the western and Indian education thinkers in terms of the aim of education is to develop a comprehensive personality, with emphasis on spiritual development. Freire's *Pedagogy of the Oppressed* and Illich's *Deschooling Society* present new visions on education.

It is worth recording that the teachers of the future have greater responsibilities on them than many other categories of professionals—teachers should master the past wisdom, knowledge and skills, should assimilate the present technological inputs into the field of teaching and learning and should be capable to foreseeing the shape of things to come, so that they are not awed by the new developments which present new challenges to them. It is in this contex that the educational wisdom of the philosophers, in the book: *"Doctrines of Great Educators"* is relevant to teachers to acquire knowledge, develop skills, enhance competencies and become educationally wise for teaching in the school system of the twenty-first century.

The author is grateful to Dr Sandeep Berwal for contributing a chapter on Bhagat Phool Singh and to the writers who—and other sources— which have been quoted in this book. It is hoped that teachers-in-trainning and their instructors will benefit from the study of this book in which the author has presented and analysed the quintessence of the educational wisdom of the world—past and present.

With sincere humility, the author wishes to claim that the book is unique in the world of books by virtue of its wide coverage of philosophers of education, critical analysis of their views, the simple style of presentation and critical summary.

A. S. Thakur

PART I
WESTERN PHILOSOPHERS

1

Greek Philosophers: Liberal Education

The Greeks defeated the Persians in battles fought between 490 B.C. and 479 B.C. Not only did the Greeks continue with the democratic principles, but also they enriched the world through their contributions to political, literary and artistic fields. Towards the changes and innovations, philosophers like *Socrates, Plato* and *Aristotle* made their unique contributions.

Pre-Socratic Philosophies

Indian and Persian philosophies were ancient but philosophy in the west seemed to have begun with the Greeks. As there was absence of religious dogmatism in Greek philosophy, the philosophers produced impartial and scientific explanation of the world. Again, their morality was not fettered either by authority or revelation.

Greek philosophy, like Greek art and poetry, grew out of the minds of the people, forming an organic component of the Hellenic culture. The pre-*Socratic* philosophy was a cosmological inquiry or philosophy of nature. The Greeks asked: what was the permanent element in real existence? *Thales* seemed to have answered that water was the material cause of all things. *Anaxagoras* called the cause to *Mind* or *Nous. Anaximander* was of the view that the material cause and first element of things was infinite: things arose and returned to it. *Pythagoras* advanced the theory of transfiguration.

Parmenides argued that only that could be which could be thought, for thought existed for the sake of what was, thereby rejecting "Non-Being". The sophists moved into the field of humanism. *Protagoras* said that man was the measure of all things.

Socrates (470-390 B.C.): Know Thyself

It is mainly from *Plato's* writing that we know something about the great philosopher, *Socrates*. He did not leave any writing of his own for the succeeding generations. It was recorded that he married late in life and left three sons who did not prove to be men of significance. *Socrates* started as a sophist, but broke company of them, for he found them too selective.

Philosophy

Socrates believed that truth was absolute, and it was through asking questions and testing ideas that one could arrive at truth. His message was: "know thyself". It was through knowledge that man got the correct picture of himself, of the universe, he lived in, and of God. According to him, knowledge led to virtue—it meant that an educated man was a noble man. The idea that knowledge was virtue, has been criticized as a "*Socratic* fallacy".

The Athenian youths liked *Socrates* for his modesty. He did not claim to be wise: he described himself as a seeker of wisdom. He concluded that, perhaps, he was called wise because he recognized his own ignorance, whereas many others did not recognize their ignorance.

He discussed abstract concepts of virtue, truth and immortality in the parties and in the market places. He questioned all those who laid claim to knowledge—poets, dramatists, statesmen, philosophers. Particularly, he criticized politicians and philosophers. He thought that the politicians were ignorant and the philosophers were arrogant.

Socratic Method

Socrates would enlist anyone who would be ready to listen to him. He would go from man to man, enquiring and questioning. For example: if some one talked of "justice", he asked him what justice was. Further questions were put until clear concepts emerged. Similar questioning was done about abstract words like virtue, morality and patriotism. He believed that questioning led to clear thinking. The method has come to be known as the "*Socratic* method". As far as aesthetic sense was concerned, *Socrates* loved beauty, including the beauty of human body. He, however, expected the beautiful human body to have a noble soul. In the *Symposium,* the spirit of *Socratic* teaching was brought out when *Plato* wrote:

> Evil is the vulgar lover who loves the body rather than the soul, in as much as he is not even stable, because he loves a thing which is in itself unstable, and therefore when the bloom of youth which he was desiring is over, and he takes wings and flies away, inspite of all his words and promises; whereas the love of the noble disposition is life-long, for it blooms one with the everlasting.

Sense of Humour

The Greeks were lovers of beauty of soul, nature and human body. *Socrates* managed to be humorous even for his own ugly body by the Greek standards. He had open nostrils with which, he said, he could smell better; he had flat nose with which he said, he could see better; and he wished his eyes were protruding to enable him to see all round. It appeared to be a genuine attempt to laugh at himself rather than one at a defense mechanism: very few people genuinely laugh at themselves–many laugh at others.

Views on Education

Socrates treated education as a spontaneous process which did not require a school or a class. Knowledge was a search for virtue through discussions, conversations, questions and answers. Virtue could be taught. A person who claimed to hold knowledge was questioned by him. He was made to give reasons to support his belief and see the deficiencies and contradictions. He was made to examine his opinions, and reconstruct his experiences to justify his beliefs and opinions.

Role of the Teacher

(i) Socrates advocated that the function of the teacher was to pursue truth, even in the teeth of opposition and to awaken the average man by helping him to shed his half truths and illusions. The teacher was expected to be the leader of civilization. He believed that knowledge was intuitive. It was the function of the teacher to bring out knowledge by stimulating thought in the learner and by encouraging investigation. Students were to be enabled to think for themselves.

(ii) ***The Curriculum*:** He was not an ardent defender of liberal studies, nor was he greatly interested in studies which were useful for a work-a-day life. For him, a subject like geometry was for practical application, astronomy had value for predicting seasons and arithmetic was useful for business. But the job of the thinker, the lover of wisdom, was to clarify, to fix general concepts and to introduce precise thinking into intellectual inquiry.

Limitations of Socrates

Criticizing *Socrates* will be an attempt at criticizing a god-head. Yet, critics felt that his view that a wrong committed in full knowledge was superior to a wrong committed unwittingly and that known bad was superior to unknown bad could have serious implications. For example, is deliberate shooting dead a person pardonable and an accidental killing punishable?

Conclusion

Socrates remained poor throughout his life. In his old age, he was condemned to death by Athenians on the charges of impiety and of corrupting the youth of Athens. He chose to drink hemlock (poison) and died.

The last words of *Socrates* in *Plato's Apology* are repeated here for their emotional appeal. "The hour of departure is arrived, and we go our own ways I to die and you to live: which is better God only knows." The lines from a poet: "Men may come and men may go. But I go on for ever" suit *Socrates* as his modesty, faith in knowledge and virtue, love for his country, upholding of great moral values and timelessness of his ideas inspire us even today.

Summary

Socrates' ideas were recorded by his disciple, *Plato*. His philosophy was that knowledge was virtue, and virtue could be taught. Love of the noble disposition was life-long. *Socrates* was a great teacher. He fought for righteousness. Knowledge was also a search for virtue. His discussions developed into *Socratic* method of teaching. Socrates was one of the greatest philosophers of all times.

2

Education: A Life-Long Process

Plato (428-347 B.C)

Plato was one of the greatest philosophers in the history of European philosophy. As there was no written record of the wisdom of *Socrates,* it was through the writings of his disciple, *Plato,* that the world came to know of the wise, virtuous, patriotic, fearless and inspiring *Socrates*.

Life Sketch

Plato was born into a family of aristocrats. He befriended *Socrates* when he was a young man. He travelled to other countries and discussed *Socratic* ideas. After his travels abroad, he opened institution of learning–a school–called "academy", and started teaching in it.

Plato's ideas are found in his books. Two of these books: *The Republic* and *The Laws* are famous and contain his views on life, politics and education. He upheld many of the Athenian traditions, although he advocated new ideas also.

Philosophy

Inspired by *Socratic* teaching of the Concept or the Idea, *Plato* developed his Idealism into what could be called the World of Ideas– the characteristics of the ideas were:

(i) The fundamental characteristic of ideas, from which all other could be deduced, was that they were substances, self-consistent and self-contained as against the sensible objects which depended on the ideas in order to be known. The point was explained in the allegory of the cave in Book VII of *The Republic.*

(ii) The ideas alone were real, whereas the sensible objects were phenomenal.

(iii) The ideas were universal, and not particular, which was explained thus: we came across tables in the world of sensible experience. The idea of table was not anyone particular table among such tables, but it represented the general or common attributes found in the whole class of tables.

(iv) The ideas were essential, while the sensible objects were accidental. For example: the idea of man was what was common and essential to all men, irrespective of their differences.

(v) The ideas were perfect, while the sensible objects were partial and imperfect. The ideas were the models or archetypes, containing everything that was essential.

(vi) The ideas were eternal and immutable, while the sensible objects were fleeting and changeable. As forms of intelligibility, ideas were to remain the same without being affected in the least by the conditions of space and time.

(vii) *Plato* emphasized that the highest of all ideas was that of the "Good"—the very excellence of a thing. Whatever was true with regard to one idea, could be applied to all of that category of objects. The "Good" admitted of degrees as one idea was more comprehensive than the other. As we ascended higher and higher up the scale of ideas, we were left with the idea of the "Good"—the quintessence of all ideas.

For centuries together, philosophers have debated the Ideas in respect of whether these concepts were that of *Plato* or *Socrates*. Again, whether their metaphysics and epistemology were intellectually viable. That *Socrates* and *Plato* were mutually inspiring and the latter owed a lot to his teacher could not be denied. However, many writers did not accept *Aristotle's* criticism of *Plato's "Ideas"*, which the former called "causes". It could be said that there were no differences between the two: the differences were in the poetic temperament of *Plato* and scientific temperament of Aristotle. The Philosophy of Idealism as it developed in the western world, and the contributions of *Plato* to it, adequately justified the metaphysical and epistemological positions of *Plato. Hegel* also said that ultimate reality was of the same stuff as ideas, and he agreed with *Plato* that man could achieve truth by examining his own ideas and testing their consistency.

Views on Education

Plato's views on education sprang from his political ideals. He believed that justice was an important virtue of the state and could only be achieved in a certain type of state. The state was to contain three classes of people-the guardians, the auxiliaries and the common people. The guardians were to be highly trained philosophers who were to rule the city. So to say, they were to be the philosopher-kings. The auxiliary constituted the military class, which was to defend the city. But out of the military class were recruited the guardians. The common people, the great mass of the population, were to be employed in business, the art or manual labour.

Education and training depended on the different classes, and on the roles played in the state. Each role called for certain virtues and certain types of education. For example: four virtues–wisdom, courage, temperance and justice–were supposed to be found in state.

Wisdom was the particular virtue of the guardians and courage was the particular virtue of the auxiliaries. Temperance or discipline was a virtue of the state as a whole which was displayed when there was a harmonious relationship between rulers and ruled. But justice belonged to all classes. It consisted in each person fulfilling his particular function in society.

(i) Scheme of Education: For the ruling class, *Plato's* aim of education was to train the whole personality so as to produce good citizens. Such citizens were to be wise. Thus, the training of the future rulers started from the nursery. Children were to learn by imitation and by listening to folk tales. The old-world fables and myths that children heard from their nurses and later on the poetry and music that they learnt from their teachers introduced them to great human interests through beauty and goodness. He believed that beauty and goodness appealed to children's imagination. The rhythm and harmony made the soul graceful and prepared the child to receive the good and reject the bad. However, myths and fables were to be selected for their suitability. For example, effeminate and sensuous music was not allowed; martial music was encouraged.

(a) First Stage: Formal education started from the age of seven. The traditional approach to teaching reading and writing was retained. Gymnastics and music were emphasized. But both types of studies were meant for the soul. Counting was also taught as a preparatory object to mathematics and later to dialectic. For *Plato*, it was not so much the mastery of the subject that mattered but the spirit with which these were taught and the environment in which they were imparted.

(b) Second Stage: The next stage in education started at the age of adolescent period. At the thirteenth or fourteenth year, music, literature and mathematics were taught. Then followed a period of about nine years during which gymnastics, arithmetic, geometry, mathematical theory of music and astronomy were taught. Importance was attached to mathematical studies, for, he believed, that these developed the soul by promoting reflection and by intellectually and spiritually developing the learner a stage further.

(c) Third Stage: The bright and promising learners were to be educated for a period of five more years through the study of dialectic which meant the right method of reasoning for the discovery, the communication or the demonstration of truth to complete the knowledge. It was considered to be the study which examined the nature and validity of assumptions which other sciences including mathematics were to accept. He believed that a mathematician could not prove the first principles on which his subject was based until he had studied dialectic. Over and above, *Plato* emphasized that the study of dialectic led to an understanding of the "Form of the Good". The qualities that he assigned to the form of the good were

those assigned by some religions to God, although he considered the form of the "Good" to be superior to God. After the completion of the study of the dialectic, the student was expected to be in a position to see all things as part of an ideal system.

(ii) Theory into Practice: Having gone through the elaborate system of education and training, the citizen took part in the government of the city between the age of thirty-five and fifty. At fifty, when the citizen had gained a lot of experience in the service of the state, he was to raise the eye of the soul to the universal light which lightened all things and he was to behold the absolute "Good". The aim of higher education was the conversion of a soul from the study of the sensible world to contemplation of real existence.

(iii) Growth in Ideas: *Plato* advocated state control of education. In *The Republic,* the superintendent of education was expected to be a mature man of fifty, married, father and duly elected for the office. In *The Laws,* he made education available to all the inhabitants of the city. He also made it compulsory. However, the main concern remained with how to choose the rulers. Emphasis was laid on pre-natal care. The childhood education was to be given through set games. Boys and girls were to be educated together up to the age of six. The more serious education started after the children were separated. They were to be made skillful in the use of both hands. Music, gymnastics, arithmetic, geometry and astronomy were to be taught. These sciences were meant to be studied by all, but brighter children were expected to make their study in greater depth. Boys and girls were to receive the same type of education.

Plato, in *The Laws,* advocated that schools were to have salaried teachers. The minister of education was to be a mature man, at least 50 years old. He was to manage all the schools and make regulations for their conduct. The state control over education, stated in *The Republic,* was re-emphasized in *The Laws*. He believed that the object of education was the personal insight of the learner rather than his ability at rote memory.

Influence on Education

Plato had a great respect for tradition. He believed that the decay of the city. was due to giving up the simple customs of the forefathers. It is interesting to note that even after centuries, the views of many societies on the value of traditions are similar to those of *Plato*. For example: in Africa and Asia, tradition is highly regarded. In spite of the western type of schooling, traditional ways of life play an important role, and continuing these is considered essential to the preservation of the culture of the people.

He greatly influenced education in the western world. The organization of schooling followed the *Platonic* concepts, resembling stages like elementary, secondary and higher. The curriculum was also graded into stages of difficulty.

The western concepts about the curriculum and structure of education influenced English-speaking countries through their colonial experiences, and later the former colonies.

He advocated state control of education. Of late, there have been moves by the governments to take full control of education through financial, policy making and inspectorial means.

Plato's importance lies not so much in presenting ready made answers to the issues concerning life and education, but in raising questions which philosophers over the centuries have been trying to answer.

Limitations

1. Plato limited liberal education to the upper classes only and that violated one of the important principles of idealism to impart education to all, as every man was the noblest work of God.
2. Plato's education lacked variety and does not take into account the individual differences.
3. His view of the society comprising three classes was static and a straitjacket in nature. There was no scope for upward social mobility. Crafts, the basis for technical education, were assigned to lower status.
4. Censorship of curriculum was likely to have a deleterious influence on social growth.

Conclusion

Had there been no *Plato*, we would have been deprived of the philosophy of *Socrates* and, perhaps, Aristotle and other philosophers would have had little material for criticizing the World of Ideas. Plato drew a road map of structure of schooling from elementary to higher levels, which after centuries influenced the educational ladder of Europe and later the larger parts of the world.

Summary

Plato was the disciple of *Socrates*. He was an idealist in that he considered the World of Ideas to be self consistent and self-contained. His works: *The Republic* and *The Laws:* contained his views on life, politics and education. State was to divide people into three classes: the guardian, the auxiliaries and the common people. Education depended on the classes. *Plato* laid down structure of education from early childhood to adulthood. He described appropriate subjects for each stage. He influenced education in the western world and through it the former colonies, which adopted western type of education.

3

Education For Human Excellence

Aristotle (382-322 B.C.)

Benefiting from the wisdom of *Socrates, Plato* and other Greek philosophers, *Aristotle* followed a good deal of the Greek tradition, but added to the Greek heritage his own unique contribution as is briefly described in this chapter.

Life-skecth

Aristotle was a physician and biologist. He was the tutor of *Alexander* the great, and had the opportunity of receiving information about many countries which *Alexander* invaded. *Aristotle* is still considered as one of the best educated men of all ages, for, perhaps the range of his writing has been surpassed by only a few scholars. He wrote on almost all the subjects, known in his times. Some of his views were given the philosophical label of "Metaphysics".

Aristotle's views on education were mainly found in his two works: *The Ethics* and *The Politics*. His basic philosophical assumption was that education of a liberal man was contingent upon natural endowments and habitation. Education by habit came before education by reason. He considered "Nature" as the starting point of all philosophizing.

Metaphysics: Doctrines of Four Causes

In his metaphysicalviews, *Aristotle* rejected *Plato's* world of ideas as nothing but a reduplication of world of sensible objects. He questioned the feasibility of finding system and unity in a world where there was multiplicity of ideas.

Aim of Education

Aristotle treated education from the point of view of an individual as well as the society. The aim for an individual was "self-realization". Education was to develop physical, moral and intellectual capacities of the learner. In the process of education for self-realization, man cultivated his reason and thus became a rational being. On the social side, education was an art which was subordinate to the art of politics. Both aims were realized simultaneously and were expected to lead men towards happiness.

However, happiness was not a state of mind or body: it was a process, an activity of the soul. Education was to produce men and women with

5

Christianity: Education for Here and the Hereafter

St. Augustine and St. Thomas Aquinas

After the collapse of the Roman Empire, the Christian influence on life and education acquired a new significance. Although the period from 500 A.D. to 1000 A.D. was called the "dark ages", some educational activities did go on during this period. Particularly, Christian education got better organized, and philosophers like *St. Augustine* and *St. Thomas Aquinas* made their unique contributions to philosophy and education. In chapter-5, an attempt has been made to discuss briefly education during the middle ages, before presenting the thoughts of *St. Augustine and St. Thomas Aquinas.*

Education during the Middle Ages

To understand the structure and the trend of education during the middle ages, it is important to study the essence of the cultural and social developments during this period. During the early middle ages, education was in a chaotic stage due to the overthrow of the Roman empire by invading barbaric nations. This resulted in the era (500 A.D. to 1100 A.D.), quite often referred to by historians as the "dark ages" in the European history. Because of the confused situation at this time, there was a decline in learning and general culture. The old Greek and the Roman contributions to civilization were termed "*pagan*" by the new culture of Christianity.

Christianity and Education

The Christian church rose to power because of its hierachical structure, with the powers concentrated at the top in the hands of a single agent, the Pope, held to be responsible not to man, but to God. It followed, therefore, that the person who sat in the place of the highest authority had been placed there by divine will and, thus, deserved the unquestioning obedience and support of all who had been assigned lesser stations by the same power. Also contributing to the rise of Christianity were its high moral and ethical doctrines and the intensity of the faith of its adherents. Learning was strictly preserved and guarded in the monasteries. The church exercised great control on education throughout Europe by authorizing

the right kind of intelligence, ability and character. He laid high expectations about the statesman. His supreme end was to ensure well-being of the community. The statesman gave instructions about how all were to practise their respective arts, politics, education, commerce and war. It was through such fulfillment of duties and obligations that the well-being of the community was ensured. It is noteworthy here to point out the contradiction and the irony in the *Aristotelian* state which demanded that the teacher as an officer of to the state was not to work to change the *status quo* but was to teach loyalty to its institutions and obedience to its laws.

(i) Process of Education: The basic *Aristotelian* concept was that state came into being for the sake of life but continued to exist for the sake of good life. Thus, state was to take practical measures to make good life possible for its citizens. Education was to be under state control to achieve this objective.

Up to the age of five, children were not to be given set lessons, but they were to be provided with healthy play. Between the ages of five and seven, they were to imitate older children. Care was taken about the company, children kept. They were not to consort with slaves and servants for fear that they might absorb low tastes and vulgar habits. State inspectors of education were to watch the children always. It was made sure that the stories told to the children were proper and well supervised. The aim was to promote physical health through exercises and ennoble the mind through literature, art and music.

(a) First Stage: Elementary education started at seven. Liberal studies were recommended for citizens and illiberal studies–art and craft—for the slaves. *Aristotle* could not arrive at any definite conclusion whether the aim of training was to be its usefulness in life, or higher knowledge for its own sake. Two other important aspects of education deserve mention. One aspect was that the children were to be taught to speak the truth before they knew why it was right to speak the truth. In general, the moral judgement on the goodness or badness of an action was to take into account the motive of the agent and the spirit in which the act was performed. The just or temperate deeds were the deeds because these were done by just and temperate people.

(b) Second Stage: From the age of seven to puberty, the child was exposed to a rich curriculum. Music, gymnastics, reading, writing and arithmetic were taught. From puberty to the age of seventeen, the youth was to study rhetoric, grammar, literature, geography, instrumental music and mathematics. The emphasis was on the mastery of the exact knowledge.

(c) Third Stage: His scheme of education reached its climax when at the age of twenty one, the superior students were exposed to still more

extensive curriculum. They studied biological and physical sciences, psychology, ethics, rhetoric and philosophy. The aim was not the memorization of these subjects, but a thorough understanding of them so that the learners became wise. The wise man, according to *Aristotle*, would combine theory and practice, and intuition and scientific knowledge, and come with originality, or the discovery of new ideas and concepts in the universe.

He attached great importance to the study of ethics. It was through the study of ethics that man could become good. Goodness was the condition of the soul–a mean between excess and defect. As far as methodology of teaching was concerned, he highlighted the importance of systematic presentation of knowledge. He recommended that knowledge was to be presented from the particular to the general, and from the specific to the universal. He drove home the point on the importance of methodology when he said that without correct method, no progress could be achieved in education and philosophy.

(ii) Education for Leisure: Leisure, for *Aristotle*, was not amusement or relaxation. All work and business, and the activities of war and public life were pursued for enabling man to live in his leisure the highest kind of life that was possible for him. Such highest kind of life was lived in the disinterested pursuit of knowledge and wisdom. The activity included not only study and research but also all creative efforts in art and literature and appreciation of the perfect and the beautiful. He believed that when engaged in the pursuit of knowledge and wisdom, man enjoyed the bliss which was God's eternity.

Relevance of Aristotle's Ideas

The concept of liberal education was practised in Europe, particularly after the renaissance. The concept has affected education in India due to Anglo-American influences. For example: even as recently as in 1986, the National Policy on Education in India emphasized liberal education as part of the life-long education. *Aristotle's* ideas relating to morality, rationality and nature-nurture aspects of personality development of learners are relevant to India of the present times.

Summary

Aristotle was a physician and biologist and benefited from his travels with *Alexander the Great*. He remains one of the best educated persons. His books: *The Ethics* and *The Politics* contain his views on education. For him, the aim of education for the individual was self-realisation and for society, it was an art, subvrdinate to politics. He stood for state control of education and the censored curriculum for children.

4

Eloquence and Character: Roman Education Training for Practical Life

Quintilian (35-95 A.D.)

Roman education dated back to 800 B.C., and it was family-centred. Later on, community and state took over from the family. In the period from 275 B.C., Greek influences affected Roman education. Even though Rome did not produce great philosophers like *Socrates, Plato* and *Aristotle,* the names of *Cicero, Plutarch* and *Quintilian* could not be ignored. Here *Quintilian's* views on education are presented.

Background

If we review the earlier period 800-275 B.C., we find that the Romans were rural people and their society was simple. Customs or traditions were the basis of education. The family was the chief educational agency. The mother trained children for a few years after birth; then she continued with the training of the girl so that she became a good house-keeper and a wise mother later in her life. The father took charge of the boy and tutored him in moral excellence and high sense of duty. Reverence for the family and its traditions was also instilled in the boy. Further training for the boys was given by the community and the state. If the boy was to be prepared for public life, he was expected to master the Twelve Tables of the Roman Law.

As far as the schools were concerned, they taught the three R's and moral values. Public apprenticeship took place under a man of high public position, wisdom and experience. The common virtues demanded of the learners were modesty, firmness, prudence, piety, courage, seriousness and regard for duty. For spiritual development, fire-side deities and deities presiding over activities of the state were worshipped. Physical fitness too was taught and practised. Wrestling, ball games, running, jumping, hunting, swimming, dancing and riding were some of the important activities, undertaken to ensure physical fitness. Education was to prepare learners as soldiers, governors, builders and citizens.

During the later period, (275 B.C., to A.D. 300,) education in Rome was influenced by the Greek scholars. After 279 B.C., many Greek

scholars, some of whom were captives, came to Rome and translated Greek works into Latin.

Three types of schools emerged in Rome. These could be equated with what we now understand as primary, secondary and tertiary. At the primary level, elements of reading and writing were taught and moral instruction was given. Teachers were said to be good imitators but poor innovators. At the secondary level, liberal arts, literature, grammar and history were taught. At the advanced level, rhetoric, law, medicine and philosophy were taught. In all types of institutions, teachers were paid low salaries. Nevertheless, the administration of schools was under strict state control.

Among the Roman educators, *Cicero, Plutarch* and *Quintilian* stood out. *Cicero* wrote *De Oratore*, or the Education of an Orator. In it, he laid the foundation for an orator's liberal education. He stressed the significance of broad and dependable knowledge. Such knowledge was to form the context of any speech.

Plutarch contributed to educational theory by his '*Moralia*' or 'The Education of Children'. According to him, a wise teacher was expected to cultivate memory, correct habits and intensify instruction. Discipline was considered essential to the progress of a student, and teachers were expected to be models for their students.

However, *Quintilian* was the top Roman educator, for, not only did he lay down the theory of education, but also taught a school to put his theories into practice. His views on education are found in *Institution Oratoria* or 'Institute of Oratory'.

Quintiliant's Views on Philosophy

To *Quintilian,* the only worthwhile life was the life of action. Contemplation was an escape from reality. Incidentally, this view was traditionally held by many Romans. He thought that the philosopher was bound to fail if he tried to reform the society according to his own ideals. He divided philosophy into three areas and considered these areas important to the orator. The areas were: dialectics, ethics and physics. The first area concerned the study of dialectics–the laws of reasoning. The second area was the study of ethic–the laws of justice. The third area related to the study of physics–the ways of providence. He, however, considered the philosopher inferior to the experienced statesman. Thus, his views were different from those of *Plato* and *Aristotle* who attached great importance to speculation and disinterested pursuit of knowledge and wisdom.

Aim and Process of Education

Quintilian's aim of education was to produce an orator. Such an orator was to cultivate not only eloquence but also his character. He was to be a

good man as well as an experienced speaker. The orator's main motive was to be the public interest which he was to serve all the time. However, he believed that orators were not born; they were made: but they could not be made out of nothing. Thus, selection of the right type of people was necessary. Then, the function of the teachers was to correct the weaknesses of nature.

He advocated that the education of the orator was to start early in life. He considered it absurd to say that children could not learn before seven. To start with, the nurse of the children was to be carefully selected so that she could speak properly. He laid down some important principles for teachers.

Principles for Teachers

Quintilian was against the corporal punishment, for, he considered it disgusting and fit only for slaves. He thought that children were easily victimized. Instead of punishment, he advocated "motives" like competition between students, commendation by teachers and interest of the subject as important factors. The main consideration was the child's enjoyment of learning. Teachers were to make sure that knowledge was dropped in and not poured into the learner. He pointed out that knowledge was difficult to acquire, but it could be hardly acquired, if it was not given systematically. He believed that the average child was eager for knowledge. If the child became reluctant to learn, the fault was of the training. Thus, in the early stages of learning, work was to be in the form of amusement. He suggested ivory shapes of letters to handle, and the use of stencils to guide learning of shapes alongwith names.

Teaching was to suit the power and the individual characteristics of the learners. He appreciated the individual differences of learners and wanted teachers to recognize them. He cautioned against over-teaching and against needless intervention by teachers between student and his study. He recommended moderate relaxation and amusement for children, but attached great importance to games as these were considered valuable guides to character.

He also expected teachers to be of good moral habits, which included self-control. With his pupils, the teacher was to be friendly but not familiar; he was to be stern but not melancholy; and he was to be generous in praise but was not to overdo it. He was to exercise patience and quiet insistence in getting the work done. The teacher was to be well educated and he was expected to continue his education. He also identified that sort of teacher as worst who was not conscious of his own ignorance.

The Curriculum

Quintilian laid down a very rich curriculum for the education of the orator. Grammar, music, geometry, dancing, physical education, rhetoric, natural

philosophy and moral philosophy were to be taught. Grammar consisted of language and exposition of poets, geometry including arithmetic, algebra, geometry and astronomy. Rhetoric included reading and expounding prose authors, declamation, theory and practice of rhetoric, logic, history and dialectic.

The training of the orator fell into three stages. Up to the age of seven, he was to be educated at home. Then, he was to enter the grammar school. After the general education at the grammar school, he was to receive the specific training in rhetoric.

Rome contributed law and government to civilization. Additionally, Rome contributed alphabet and speech, and practical knowledge in agriculture and mechanical arts. The immediate beneficiary to Rome's contribution was Christianity.

Relevance of Quintilian's Ideas

Quintilian is an important figure in the history of educational theory and practice. He influenced the European thought and practice in education during the renaissance. We can still identify many aspects of his education that apply to India. The dominant speculative aims of education are being supplemented by aims which are also utilitarian. For example, the expectations of the role of teachers, envisaged by *Quintilian,* are well reflected in National Policy on Education, 1986. The aim is to produce highly motivated, conscientious and efficient teachers; teachers who have inquiring minds and are creative; teachers who are committed to the profession, and are ever willing to admit their shortcomings and to undergo in-service training courses in order to improve and update their knowledge.

High moral standards are expected both of the teachers and learners. The voluntary agencies, the various governments and religious organizations have been laying a great stress on the inculcation of good moral and spiritual values. Eloquence is through debates and discussions.

Limitations

It is worth recording that *Quintilian* emphasized methodology in education. Education is more than mere methodology; it is man's vision of his potentialities and powers in the intellectual and moral fields. Indian philosophy of education is geared towards self-realization, better human relationship, individual and national efficiency, effective citizenship and national consciousness and unity. The Indian philosophy seems to have taken a broader view of education than was taken by *Quintilian*.

Conclusion

The Roman senate required eloqent speakers and that was the need of the times. But that a speaker was also to be a man of character was *Quintilians* great contribution to education.

Summary

In sum, Roman education was family-centred. Training was given initially by the mother; then father took over the training of the boy and the mother continued with the training of the girl. When the Greek influence reached Rome, schools on the patterns of Greece came into being. Schools aimed at the production of a good speaker. Although Rome did not produce educators and philosophers like those of Greece, *Quintilian* stood out and was somewhat comparable with the Greek philosophers. His aim of education was to produce an eloquent speaker who was also a man of good character. He laid down useful and thought-provoking principles for teachers and teaching, and prescribed a broad-based curriculum for the orator. Some of his views are still relevant to education in India and elsewhere.

the establishment of schools and supplying members of the clergy as teachers. The instruction offered in the parish and charity schools, as they were called, was designed for the laity. The method of instruction consisted of having pupils repeat after the teacher, word for word, the Latin versions of the creed and the Lord's Prayer until these had been memorized. Instruction in the Latin schools was the same, but more sophisticated, touching all the areas of knowledge, and the development of each competency which the clerical calling required. The most important subjects were singing, reading and writing, togetherwith the knowledge of Latin grammar (the language of the church) and the calculation of the holy days. There was also increased interest in liberal arts and medicine.

Medieval education was a result of the attempt to resolve the conflict between the old classical Roman schools, often of very poor scholarship, built on the Greek pattern, and the new emphasis on the other-worldiness of Christianity. The Latin books were the final authority. The better books of the past had been lost or were ignored. The process of education was largely one of being certain that the exact subject matter of the text book was mastered, or rather, memorized by the students.

This was an age where there were very few books, and those few were held in great reverence. Whenever words were written down, they were held to be authoritative; consequently, education was extremely bookish in nature. The schools were no better: they were set to cultivate in the pupils the qualities of submissiveness and blind obedience. There was little or no attempt to use education, or books for the purpose of developing the individual or enabling him to better prepare himself to live in the society outside the church. Such things as healthful socialization, participatory democracy etc., which were very important in the educational theories of the Greeks as well as the Rome of the time of *Cicero* and *Quintilian* were overshadowed by the almost fanatical religious emphasis of the church.

Schoolmen and Education

The heads of the individual schools were designated as *rector scholarum* or *scholariun* (schoolmen). Through the schoolmen, the church developed and exercised a monopoly over all educational activities. For example: without a license from the schoolmen, nobody was permitted to teach any subject to any body anywhere.

As long as the Christian tradition was based on a specific body of knowledge and beliefs which were said to have been revealed, the individual Christian had no alternative but to accept those beliefs literally and as acts of faith. The schools strongly fostered unquestioning acceptance of traditions, beliefs, and the Church's interpretations of everyday phenomenon. The medieval man lived by faith and found no need to cultivate intellectual powers to help him interpret what was said to have been revealed to man in the beginning and had been preserved for him by the church. This kind of absolute control on thinking could hardly stand the test or any strong outside view that was contrary to that of the church.

The Later Middle Ages

During the later middle ages, political authority was gradually transferred into the hands of the kings in many countries. The later middle ages witnessed the development of the middle class which had acquired sufficient kind of education. The church had also grown considerably both economically and politically: historians have recorded that in the area of economic power, for instance, the church at one time in the thirteenth century owned nearly one third of all the land in Europe.

One of the tasks, faced by thinkers of the later middle ages was how to reconcile the religious and spiritual aspects of the church with the secular interests which kept intruding at all the times. Another serious intellectual problem of this period was to reconcile the sacred literature of the Bible and its interpretations by the Church Fathers with the secular literature of the Greek and Roman classical writers. Since early attempts to discount the old "pagan" culture had failed, efforts were made to adapt some of the thoughts of *Plato, Aristotle,* and others to support Christian teachings. In the realm of philosophy, scholars battled with the problem of trying to settle the claims of human reason or logic with the claims of the Christian Fathers. Such claims were more often than not seemingly illogical and paradoxical.

Fortunately for the church at this critical juncture in history, she was graciously aided in her search for philosophical reconciliations by the scholarship of her foremost thinkers of the period—*St. Augustine and St. Thomas Aquinas.*

Saint Augustine (354-430 A.D.)

Teaching as Stimulation of Ideas and Experiences

St. Augustine was generally regarded as one of the most profound and influential of all the Christian philosophers. He was born of a Christian mother and a pagan father. He accepted Christianity after much skepticism and hesitation. His religious pilgrimage reflected a wide variety of course. After going through disillusionments with the Manicheans, the skeptics and the Neo-Platonists, he came in contact with *St. Ambrose* who was a major influence in his conversion to Catholicism. After his conversion, he became a fanatical enemy of all herecies and all attempts to subvert Catholic dogma. *St. Augustine* built his philosophy upon two basic principles: the existence of God and the immortality of God.

Philosophy

(i) The Existence of God: *St. Augustine* maintained that the existence of God could be proved intellectually because the order of the universe naturally indicated a creator, and our conscience led us to believe in a divine, moral force. Creation itself indicated contingency and demanded necessary cause. Also, our knowledge was relative and finite. We could not be certain of anything unless we had an absolute standard of truth, which was God. He preached that more important than the pursuit of knowledge was the love of God. To him, the love of God was the beginning of wisdom. He believed that in the highest stage of knowledge, we experienced a mystical presence of God. We felt the presence of divine light which revealed the splendour and majesty of God. The person who experienced this illumination realized that scientific analysis of the existence of God was secondary. We could only tell the presence of God: we could not describe it in intellectual terms.

(ii) The Immortality of God: Together with the existence of God, the spirituality of the soul was affirmed vigorously by *St. Augustine*. He denied that the soul was material and that it existed in another form before man was created. The soul itself was a copy of the Divine Trinity. Its manifestations—memory, understanding and will—corresponded to the three aspects of Trinity. He believed that the immortality of the soul could be established by reason. He claimed that the soul was the principle of life and was superior to the body: hence, when the body died, the soul continued. Identifying soul and reason, he maintained that reason transcended the limitations of matter.

The philosophy of *St. Augustine* depended on the authority of the Church which he was vehemently defending throughout his lifetime. With all his power, he led the fight against individualism within the church. His political ideas were best represented by the *City of God*. He was deeply pessimistic regarding human merit. In fact, he believed that since the fall of *Adam*, all of us had deserved damnation. Sin represented a rebellion against the majesty of God. His doctrine of predestination at once caused much controversy, for it made God's will arbitrary and contradicted the freedom of the will.

St. Augustine was greatly influenced by *Plato*. He believed that truth could be understood only by the few. Truth was not relative but absolute, and it was taught through the church. The task of education was to avoid independent judgement and to subordinate private ideas to the ecclesiastical organization. Real truth could be found through mystical knowledge, when our mind had been purified by prayer and contemplation. Most individuals were guided by their senses and, thus they became victims of illusion and falsehood.

Views on Education

The educational record of the experience of *St. Augustine* was clearly set forth in *The Confessions*, one of the masterpieces of religious autobiography. He examined his life and his actions, and came to the conclusion that they were sinful, hence his Confessions. In it, he naturally exaggerated in self-accusation. Especially significant for the present purpose, however, was his treatise on education.

***(i) Physical Punishment*:** He described with great eloquence the harsh educational system which prevailed in his childhood. He wrote that if he proved idle in learning, he was soundly beaten, for this procedure seemed wise to the ancestors. As a boy, he prayed that he might not be beaten at school, although his prayers were not heard. His elders and even his parents, who certainly wished him no harm, treated his stripes as a huge joke. He continued to say that the one thing in which he reveled in was play. For this, he was punished by men who after all were doing exactly the same things themselves. But the idling of men was called business. The idling of boys, though exactly alike, was punished by those same men.

It is over centuries, since *St. Augustine* lived and wrote, yet there are still some parents and teachers who treat children in much exactly the same way the medieval schoolmen did. It is only during the last few decades that corporal punishment has been outlawed in our schools as something cruel and unusual. Yet, in some cases, the principal reserves the right to administer corporal punishment. In some countries, educational laws lay down procedures in relation to corporal punishment. We are just beginning to find out through research that children brought up under strict discipline and corporal punishment experience great inhibition, shyness and delayed maturity during their late adolescent years. They are also the most likely to give out corporal punishment to others.

Children, we now know, are very good "psychologists". They learn more by imitation and by the example of their peers, tutors, and parents rather than by threats, or fear of punishment. Hence, educators and parents are now being urged to set good examples for the children by actions rather than by word, and to avoid dual, and sometimes conflicting, statements and standards of behaviour and justice. Also, the role and importance of play, drama, and manipulative objective, in the learning processes of young children cannot be over-emphasized in modern curriculum theory and practice. We learn through all our senses, and none of them should be ignored in any sound educational practice.

St. Augustine hated Greek because of the threats and savage punishments of his teachers, and the methods of presentation of the foreign language. On the other hand, he enjoyed Latin because first, he saw the need to learn it; secondly, it was perhaps, presented to him in a coaxing and curious way.

***(ii) Christian Scholar*:** The Christian scholar was to be acquainted with literature, rhetoric, logic, arithmetic, ethics and natural philosophy. These subjects were not to be studied as ends in themselves: care was to be taken that they did not corrupt the scholar's faith. They were, however, preludes to the study of Christian doctrines. Science, in general, could be studied as a tool in combating superstition.

He warned against classical learning, pointing out that it was full of errors and falsehoods, and that it gave a man a false sense of security by unduly over-emphasizing his rational power. Furthermore, he believed that learning could not be promoted without discipline. The teacher was to control the child. Even though he was critical of corporal punishment he had received as a child learner, he recommended it for other learners. Through it, the pupils learnt to control their evil impulses and became conscious of the importance of discipline and obedience. Because he was constantly aware of the original sin, he believed that children were naturally evil; therefore their nature had to be changed by the school master through a system of rigorous education and strict discipline.

***(iii) Illumination of Innate Ideas*:** *St. Augustine* believed that a teacher did not communicate ideas to his pupils. He simply stimulated them to employ experiences and ideas which were already in their minds to form a new idea. Teaching was, thus, the activity of causing pupils to learn. He advocated that whatever was known to us was known through the senses of the body and the experiences of life. But universal truths which were grasped by the mind were divine ideas. These ideas permeated the physical world and were perceived through our experiences. The degree of perception depended on the nature and complexity of ideas, the quality of the individual's intelligence and the wealth of sense experience available to him.

Conclusion

The influence of *St. Augustine* on education today can hardly be overestimated. Many great philosophers, both inside and outside the Church, have been profoundly influenced by his ideas. Some religious existentialists have claimed him as one of their foremost saints. He indicated to us the now almost *Augustinian* exiomatic principle of life–that man's personal awareness of God was most significant, and that life demanded an honest religion of the heart rather than of the intellect. Today we are still wrestling with the same problem that worried the saint more than fifteen hundred years ago: how can we find security and love in a world tormented by hate, flux and rebellion?

Summary

As an educator, *St. Augustine* influenced Catholic, Protestant, and non-denominational ideas. By pointing out the need for discipline, he made education a rigorous process. By subordinating free inquiry to orthodoxy, he transformed education into a form of indoctrination. This view is cherished practically by all countries today. Throughout the world, education has become one of the strongest weapons for indoctrinating the youth into national ideologies whether these are capitalistic, socialistic or communistic. The scholars that followed in his footsteps were not interested in new ideas. This is understandable since they were committed to the preservation of the papacy and its orthodoxy.

But now more than ever before, our educational system needs new ideas and originality, perhaps, much more than anything else, because without these, we are desperately doomed to repetition, however meaningless, and the mistakes of the past. What use is education, if is not productive? And can one be productive, if originality is stifled? This is especially germane with education in the developing nations of Africa, Asia, and Latin America, where the gospel of "catch up" demands the greatest ingenuity on the part of the educators and the educated.

6

Teaching: Mediation between God and Man

Saint Thomas Aquinas (1225-1274)

St. Aquinas was one of the outstanding thinkers of the late medieval period whose work actually laid the foundations of Christian education. His philosophy represented a synthesis of medieval knowledge: it united the realms of reason and faith, science and theology, and nature and metaphysics.

Summa Theologica

Taking up from where *St. Augustine* left off, *St. Thomas* with logical consistency, addressed himself to the problem of reconciling the pagan Greek thoughts, as represented by *Aristotle*, with the Christian faith, philosophy and theology. His *Summa Theologica* eventually became the official doctrine of the Catholic Church, adopted by a papal decree in 1879. He carefully distinguished between what he called natural philosophy and supernatural theology. To him, philosophy dealt with the natural world where things came into existence, went through a change, and went out of existence. It dealt with everything that was open to argument, or could be demonstrated by human reason. Theology, on the other hand, dealt with revealed truth, and involved the supernatural world which was changeless, eternal and ultimate. These universal truths made up the content of faith, and they were not open to question by human reason because human reason could not have any basis for challenging them. This divine truth was created by God, and anchored in some kind of eternal reality. *St. Thomas* like *Aristotle* elevated theoretical intellect and theoretical knowledge above practical and experiential knowledge. This *Thomist* approach to philosophy continued to be the cause of controversy in contemporary educational philosophy.

Education and Philosophy

The lasting influence of *St. Thomas* on education and philosophy could be attributed to the following characteristics:

(i) He did not appeal only to tradition but freely used all the resources of his own reasoning power to the fullest. The orderliness and the logical consistency of his observations have rarely been surpassed in philosophy.

(ii) He pictured an orderly universe: there was a function for all levels and all creatures. The task of man was to utilize his reason and to glorify God.

(iii) His philosophy was antimechanistic. It meant that the universe was not governed by blind chance or by necessity: it was governed by God, and nothing occurred without his intervention.

(iv) He accepted the leadership of the Church as an institutional haven–perhaps for his insecurity, and maintained that without the Church, there was no salvation.

(v) He built his philosophy upon a definite scientific foundation of sense experience. He did not believe in the experimental approach to science. To him, as to *Aristotle*, the main purpose of science was explanation rather than the control of nature. The road to truth laid from the particular to the universal, from the specific to the general, and from the known to the unknown. He stressed that we could not merely start with innate ideas.

(vi) Reason was also unable to destroy the essential foundation of Christianity which stood above it. Like theologians before him, he believed in the immortality of the soul. However, he added an interesting argument which depended on man's desire to live after death. Thus, the good God would grant the resurrection of your soul after death with a bodily form. Reason could prove to us that God existed but it could not explain the resurrection.

Existence of God

Like *St. Augustine*, one of the *Thomist* basic arguments was also the existence of God which he carefully delineated in five natural ways:

(*i*) *The nature of motion:* It appeared that the things which we saw in motion were not self-moved. To explain motion, therefore, we needed the first mover which, naturally, was God.

(*ii*) *The nature of causation:* This was closely related to the nature of motion above. It stated that nothing in the universe caused itself. We needed a relationship between cause and effect. Since we could not accept an infinite regress of causation, we had to accept a first cause, which was God.

(*iii*) *The nature of possibility and necessity:* The possible was not autonomous, but depended on something which was necessary to make it happen. A being which had its own necessity had to be God.

(*iv*) *The nature of gradation:* There was a hierarchy of things in the universe which were related. Relative standards demanded an absolute standard. The highest principle, which was God, was the cause of lower beings.

(*v*) *The nature of divine purposes*: The teleological arrangements, revealed by the universe could not be due to accident. This purpose had to be traced back to God.

According to *St. Thomas,* God was the source of all perfection, all goodness, all existence and all truth. God created the world to mirror his own perfection. He explained that the evil that we saw in the universe was only apparent, that through it, goodness triumphed, and that the world would attain a more varied appearance.

He divided the sciences into three parts: physical, metaphysical, and mathematical. The most important of these sciences, of course, was metaphysical knowledge.

In any sense, he was a loyal son of the Church and acknowledged the absolute power of the Pope and the necessity of the Sacraments as parts of divine grace. While the eastern theologians like *Origen* and *Clement* frequently regarded *Jesus Christ* as a metaphysical force, *St. Thomas* considered *Jesus* as a living reality: *Jesus* was a supreme teacher whose methods and examples we were to emulate.

Universal Principles

St. Thomas was more concerned with universal principles than with specific facts. He felt that knowledge depended on the study of certain principles.

(*i*) *Love of God*: *St. Thomas* stressed moral education and pointed out that the most important virtue was charity. It implied not only merely giving freely to the poor, but also love of one's neighbour. The highest form of love, however, was devotion to God. Heretics were to be converted at all costs: and if necessary then lives were to be taken to save their souls.

(*ii*) *Importance of family*: He reaffirmed the patriarchal system of Middle Ages where the father was the head of the household. He pointed out that the foundation of the state was the family. It, therefore, followed that when the family had been disrupted, social chaos had become inevitable. Since the family was an indissoluble unit, divorce was never to be tolerated because it would violate the commandments of God and *Christ*, and would also socially lead to the breakdown of civilization. Birth control also would be harmful to the individual and the state; it also violated both natural and moral laws.

(*iii*) *Moral state*: The moral aspect of the nature of statehood was very much emphasized by *St. Thomas*. According to him, it was the task of the ruler to preserve the integrity of the state and well-being of the citizens. The best political unit was the small unit in which the ruler was pious, avoided warfare, and was an example to his subjects. These views differed radically from the philosophy of *Machiavelli* who believed that power was a goal in itself, that the end justified the means, and that social relations could not be governed by moral precepts. *St. Thomas,* however, felt that morality was to dominate all relationships, and that man could never negate the foundations of ethics.

Education

His education treatise entitled *De Veritate* (On Truth) summarized his educational philosophy. In it, he asserted that education was dependent on two potential qualities. One type of potentiality was actualized from the outside and demanded the instruction of good teacher. Another type of potentiality developed intrinsically. All of us were endowed with the light of reason, which indicated the majesty of God in us. To teach, then, was to mediate between God and man. The teacher was always to be conscious of the majesty of God in his pupils and, thus, attempt to develop the innate capacities of students. Right education was based on the ideals of the Church and was a symbol of divine truth. Wrong teaching, on the other hand, was alienation from God and represented vicious intellectual pride.

He also stressed that the teacher in the school was to exercise the same type of authority over his students as the father over his household. Hence, the application of the phrase, in place of the parents, (in *loco parentis*) came in vogue.

Relevance

On the whole, medieval education, as represented by *St. Thomas Aquinas,* gave us a rounded picture of the medieval world. His initiative and independence of thought in support of "a just cause" (which, in his time, was Christendom) is something worth admiring. His arguments for the existence of God have withstood the test of time for the Church. The emphasis, he placed on moral education, and the love of one's neighbour is still something which we have to wrestle with in our own civilization. We need concerted efforts to overcome the ethnic, caste and creed divisions. Many countries are trying with national integration to unite the diverse groups. *St. Thomas* firmly believed in the preservation and protection of society for the well-being of all, and for posterity. This is very well exemplified in his emphasis on the family unit as a unique basis for societal cohesion and advancement, in his views on birth control, and his moral bent on the nature of statehood. However, some societies may not agree with ideas relating to divorce and birth control *vis-à-vis* the explosion of population in their countries.

Conclusion

St. Thomas would have liked to keep off the 'pagan' Greek background, but it was not possible, the same way as we cannot appreciate English literature without the knowledge of the Bible. He demarcated between philosophy and theology- both needed in human life.

Summary

The major weakness of the medieval education, in general, was its lack of interest in the experimental sciences. Truth was regarded as an absolute standard from God. Heresy or opposite view was not tolerated. Knowledge was pursued as some sort of a rigorous task, not to be enjoyed. The curriculum was also limited when compared with the Athenian schools in the time of *Socrates, Plato* and *Aristotle:* in Middle Ages, philosophy was subordinated to theology. Above all, the lack of academic freedom and recreational activities, coupled with the stress on asceticism, caused a great amount of timidity in intellectual matters. These also hindered intellectual growth and emancipation. *St. Augustine* and *St. Thomas* championed the cause of Christian education in the middle ages. Many of their ideas are relevant to our times.

7

Education for Creativity and Individuality

D. Erasmus (1467-1536)

The passage from the Middle Ages to the period known as "renaissance" –the "rebirth of learning"–was significant in that during this period interest from the other-worldliness started changing to the natural and human worlds. Man became the centre of attraction. The restoration of the studies of the Greek literature revived the concept of liberal education. *Erasmus* represented the mood of the times. In addition to the contributions to education of *Erasmus,* this chapter contains a review of the general trends of the new awakening, called "humanism".

The Renaissance

The beginning of "modern" education might be considered to have occurred in the last half of the fifteenth century, coinciding with the period called the renaissance or "rebirth of learning". At that time, a new interest in education accompanied a new emphasis on such academic studies as ancient classical literature, architecture, arts and the sciences. Beginning in Italy, where a flowering of political and economic life had been taking place, the revival of learning spread north into central Europe, and eventually to the British Isles. The common features of the renaissance were that it laid emphasis on creativity and individuality.

Background

By the beginning of the fifteenth century, it could be said that classical Greek had almost entirely disappeared in Italy. Then, a group of Greek scholars headed by *Emmanuel Chrysoloras* came to Florence from Constantinople and taught Greek from 1396 to 1400. Many Italian scholars also went to Constantinople to study Greek. After the fall of Constantinople in 1453, more Greek scholars came to Italy, and there was a renewed interest in Greek scholarship. However, Greek never replaced Latin as the main interest in scholarship, and soon the interest in Greek began to wane.

Impact of Renaissance

The renaissance in Italy, like the age of *Pericles* in Greece, was a period of rebellion. In Middle Ages, it was thought that man's main task was to glorify God, and to escape from the temptations of the devil. All this was reversed during the renaissance. Power replaced virtue, and humanism became the keynote of the age.

The scholars of this period found a new interest in human nature and wished to free the individual from those demands which had been imposed upon him by the various authoritative institutions of the medieval period. Such authorities included the church, the guilds, the lords of the manor, and the monasteries. Since many of the scholars were primarily interested in finding out more about human nature through the revival of classical writings, they called themselves 'humanists'. It was during the renaissance period that the humanities came into existence; these were the forerunners of such modern studies as social studies, political science, government, sociology, psychology, education and languages.

One of the contributions of the renaissance scholars was their glorification and exaggerated admiration of this period. They felt that the period immediately preceding had been practically of no value. It was they who labelled the preceding period as the *Dark Ages,* a term which has prevailed down to the present time. The renaissance did not last long before it was replaced by Puritanism, and later on, by the Thirty Years War which created a wasteland in European culture. This period was characterized by the same common factors in all ages of creativity. They all encouraged nonconformity, preached intellectual tolerance, encouraged science to make rapid progress and replaced the theology: these were ages of rebellion.

Renaissance and Education

There was very little progress made in the realm of science. When the humanists did become interested in science, they would seek to substantiate their findings back in the ancient texts rather than doing investigation on their own. They were more interested in trying to find out what was said in the language of science than of scientific content and investigation. However, some gains were made during this period in basic understanding of mathematics, astronomy and physics, thus, laying the groundwork for *Copernicus* and *Galileo* and later on, in the development of heliocentric theory. *Agricola* (1494-1595), a humanist scholar, was also interested in the scientific study of mining and metallurgy. However, it was in the development of practical arts which were basic to the later scientific experimentation that the period of renaissance produced tangible results. Accurate mechanical clocks and watches were developed. Considerable improvements were made in sailing vessels. The development of better paper and ink-making, and the invention of movable type led to the development of the printing press in the fifteenth century (around 1438) through the efforts of *Gutenberg* and others. The implications of the printing press for all aspects of civilization and for education in particular were enormous. Knowledge could now be made available and easily disseminated by a cheaper method of duplicating books. This made possible the extension of popular education.

The renaissance period represented re-awakening of learning from the restrictions of the medieval period. It was largely an attempt to go back and read the ancient classics and often even to imitate them slavishly. It did not, however, represent altogether a creative period. Additionally, it was not very critical of the intellectual points of view of the times, although there was a swing away from other-world ideas to more interest in this world.

(i) Secondary Education: In general, the only kind of education of interest to most scholars of this period was that intended for the youth of the upper classes, now generally termed secondary education. The Church, of course, was interested in preparing scholars and the clergy thoroughly for its future leadership. The secular rulers were also interested in having scholars around them as advisers. Education was largely for the elite, and there was much stress on classical learning and the development of gentlemanly graces. The middle class attempted to break into the educational circles of either the church or the nobility.

One of the best renaissance secondary schools was *LaGiocosa*, established by *Vittorino da Feltre,* near Padua in Italy at the request of the *Marquis of Mantua*. The school was to cater mainly, for the children of wealthy and powerful persons, and a few children who were sons of the poor. The children ranged in age from six to twenty-seven years. The primary purpose of the school was to educate the complete citizen. The curriculum included a wide range of subjects from the classics through mathematics, physics, astronomy, history and ethics to physical education. A good knowledge of reading, a very broad background of manners and social graces and training in loyalty to Christian principles were emphasized. This was the ideal of the educated Christian gentleman. In some German towns and of France, there were some provisions for the education of girls at the elementary level.

(ii) Vernacular Schools: The development of the vernacular language and the relative increase in the well-being of the common people led to some demands for the establishment of vernacular schools, but these were of very poor scholarship: the vernacular writers had not yet developed any good literature. Later on, these schools became important foundations in the national spirit of education.

(iii) Universities: During the renaissance, most universities were neutral or antagonistic towards the changes that were being introduced by the humanists. Some universities such as the University of Florence

which were strongly humanistic, did not have the reputation of the older universities which were strongly scholastic and medieval in background and outlook. In England, however, the Oxford Reformers, a group of orthodox Catholics who tried to reform the church and society from within, did accept the new learning and were able to bring it to the universities in England.

The humanists stood in the position of being the liberals or radicals in the educational controversy of the time. It was interesting to note that in the eighteenth and nineteenth centuries when science was trying to get into the school curriculum and into the scholarly bodies, the humanists were then in the position of conservatives, attacking the new. It was also significant to note that whenever there was a challenge to the older traditions, there was usually a stimulating effect upon the individual student. He then had the opportunity to develop more fully because the ideas found in his culture were being challenged and refined to make them withstand the test of time.

Erasmus and Humanistic Education

Among the northern humanists, and certainly above most of the others in terms of the depth of scholarship and creativity, was *Erasmus* of Rotterdam. He was probably the most outstanding scholar of his age. Although most of his scholarly productivity came after the end of the period under discussion, he represented the embodiment of the best of the humanist and of the renaissance movement. He taught at the universities throughout England and France and travelled widely, lecturing about the advantages of the humanist point of view. He edited many of the Greek and Latin authors, including the work of the Church Fathers, such as *St. Augustine,* and *St. Jerome's Vulgate* edition of the New Testament. His scholarly Greek translation was later used as the basis for the *King James* English version of the New Testament.

Erasmus was a Roman Catholic priest, educated in the Netherlands, and the University of Paris, and in schools in Italy. But it was his work at *St. Paul's* School in England and at Cambridge, where he instituted a humanistic curriculum with an emphasis on classical languages and literature that had the most direct influence on the educational system in England. His efforts in the English academies, and this type of institutions, which stressed sciences and as well as the classics, eventually became the pattern of schools transplanted in most of the British colonies throughout the world.

He believed that man was the centre of the universe. He had strong faith in God, but hating superstition, he fought a constant warfare with his fellow theologians. He felt that hypocrisy governed most of mankind and that the educator was to beware of conceit. He advocated that the study of the classics was to be used for the purpose of broadening knowledge and taste, and for developing the ability to make intelligent decisions. He felt that the interest of boys was to be aroused by the work itself rather than imposed by strong discipline.

The issue of relevance of subject matter is an issue that is, perhaps, one of the most crucial ones in our educational systems today. Critics and educators alike have been drawing our attention to the lack of relevance in our school curriculum and text books, and to the rigid formality and blind adherence to the transplanted colonial system of education some of whose elements are probably still as they were first introduced by *Erasmus* at *St. Paul's* School. Gradually, most new governments in the former colonial countries are beginning to scrutinize this transplanted educational system, and to take concrete steps aimed at indigenous reform of the syllabus in content and methodology, so that education will become more down-to-earth and appealing to our students.

Works on Education

From the educational point of view, *Erasmus's* masterpieces were: *On the Education of a Christian Prince, On Christian Matrimony, Colloquies, Upon the Method of Right Instruction* and *In Praise of Folly*. These are of special importance to us in our attempts to understand and improve our educational systems. Unlike *Machiavelli, Erasmus* believed that the prince was to be a moral example for his subjects and that he was to cultivate the arts of peace rather than those of war. *Erasmus* believed in the education of women in order to strengthen family ties. He urged for the systematic training of teachers. Since wisdom, according to him, was nothing but an applied knowledge, it then followed that the students' innate capacities had to be simulated and guided by nature, aided with constant love and guidance from the teacher and the students' own continuous practice of what he wanted to learn. Like many of our better modern educators, he proposed that the aim of education was to promote independent judgement, which combined honesty with real knowledge. He emphasized that one was not to rely fully on the ancients for all the answers to the present problems; rather one was expected to learn to stand on one's own feet through the wisdom of the ancients, and be able to deal intelligently with the problems of our own time.

(i) Teacher's Role: *Erasmus* made one of the first important contributions to the study of motivation in educational psychology. He observed that if a teacher used force and coercion, he would motivate his students in a negative manner. On the other hand, if he set a scholarly example, he would produce a positive influence in his students. He maintained that it was easy to use the rod as a tool of discipline; yet it was far more important to use moral inspiration so that the student might want to learn. Teachers spent a disproportionate amount of time and energy making students learn. Since students placed more premium and pride on what they discovered for themselves, the teachers' task would, therefore, be made easier if they attempted to make students to want to learn to bear the onus of learning rather than attempting to force them to learn.

The task of the teacher, he observed, was to develop a Christian philosophy of education which could be understood by all. To him, other philosophies were either too difficult or too removed out of the range of most minds; but he thought that no age, no sex, no condition of life was excluded from comprehending the Christen philosophy of life which was too common and open to all as the sun itself. He wanted the sacred scriptures translated into every language so that it would be less difficult for people of all walks of life to understand and practise the message in the scriptures.

(ii) Functions of Education: He outlined four principal functions of education. These were:

(a) Piety,
(b) Love and knowledge of the liberal studies,
(c) Knowledge of the duties of life, and
(d) Habit of courteous manners.

In these principles, he very skilfully grafted *Plato's* liberal education on to a stem of Christian ideals. He accepted the *Aristotelian* evaluation of reason as the guiding force in human nature but added that the function of education was to enable human beings to enjoy life to the fullest. However, as both nature and ability varied from person to person, education could not be expected to achieve success by employing mass methods, particularly, those methods which engaged punitive measures for the student.

In *The Order of Study* (*De Ratione Studii) Erasmus* maintained that the manner of studying classical authors was the same as the great classical teachers had laid down. However, he wanted human interest and value considered along with the life and times of each author. Additionally, author's personal attributes and characteristics of the writings were to be carefully examined in terms of Christian values.

(iii) Rules on Teaching: In his later educational work, *The Liberal Education of Children, De Pueris Statimac, Liberaliter Institutuendis, Erasmus* gave some simple rules on teaching which are still considered very basic today. The rule was not to hurry, for learning came easily when the proper stage was reached. In the second rule, he advised teachers to avoid a difficulty which could be safely ignored or at least postponed. The third rule was that when the difficulty had to be handled, the teacher was to make the boys' approach to it gradual and interesting. At a time when the practice of rote learning was no less prevalent than it was in the era of cheap education for the masses, *Erasmus* pointed the way to true study and learning by insisting that the gaining of knowledge could be achieved only by intelligent, purposeful thinking on the part of the learner. His theory of learning process was: "understand, arrange, and repeat": the theory is not inconsistent with our modern psychological theories of learning.

An analysis of *Erasmus's* views showed that he did not invent any new theory; but he did graft the best of what he found in classical learning into the new doctrine of humanism, prevalent at that time. He could not accept as either human or fruitful the cruelty of the lifeless academic system, he had endured as a boy, and which he still saw being vehemently practised in the sixteenth century schools. He was ahead of his times. His plan for ending cruel practices was perhaps his greatest contribution to education. He pleaded that the rod used by teachers was to be the rod of guidance or rebuke, such as a free man might obey and that the discipline was to be of kindness and not of vindictiveness.

He firmly believed that education was no less important to a nation than military defense–a concept still not fully accepted by many nations today. In *Benueris*, he emphasized that teaching was to begin at a tender age, preferably before seven. The early start was desirable, not only to inculcate the maximum amount of knowledge during childhood, or the formative years, but also to train children in good habits of study, and to leave them no leisure or opportunity to imitate bad examples. He maintained that the skill of the teacher lay in guiding the individual pupil by reason, training him along desirable lines, and giving him practice in acquiring knowledge and experience. Such teachers, he admitted, were rare to come by and it was here that the state was expected to help to seek out and train good teachers. From this, we could see that he was one of the first educators to realize the importance of teacher training institutions as a sure way of obtaining and retaining good teachers. One of his remarks to teachers was heeded, but, by a few during the next four hundred years:

> wholly wrong are those masters who expect their little pupils to act as though they were adults.

Erasmus advocated no rote-learning. However, he would abolish from the schoolroom games such as chess which wasted time to no purpose, nonsense such as riddles, and all songs and stories that were related to the vernacular, and particularly to folklore. These restrictions showed his shortsightedness in many aspects of teaching and educational aims and objectives.

He had a genuine faith that a universal language, such as Latin, would help to bring men and nations closer together, and he set out to foster education for world citizenship, which he believed, could be achieved by classical literature as the instrument and with the knowledge of Christ as the aim.

Conclusion

As far as the western type of schooling is concerned, we can identity humanistic tendencies emerging more clearly in a document like the National Policy on Education, 1986 in India. The Policy aims at the all round development of the child by trained and humane teachers through exposure to arts, sciences and humanities. Like many other humanists, *Erasmus* showed us that life in the world was worth living and education was to be applied to solve problems of life.

Summary

Erasmus, like many educators before and after him, emphasized that lasting change was only to come from within the individual, and it was to be based upon sound ethical principles. He boldly and uncompromisingly attacked the follies of his times, especially those which he found in ecclesiasticism. He strongly advocated a good education for all people because he thought that scholarship would create a brave new world of peace and understanding. Education was considered an attempt to relate ideal to reality. He strongly maintained that education was meant to appeal to man's creative possibilities. Condemning all forms of orthodoxy and conceit, he believed in man's guided individuality and originality, maintaining that one became wiser not as one imitated the past, but as one lived for the future, and learnt from the lessons of the past. It followed, therefore, that receptivity to new ideas which anticipated the future was to become one of the distinctive traits of any progressive educational system. Like many other humanists, he showed us that life in this world was worth living. Relevance of education to real life problems, and the application of knowledge to useful ends, the proper training of teachers, humility among educators, and careful understanding of how children learn are all but parts of what we owe to *Erasmus* as one of the major proponents of humanism in education.

Historians have recorded that during his time, he was perhaps the most liked and hated man in Europe. He received pensions and presents but he also received furiously hostile abuse.

8

Perfection of Reason: The Tutorial Conception of Education

John Locke (1632-1704)

The seventeenth century was the age of realism. New discoveries and explorations opened new avenues between knowledge and social progress during this time. The principal innovators of the century were *Descàrtes, Galileo, Newton, Gilbert, Stevin, Boyle* and *Kremer.* These scientists and educationists revolutionized the fields of mathematics, science, geography, biology and medicine. Then the content of education was not left limited to the traditional authority. School practices were re-examined. Efforts were made to bring changes in the school programme by reversing the curricula and reforming the pedagogy in order to bring about a natural learning process.

Background

Realism took different forms in the hands of scientists, social reformers and educators. But, in spite of the different emphasis, laid down by these reformers, there was some common ground found with each of them: it was that learning was to come to grips with data, and furthermore, the school-curriculum was to be valid, meaningful and of practical application. Most efficient teaching techniques were discovered for producing the goals of decent education.

New ideas to make the use of language more effective were experimented. A humanist-realist like *John Milton* thought that although science was the key to producing dependable knowledge, language was still the means of communicating it. So school curriculum was to consist of language and literature which would be flawless and effective, and also useful for intelligent discourse among learned men. *John Locke* played quite an important reforming role alongwith the other realists by adding an empirical dimension to pedagogy. His influence on the thought of later centuries was perhaps even greater outside than inside the educational arena.

Life Sketch

Locke was born in Warington, England. He received good education at Westminster School and at Christ Church College, Oxford. He was not a robust boy, and as a weak student, he hated Westminster School and its rough-and-tumble life. Later, as a reserved young student at Oxford, he criticized the university practice of disputation, partly because of its artificiality and falsity, and partly because he did not enjoy such enforced discipline.

His intellectual qualities were such that these brought him much success and after taking his Master's degree, he became a tutor at Christ Church, Oxford. It was interesting to record that he entered Oxford at the age of twenty and was still there when he was fifty, working on a studentship. After stay at Oxford, he was drawn towards philosophical studies and found Cartesian ideas particularly acceptable. But his father left adequate property for him and thus, he was able to take his time in deciding on a career. He considered holy orders, medicine, and public affairs, in turn. Finally, he studied medicine. Although he lacked paper qualifications, he was considered quite a skillful doctor. This brought him the friendship of many a reputed persons.

Thus, locke got opportunities to practise his educational ideas on his pupils who mainly belonged to the noble class. During *Locke*'s period, teachers were determined to make their students ornaments of erudition. They honoured all signs of intellectual progress and neglected physical training. *Locke* had definite notions about this sort of neglect.

His theory of education was mainly concerned with specific directions for physical, moral and intellectual training. In his works, *Some Thoughts Concerning Education* and *Of the Conduct of the Understanding*, he wrestled with the issue of cultivating man's rational element, which he thought could be best tackled by school masters. He was of the opinion that teachers played a great role in perfecting reason but as the process began much early, parents were the most important directors, and then carefully selected tutors were to take their place.

Locke preferred the auspices of a tutor. Indeed, for the most part, his pedagogical affirmations must be weighed in a tutorial context. In *Some Thoughts Concerning Education*, we find that Locke had no thought of writing about the education of ordinary people. In his letters to one of his friends, *Edward Clarke*, he made it clear that his methodology was intended for an individual system of instruction. It was not meant for the teaching of a large number of students in a class room. *Locke* in his methodology, considered the following to be most important:

(i) There is to be no compulsion in learning.
(ii) Teaching has to be attractive.

(iii) Games or the spirit of play is to be introduced while instructing.
(iv) Teaching is to proceed from simple to complex, and
(v) Some sort of diversity was to be planned in teaching

His educational aims were threefold:

1 Vigour of body;
2 Virtue of the soul, with its manifestations in good breeding and wisdom in conduct, and
3 Knowledge, or mental acquirements: The knowledge aim was considered to be subordinate to the two former aims.

Let us discuss these aims one after another.

Vigour of Body

Being a medical doctor, and in addition, hampered by a frail constitution, *Locke* naturally devoted his attention first to care of the body. In order to fashion the body into a strong and vigorous organism, nature was also to be given a full scope of action besides parents care of the children. *Locke* clearly warned parents against spoiling their children's constitution. He thought that the strength of the physical organism could be secured only by the endurance of hardships. His main theme was that a person could bear anything to which, from the beginning, he had become habituated. In line with this thought, he advised that children were to be taught to tolerate temperature changes by not dressing too warmly in winter. They were to spend as much time as possible in fresh air, take bath in cold water and sleep on hard beds. He advised that wholesome but simple meals, preferably bread and milk, were to be taken during the entire studentship period. Locke had a sincere conviction that physical hardness was a prerequisite to the attainment of self-denial and self-restraint, both of which he considered as essential attributes in the life of a gentleman. *Locke* recommended plenty of open air, exercise, sleep, plain diet and no wine or strong drink. Too much of warm clothes were to be avoided and the head and feet were to be kept cold; the feet were to be made used to cold water.

In *Locke's* days, teachers were determined to make their students ornaments of erudition. They honoured all signs of intellectual progress and neglected physical training. He had definite notions about this sort of neglect.

Virtue of the Soul

Locke thought that having strengthened and disciplined the body to ensure its obedience to the dictates of mind, the educator was then to turn to the next task, which would be to set the mind in right order. He attached much importance to the formation of virtuous habits. In his view, a sound mind did not mean necessarily a well-informed mind. A pupil might be well schooled in language, philosophy and literature, and yet he might be badly educated. Virtuous habits and social qualities went by the name of good breeding. Character, virtue, wisdom and breeding, according to him, were the marks of sound mind. He thought, learning was secondary to 'good breeding'.

He discovered all virtue and moral power in the achievement of the ideal of good breeding. He stated that a man was able to deny himself his own desires, cross his own inclinations and purely follow what reason directed as best, though the appetite might lean the other way.

He did not approve of the breaking of children's spirits by excessive rigour in discipline. He would rather have the child at ease and free. At the same time, he thought that right from the infancy, a child was to be made to realize that there were things, he might not do and things, he might not have.

Most important in the formation of good habits and virtue was the early recognition of parental authority. From the early years, the parental authority would ensure good behaviour, but reason was also to be carefully guided. A good teacher was expected to be an example of virtue and one who was to make the child comprehend it. He opposed public education and favoured private or tutorial arrangement for he believed that it would help the pupil to achieve virtue easily, since he would get more chance to stay with a virtuous teacher.

If we turn to consider the 'special virtue' that *Locke* had held to be most necessary for a young gentleman, we find that he emphasized the social virtues and the social side of virtue. Thus, good breeding was the surest sign of a gentleman. With all its limitations, his theory was really one of moral education. He was quite definite in placing moral formation above intellectual formation in the hierarchy of educational purposes.

Knowledge of Mental Acquirements

He thought that the education of his times was out of date and directed his most sharp criticism against the classical languages which had continued to dominate the school curriculum for a long time. He thought that Latin, Greek, grammar, rhetoric and literature were of little use to the man of affairs in his practical life.

Curriculum

Locke prescribed the following curriculum for the primary and secondary school children: as soon as the child began to talk, the teaching of reading was to begin. The start was to be in the nature of play and a few letters were to be introduced at a time until the child had command over the entire alphabet. Letters were then to be turned into syllables, and before long, into words. But the whole process was to appear like a game. When the child began to read, he was to be given simple and pleasant books such as fables. When reading facility increased, the Bible stories were to be added to his reading material. Reading was to be followed by writing.

In all schooling, the mother tongue was to be given first attention. When the gentleman carried on his oral and written discourse in the vernacular language, the second language, French– which was preferred to Latin—was to be taught as French was accepted as a living language. But it was to be taught early. The method of instruction for all foreign languages would be the same—that was: conversational. There would be no need to teach grammar then. Normally, grammatical studies were not to be undertaken until the student was quite mature and would understand these well.

In addition to vernacular-language study, *Locke* added arithmetic, astronomy, geometry, chronology, history, ethics, law and natural philosophy to the curriculum. Other accomplishments included dancing and music. Though he recommended fencing, he preferred wrestling to fencing. One more addition, which he mentioned later on, was the inclusion of a trade. He recommended gardening or husbandry in general, and working in wood as a carpenter and joiner or turner. He considered healthy recreation suitable for a man of study or business.

He condemned memorizing, for it did not serve any useful cultural or educational purpose. With regard to reasoning, he, in his book, *The Conduct of Understanding*, stated that the mistake was that a person, who was found reasonable in one thing, was concluded to be so in all things. To think or say otherwise was thought to be insulting and thus nobody ventured to do that.

His gentleman was, therefore, expected to be always first a useful man. For this reason, he commended the study of various subjects at different stages. He recommended arithmetic to help in building the first sort of abstract reasoning. He approved dancing, for it would create graceful movements. Fencing, riding and extensive travelling were recommended as means of good breeding.

Travelling, he thought, would broaden the outlook of persons and make them mature. Gardening and carpentry were considered important as these might promote good health.

This programme of study, he thought, was to be completed at about the age of twenty. After this, a gentleman might marry.

Contribution to Education

Locke's important ideas which influenced education were as follows:

(i) He suggested that instead of having uniform classical training for all, education was to be designed to fit the prospective mode of life of the pupil.

(ii) His vocational outlook on education consisted of a pragmatic attitude. He thought that no good could come out a system which was not based on the principle of utility.

(iii) He wanted education to enlighten the educated person to the knowledge of his Maker and bring into him the sense to understand his duties. It was also to provide the knowledge of all those things which were most necessary and advantageous.

(iv) He desired that education would provide the pupil a sound mind and a sound body. He thought that the pupil who had these two had nothing more to wish for. Pupils were to be hardened physically by providing them a natural immunity against the hot and the cold weather.

(v) He wished that during the course of the educational experience, his gentleman pupil would conceive of four ideal qualities: virtue, wisdom, breeding and learning.

(vi) He clearly anticipated the play-way method in education. All instruction was expected to begin only when the pupil was in the right mood and could do the task with delight.

(vii) He disapproved of any punishment to the pupil. The rod was the most unfit instrument to educate the pupil. This sort of correction would naturally breed an aversion to education. He insisted that beating was the worst and, therefore, the last means to be used in correction of children. It was to be used only in cases of extremity and after all gentle ways had been tried and had proved unsuccessful.

(viii) He, before *Rousseau*, could be designated the father of the child-study movement. Children's natures, their aptitudes, their native stock and all that would be fit for their improvement were to be taken into consideration by the teacher.

(ix) He rejected the doctrine of innate ideas which held that certain abstract propositions—or even the ideas of God—were innate. He said that if there were innate ideas, all people would have them in common and would keep faith in God but, that was not the position always. Thus, he reflected that the only source for ideas was experience, and no innate ideas existed.

(x) From the rejection of ideas, *the Tabula Rasa* theory started getting attention and acceptance. According to this theory, man's mind was passive and, like a wax tablet, it could receive all impressions, made on it. So *the Tabula Rasa* theory, which meant that man's mind was like a clean slate, drew the attention of many educators of the day. If man began with no innate ideas or original impressions, then whatever he was to become depended on his experiences. This led to the acceptance of the doctrine of equality of educational opportunities.

Influence on Indian Education

It is of interest to observe that through the theory and practice of the western type of schooling, the potency of *Locke's* influence on Indian educational system can be easily identified.

Most of his important ideas, which have greatly influenced educational systems far and wide, except for his ideas about private tutoring, are acceptable in the Indian context. His impact on India can be examined in the following areas:

(i) He suggested that education was designed to fit the prospective mode of life of the pupil. This led to vocational outlook on education. In India, besides the existence of the diversified courses, vocational schools also thrive. These provide a wide range of courses for the pupils, and present opportunities of getting training in the choice of one's vocation.

(ii) His idea that child-study was a necessity is getting popularity and education is being redesigned and replanned in the light of the children's interests and aptitudes. The child's personality is getting more attention today than what it was in the past.

(iii) In spite of the doubts about: "spare the rod and spoil the child", *Locke's* disapproval of any form of punishment is getting much attention. The notion that punishment to the child would do little good to him is getting stronger day by day. Administration of punishment is governed by educational laws in all the countries.

(iv) His views that instruction was to be planned to suit the needs and interests of children are widely accepted. Games and play have been gradually occupying more space in time-tables today than before.

(v) His faith in God as one of his aims of education has plenty of educational implications. The need for moral and religious instruction in schools has always been accepted as it leads to building of the pupil's character. *Locke's* concept of 'hardening', which has the implications of self-denial and self-restraint, is quite acceptable, as it leads to a moral life.

Conclusion

Locke's singular contribution to education is that knowledge is not innate: it comes through the senses. The senses set impulses in motion to reach our minds. It is the experience that brings about knowledge.

Summary

Locke was known as a many-sided thinker and educator. He was the one who converted realism into empiricism. He advocated that educational process was to centre round the child and was to keep in view the individual tendencies and capacities.

He was most often remembered for his theory of *the Tabula Rasa* and for his rejecting the doctrine of innate ideas. He helped to formalize education through his judicious choice of a wide variety of subjects to be included in the school time-table and his insistence on formal discipline procedures.

His influence on India can be traced in various directions. His ideas, backed by the principle of utility criterion, are accepted facts. Gardening and carpentry have occupied important place in school curriculum and the study of a craft at school is being recognized as imperative.

9

Follow Order of Nature

J.J. Rousseau (1712-1778)

The eighteenth century made a break with the authority-centred traditions of the middle ages which had managed to survive. A great importance was attached to reason. But the situation in the educational field was not very encouraging in Europe, both in terms of quality and quantity of education. Thus, scope for reforms existed and these were indeed carried out. However, a novel thinking in educational theory and practice was done by *J.J. Rousseau*, the advocate of naturalism in life and in education. In this chapter are presented and evaluated his views on education in general and those embodied in his work: *The Emile:* in particular. The relevance of his ideas to modern times is also highlighted.

Background

The beginning of the eighteenth century did not reflect a very healthy picture in education. Weaknesses in educational opportunity and practice were commonly recognized. There was a demand for better schools and more fully prepared teachers. Besides, a general awareness that education was to be linked with society seemed to have been growing.

It was at this time that in England, a Charity School Movement was sponsored, and the teaching of reading, writing and the catechism, including the prayers for all children, became popular. The influence of the Church of England on education seemed to have increased and the Sunday School Movement had begun to gain popularity. The idea of the Sunday School was to offer instruction in reading, writing and religion to children who could not come to school during the week because they were working for their livelihood.

In Germany

The need to reform education system was felt even more strongly. *Fredrick William-I, King of Prussia,* was one of the European rulers at that time, who appreciated that education was the genuine need of the common people. It was in 1717 that he decreed that attendance in the elementary school was to be compulsory. Thus, the need for education gradually became so conspicuous that in 1763, *Fredrick* the Great issued the famous general school regulations which made attendance in schools compulsory for all children between the ages of five and fourteen.

Purssia's example of making attendance in schools compulsory had far reaching effects in Germany. The higher schools felt its impact in many fields. The new curriculum in the higher schools was permeated with the spirit and method of science and modern philosophy.

The freedom of the teacher to study and teach, and the freedom of the student to study and learn were accepted as fundamental principles for university life. The old method that had recognized the practice of lecturing on standard works was replaced by the new method which consisted of presenting the facts and interpretations of scientific findings in lectures. The university began to serve the rising spirit of nationalism. This led to a greater use of vernacular. It was then that higher education began to affect the air of independence and progress which had never been so much witnessed.

Enlightenment

In the main, the enlightenment was a revolt against the established order, it was critical of existing theories and practices and it was even destructive of some of them. It was individualistic in that man was free to express himself. However, it was very difficult to trace the educational effects of the enlightenment. It was not easy to reckon distinctively any leading figure in the movement who could be called a prominent educationist: all of them were. But there was something common in all the men of the enlightenment: it was the affinity of the ideas. One aspect of this affinity was the rejection of the authority, and this helped to hold the men of the movement together. Anything which could be recommended by reason or common sense was accepted. Thus, the enlightenment was mainly critically rationalistic in its outlook. *J.J. Rousseau* was, nevertheless, reckoned as a reactionary to this movement. Historians said that he became a reformer who was to reform the reform.

Life-sketch

Rousseau was born on the 28 June, 1712 in Geneva. His father was a watch-maker. His mother was a niece of a Calvinist minister. His mother died a few days after his birth. But his education began exceptionally. At the age of six, he was reading books from his father's library. In 1722, his father went into exile and he was left in the care of his maternal uncle. Soon he was sent to live outside Geneva with a minister who taught him the classics. He left the minister after sometime and came back to his uncle and began to work as a clerk.

After a few years, he left the clerical job also and went to Annency in Savoy where he happened to meet *Mme de Warens* who managed to send him to Turin. Between 1729 and 1733, he had no job practically. It was in

1733 that *Mme de Warens* offered herself to him as his mistress. He accepted it, though he felt himself more her son than her lover. (He was however, soon superceded by another lover). He then had reached 21 years. He stayed with her until 1740 when she found him a good position in the tax office of Chancery.

It was some time in 1742 that *Rousseau* went to Paris. It was then that he composed an opera and published *Les Muses Galantes,* a comedy, and some works on chemistry. This brought him fame as well as wealth.

From 1745 to 1752, he was employed as a secretary by the *Dupin* family. He also did some research for *Mme Dupin* who was preparing a book on the subject of women. At the same time, he was working for himself also. His essay: *Discovers Sur Les Sciences et les Arts:* got him the first prize offered by the Dijon Academy in 1750. Its publication made him more famous.

The *Discours* provoked many disputes which continued for a couple of years. Taking advantage of his position, created after the publication of *Discours*, he published his *Observation* in 1751, wherein he strongly noted that the primary source of evil was inequality. The words, rich and poor, were relative terms only. As a result of the criticism of the French government, he was placed under surveillance in 1753. It helped him further to express his true political thoughts.

Three more of his publications are further noteworthy. *Julie*, a novel with moral, philosophical and religious convictions was published in 1756. His famous work, *The Emile*, a long reverie about education and an advice to the parents to follow nature, was published in 1762. His Du *Contract Social*, containing his political principles, was published immediately after the publication of *The Emile*. He died in July 1778 in E:menpnville.

The Emile

When *The Emile* was published in the year 1762, *Rousseau* was fifty years old. The book reflected his fundamental idea that all the essential liberty of natural man was to be safeguarded by education. *The Emile* was organized in five parts. Book I dealt with the years starting from infancy to age five of *Emile's* life. Book II dealt with life from age five to twelve; Book III, from age twelve to fifteen; Book IV, from age fifteen to twenty-two years; and Book V was devoted to the education of women. In fact, *The Emile* was a hypothetical case. It dealt with the story of a child, *Emile,* selected for experiment. *Emile* was educated in three ways by nature, by things and by men.

Book I of *The Emile* dealt with how a child's life was to be made simple, and *Rousseau* stressed that there were two important points for life and happiness. These were self-knowledge and self-control. These were to be achieved by the child at this stage with the help of an exceptionally well-qualified and educated teacher. He advocated tutorials and stressed that no teacher was to have more than one pupil.

In Book II, where education from five to twelve years of age was to be given, he suggested that the child was to be allowed to discover his own personality and construct his own value system. He condemned every thing in the conventional practice and exhorted to do nothing and allow nothing to be done. By this, he meant that children were to be protected from the evil of organized society. He wanted to provide almost an unlimited freedom to the child who was to learn according to his interests, while surrounded by meaningful things for experimentation and discovery. He advised teachers and parents to encourage children to be themselves, to allow them to indulge in their sport and to let them find their own pleasures.

Book III contained his three important criteria which governed the period of a child's life when intellectual education was necessary for him. Necessity, usefulness and moral suitability were the three criteria which were to be kept in mind while educating the child at this stage. Truth was considered very important, but whatever truth resided outside the context of necessity and use was to be ignored. He advised teachers and parents that the great danger in life and education was not ignorance, for ignorance never harmed anyone: it was error, which, if allowed to go uncorrected, could be fatal. Of the three criteria to be followed to impart intellectual knowledge, the most important was the principle of usefulness. He cautioned that nothing was to be told the child which was not important and which he was unable to understand. A teacher was expected to cultivate a desire for learning and to teach the child to learn on his own.

Book IV comprised those educational ideas which dealt with ethical and moral training of *Emile* from fifteen years to early twenties. What moral objectives, he had in mind, he did not enlighten us much about. According to him, to be moral meant to act according to the dictate of one's own heart. He wanted moral teaching to begin with two great truths: God and man's soul. With these, the child would seek directly self-love and love for the welfare of mankind.

Rousseau had humanitarian tendencies but he did not approve institutionalized religion. He was religious in a very broad sense, and though he wanted *Emile* to be religious, he also wanted him to stay away from churches. He thought that morality could be formed naturally. He expected that *Emile*, having realized that all men were fundamentally alike, would possess a love for the human race. This love could then easily be translated into sound ethical action. Direct moral teaching found no favour with *Rousseau*. He thought that *Emile* would become aware of his own weaknesses, not by being told of them but from experience, and he would become moral in a natural way as he followed right living.

Book V was concerned with the education of girls. The differences in sexes made him think of providing a different kind of education for women. The education of women was to be planned in relation to man, for she was the source of his early education as mother. A woman's education was to be planned in such a way that she became pleasing in man's sight to win his respect and love. *Rousseau* thought that a woman was less governed by reason, so she needed more authority and guidance in education. She needed to be taught to love duties and cultivate self-control.

Rousseau's Negativism

There are three divergent theories of education. One considers that the main purpose of education is to provide opportunities of growth by removing hampering influences. A second theory maintains that the purpose of education is to give culture to the individual and to develop his capacities in the best possible ways. The third theory holds that education is to be considered in relation to the community and its main function is to train useful citizens.

Commenting on the first theory of education, *Bertrand Russell* expressed the view that there was more truth in the first theory which gave negative view of education. The negative view had been dominating much progressive thinking on education. It had become part of the general creed of liberty which had impired liberal thought since the time of *Rousseau.*

In fact, *Rousseau* approached the problem of educational reform from the point of view of social theory. He clearly expressed in *The Emile* that in order to remould society, the individual needed to be remoulded. In Book I of *The Emile*, he declared that God made all things good, man meddled with them and they became evil. As mentioned in Book II, he advocated nothing and allowed nothing to be done. These ideas related to his doctrine of negative education. What he meant was that the children needed to be protected from the evils of the organized society which was full of corruption, and that good education provided at this age would form a shield against vice and error.

In the context of natural education, *Rousseau* opposed both authoritative teaching and all kinds of bookishness during the adolescent years. In Book III, he advised parents and teachers that children were to be protected against error. The great danger in life and education was not ignorance but error, which if allowed to go uncorrected, could be fatal.

His negativism was equally prominent in Book IV where he expected *Emile* to have social education by right living. *Emile* would become aware of his weaknesses, not by being told of them, but from experience. He would become moral in a natural way only. His replies to *Madame d' Epinay's* letters contained his ideas on how a parent was to deal with his children. They were to be told stories and fables in which they could find out the morals and apply these to themselves. Generalities were to be avoided for one only arrived at poor results or at none at all, by putting maxims in the place of facts.

He would have the children educated at home by the mother. He approved even of co-education. He thought that original nature of the child was good and initial equalities among the pupils had to be maintained. He advised all to live according to nature, and follow the order of nature in educating children. Here, he regarded nature as equivalent to endowment, the inherited disposition of the individual. Education, according to nature meant the spontaneous development of the innate tendencies of the child. He emphasized in *The Emile* that to train a natural man did not mean to make him a savage and to send him to the woods but it meant to educate him so that he was not carried away by the social passions and prejudices. Defining nature further, he gradually developed an anti-social attitude. That was the theme of his negative education. Society, for *Rousseau*, was not a natural but an artificial outcome of a contract. So, what was conventional was evil and what was natural was good. A natural or negative education did not mean any education: it simply meant a non-social education, a preventive education.

Rousseau wished *Emile* to attain liberty for which education was to act both negatively and positively. The negative education consisted of restricting the child's desires and the positive training meant to supply him with the strength, he lacked to achieve freedom. Freedom would come to the child not by forcing him to learn but by creating in him a desire to learn and by providing direct awareness of objects or the immediate experience of a situation.

He wanted *Emile* to be guided, rather than taught, by a teacher. So he preferred to call the teacher a master, since he guided rather than instructed. It was, perhaps, because of *Rousseau's* influence that *Montessori* later on described her teachers as 'directors'. He said that the art of teaching consisted in making the pupil wish to learn.

The moral aspect of his education consisted not in imparting knowledge of virtue by the teacher, but in saving the heart from vice and error. Children were never to be punished but they were to learn by the natural consequences of their faults. During the adolescent years, education was designed to prepare *Emile* for the moral and social order. The social training which he would need was to be acquired through the experience of others and was to be indirect through the study of history, fables etc. Thus, he gradually developed his moral and religious concepts alongwith a full appreciation of proofs of God's existence.

The positive education of the childhood period comprised physical training. *Rousseau* recognized in *The Emile* the importance of physical exercises. Games and physical exercises had their moral values and the social training as achieved from participation in common games. The other aspect of the positive education during the childhood period was the training of the senses which would lead to the development of reason.

One of the outstanding features of *The Emile* was that there was no predetermined curriculum because *Emile* was to be educated through activities and by first-hand experience until he reached the age of twelve. But between twelve and fifteen, the lost ground, if any, was to be recovered and *Emile* was to be educated well. His training was now restricted to what was useful. The occupations rejected at the previous stage were now to be considered in the light of their utility.

Emile was exposed to situations which were challenging. Perhaps *Dewey* later on conceived this idea in the form of a project. *Rousseau* wanted *Emile* to study science but the apparatus, *Emile* would use, was to be self-invented. He was not to be taught truths but simply to be guided to discover them by himself.

Commenting on the other aspects of the curriculum, *Rousseau* contended that geography was to be learnt by observation of the natural phenomenon and a trade would be prescribed for the pupil so that with any changing of fortune, he might be independent economically. The trade which most satisfied him was that of the carpenter because it was clean and useful and gave enough exercise. Thus, the principle governing *Emile's* education during the transitional years was that of learning by doing.

His views about educating women were unique. In The *Emile,* he said that man was to be strong and active, the woman was to be weak and passive, for a man sought to serve, a woman sought to please. What were wanted in a woman were gentleness, obedience and submission, and her education was to be planned accordingly. His views on national education were in accord with the Greek theory and Spartan educational practices. *Rousseau* agreed with *Aristotle* that service to the state had a single end, and that education of all was to be one and the same, and that supervision of this education was to be public and not private.

Rousseau's Influence

Rousseau's influence on education in India has not been very great, but whatever influence, he exerted can be traced in the followed ways. There is more consciousness to respect the child's personality now than what had been in the past when the child was regarded as a passive receiver who had no say in the school matters. Punishment was considered imperative, and child's likes and dislikes were never reckoned important. But now the child's personality is considered of greater value. More opportunities are provided for him to enrich his life. The idea of punishment is being questioned and it is gradually replaced by better care, respect and love for the child.

There is greater emphasis on learning by doing today and educational programmes are far more diversified, interesting and fascinating. Regular games and physical exercises are now the core of the curriculum in most schools.

Although learning of a craft at school was not considered important in the pre-independence era in India, now both at the primary and post primary levels, some kind of craft has been formally introduced and children are taking great interest in the activities. Children enjoy far more freedom in schools these days. The parent-teacher associations have bridged the gap between the school and parents. The parents are now becoming more aware of the role of the school in the community.

His views on women's education have never been considered of much value, for they are full of his personal prejudices against women. Education in India has been developing with a great pace and with it, equal opportunities are being provided to women. They are not treated merely as pleasing things in the man's sight; but better status is being extended to them these days. Indians have realized the importance of education as a means of upward mobility and women especially are seeking for equality of opportunity in education as in all other walks of life inspite of the machismo.

Conclusion

J.B. Butler's comment on *Rousseau* that he was predominantly a man of impulses and emotion rather than an intellectual analyst provides befitting conclusion to him as a rationalist. For him, Nature was dependant, society was fickle; Nature was good, society, was evil and crafty–foollish people did not understand nature. But his emotions appealed to educationists like *Froebel*, *Pestalozzi, Montessori* and even *Dewey*.

Summary

Rousseau had no regular formal education during his child-hood days. Since his mother died early and his father had to leave Genewa when he was very young, he suffered a lot and wandered from place to place in quest of petty jobs. At the age of twenty-one, he happened to meet *Mme de Warens* who influenced his life for a considerable number of years.

Rousseau's second visit to Paris brought him in contact with many literary figures and great philosophers. He had also been working for himself and was awarded the first prize on one of his essays by Dijion Academy in 1750. By 1762, he had written novels, books and composed operas which brought him much recognition.

One of his important books, *The Emile* (1762), a long treatise about education, brought him much eminence. But the publication of *Du Contract Social*, which contained his political principles, placed him under the French police's surveillance. In *The Emile, Rousseau* expressed his theory of negative education. He attached a great importance to learning by doing.

10

Psychology in Education—*Anschauung*: Form, Number and Name as Developmental Processes

Johann Pestalozzi (1746-1827)

Pestalozzi was about fifteen years old by the middle of the eighteenth century. With the passage of time, the new ideas which had geared reforms in the beginning of the century, started getting more crystallized. The national systems of education had developed in almost all the leading nations of Europe. The wave of humanitarianism had spread far and wide and was being felt by all the educationists of the century. *Rousseau* was still living. He had published *The Emile* and had reached the pinnacle of his fame. His doctrine of natural education was being accepted by all and it seemed almost impossible to find an educationist who had not been influenced by him.

Life Sketch

Pestalozzi was born into a protestant family of Italian origin–a middle class family which enjoyed almost all modest comforts of life. His father was a surgeon who died early in his son's childhood. In spite of his father's early death and ensuing difficult circumstances, the boy had a happy childhood as his mother took great care of him.

After completing his early education at home and the Latin school, at fifteen, he entered a college which prepared boys for professions. Here, he encountered some excellent and inspiring teachers, who treated him with love and care. But soon he started realizing that the training was less effective and uninspiring because it omitted the solid and sufficient training of the practical ability. So it was not surprising that the students of his college and the other youths joined the newly formed Helvetic Society in which Catholics and Protestants worked together for the improvement of education and for the reform of government. It was in the Helvetic Society where *Rousseau*'s Political ideas and *The Emile* were discussed at meetings. As a result of that, the young *Pestalozzi's* mind was greatly influenced by *Rousseau* and his *The Emile.* The idea of finding a right way of teaching as a 'universal remedy' for the ills of society grew strongly within him from that time.

By this time, he had given up the idea of entering the ministry completely because he showed no great aptitude for that profession. He turned to law, which too, he could not take up. It was now the new concept of freedom which obsessed him, and his studies were focused on finding a right way of teaching which would bring enlightenment to the existing social problems and help the individual to fit into the society.

His educational ideas were mainly expressed in two of his works—*Leonard and Gertrude,* and *How Gertrude Teaches Her Children.*

Leonard and Gertrude

Almost from the beginning of his venture into education, *Pestalozzi* enjoyed writing books and pamphlets, mainly on social topics including education. The first part of his most important book, *Leonard and Gertrude,* was a didactic novel. In the first part of the book, he described a village community and the conditions under which so many of the lower class people lived; in the second and the third parts of the book, he drew up a list of various kinds of injustice and tyranny that were prevalent and pointed out the remedies to alleviate the sad conditions of the village people. He condemned the existing practices in the school, and proposed that it was to stand in the closest connection with the life of the home. In the story, the old fashioned school-master was replaced by a young lieutenant who began his crusade against fifth, laziness and disorder. When the new type of education began in the story, the children did a great deal of manual work and received instruction in the three R's. In the fourth part, he described the inadequacies of the legal system and drew up lists of suggested reforms.

Throughout *Leonard and Gertrude*, he stressed two points which were fundamental to his theory of education—the necessity of extending sympathy and justice to the poor, and the importance of mother's love, personified in *Gertrude*. Teaching methods were also much emphasized in the book. How to maintain good order without harshness, how to encourage good habits and how to instruct from nature in those things which were essential were highlighted. The children were taught to pay particular attention to what they saw and heard. Accurate observation through the senses was the first step towards real knowledge.

How Gertrude Teaches Her Children

When all the four volumes of *Leonard and Gertrude* were completed, he believed that he had completed his information about how to teach children. But he was surprised to discover that he was not clearly understood. So, thereafter whatever he wrote, including his essays and *How Gertrude Teaches Her Cnildren,* he tried to explain the deeper meaning contained in *Leonard and Gertrude.* For a short while, he gathered a number of children at Stanz and taught them. These children had lost their homes because of the ravages of the French Revolution. He tried his methods on all children in the Orphanage School at Stanz. Mainly the hostility was from the Roman Catholic population, which millitated against his success. In spite of initial setback, he tried hard to create a family spirit and mutual feelings of love and gratitude in the community. By this time, his knowledge of teaching techniques and practical school problems had been enriched. He was no longer a theorist: he possessed all knowledge that a practical school master was to have. Besides, he was fully aware of the new children's broad interests as well.

Pestalozzi was mainly concerned with the teaching techniques which would cultivate the powers of attention, observation and memory. His own experience of teaching pupils had taught him that children were to draw, write and work while they learned. He felt that the oral repetition by children when they were actively engaged in another job formed their vocal cords, and exercised attention and memory. It also prepared them for doing work in life more actively.

His teaching of reading depended on one simple method of instruction. He believed the sound to be the first elementary means of instruction. So he collected combinations of syllables and asked the children to repeat them aloud. It was his contention that sounds were to be stamped on the mind before the first letters were put before the child, and before any exercises in formal reading were begun. This sort of approach was similar to the phonetic method and was different from the conventional methods. He felt that if education was to become a science and was, thus, to obey definite laws, the knowledge achieved from sense impressions could be classified and developed with the help of three concepts: form, number and name. Therefore, *Pestalozzian* method prepared the way to more satisfactory learning and knowing, and considered the earliest age of the child's development in planning the curriculum.

Pestalozzi's conception of the term *Anschauung*, for which there was no precise English equivalent, gave us more insight into his teaching methodology. It meant the mere awareness of objects or of situations. Terms used by English and American writers to convey the meaning of the term included: simple apprehension, spontaneous appreciation, direct acquaintance, first hand impressions, face encounter and the direct impact of this and persons. *Anschauung* was not, however, restricted to mere awareness of objects; it also comprised spontaneous appreciation of moral actions and direct understanding of situations.

His elementary means of instruction – form, number, and name language – which formulated his principles of teaching techniques were based on psychological principles and produced a general methodology of instruction. Therefore, according to him, a good technique of instruction consisted of three-fold a principle:

(i) To teach children to look upon every object which was brought before them as a unit, and was separated from those objects with which it was connected;
(ii) To teach them the form of every object, including its size and proportions;
(iii) To acquaint them with all the words and names, descriptive of objects which were known to them.

The Three Forms

Pestalozzi identified (i) form, (ii) number, and (iii) name as the three forms in the developmental process.

(i) The concept of "form" was developed by him mainly through drawing so that children at an earlier stage could have knowledge of proportion. He wanted to build all powers by doing, even the power of clear representation of all real objects. Drawing lines, angles, rectangles and curves would help them to build readiness in gaining sense impressions of all kinds and develop skill of the hand and muscles as well.
(ii) His concept of "number" involved concrete counting. It conformed to the general principle of concrete representation of teaching. For example, when the teacher asked: How many times was seven contained in fifty-six? The child had no real background for his answer, and with great difficulty had to work it out of his memory. Now, if the teacher put eight times seven objects before the child and allowed him to count them as eight sevens together, the child did not need to think any more about the question as he had learnt the answer with the help of concrete objects.
(iii) About "name", *Pestalozzi* argued that the child was to learn to talk before he could be taught to read. He further affirmed that the advantage of a fluent and early nomenclature was very much valuable to children. The firm impressions of names made the things unforgettable. The names were to be presented in an order based upon reality and truth. This would develop in them a consciousness of the real relation of things to each other.

He reduced language to words or names and then he turned them into sounds. He constructed formal exercises for each stage of growth. The exercises began with syllables–much after the manner of the present-day phonic method of teaching reading.

List of names of the most important objects belonging to different divisions of the kingdom of nature—history, geography, human relations which the child required to remember—were to be prepared by the teacher. The child would, then, be asked to form sentences in various ways. Thus,

Pestalozzi's method was based on sounds and not on spellings. It prepared the way for modern methods.

According to *Herbart*, the concept of name or the language aspect of *Pestalozzi* to young children, was a word; a name was not merely the sign of a thing. The word itself was a thing. The children lingered upon the sound of a word.

Contribution to Education

When *Pestalozzi* was forty years old, no one could predict that the future years would bring him great fame. A few years before his death, he was honoured by kings and heads of states, made a citizen of the Freach Republic and was recognized by philosophers and educators for his splendid work in the field of education. Every country in Europe looked to him for some advice, and changes were made in the educational patterns of different European states after seeking advice from him. His main pedagogical achievements were as follows:

(i) For him, the best aim of education could not be other than the betterment of mankind. The ideal provided a sort of much needed inspiration. From humanities, he moved in the direction of democratic education which paved the way to greater educational opportunity for all.

(ii) He advocated that education was to be a scientific study. The prevailing ways of seeking knowledge were condemned by him. Allthough, he was not a scientist, he laid down the basis for a science education. No new knowledge was to be brought to the pupils without connecting it with the already known one. He advised the teachers to proceed always from easy to difficult and from known to unknown. The teacher was to grade the lessons to facilitate teaching and learning.

(iii) The order of learning that he advocated brought out the importance of developmental psychology to teaching techniques and curriculum design. The entire movement towards child-study could largely be traced to *Pestalozzi*.

(iv) His object lesson techniques brought realistic approach to teaching. Not only did it help the child learn easily but also made him retain the knowledge for a longer time.

(v) His whole approach to education made a new kind of teacher absolutely necessary. The teacher needed to be well skilled in the art of teaching. He was also to possess good education. Thus, *Pestalozzi* laid down the foundation of formal teacher training. In fact, his object lesson techniques, though simple to administer, needed trained minds to implement in the classrooms.

(vi) Teaching methods and techniques started getting changed from the time *Rousseau* claimed freedom of *Emile. Pestalozzi, Froebel* and *Monstessori* followed *Rousseau's* line and upheld the child's interests and advocated child-centred education. There could not be a better way of meeting children's interests than offering lessons which provided them with different sorts of sensory exercises and the knowledge of the three R's. In fact, *Pestalozzi's* object-lesson techniques met children's interests in different ways. They drew objects, learnt proportions of objects and gathered satisfaction as they created. The concept of number, which normally developed with great difficulty, was presented before them with the help of concrete objects. This made them understand it easily. Again, the development of vocabulary took place at an early stage and in a sequential way. It brought about growth of language and developed listening and speaking abilities.

(vii) These object lesson techniques have brought tremendous changes in classroom teaching. In the primary schools, children draw, count and develop linguistic abilities. These practices reflect *Pestalozzian* influences—however, indirectly these may have been obtained.

(viii) With the rapid growth of education in India, the need for trained teachers is being felt more potently today. In all the states, provisions through J.B.T. and B.Ed are being enhanced, yet shortage of trained teachers persists and is likely to persist as the base of the educational pyramid is getting broader.

(ix) The curriculum is being constantly and carefully scrutinized and efforts are on the way to make education a scientific study. As a result of this, curriculum at primary and secondary levels is far more graded and pragmatic today than what it used to be in the past.

Conclusion

Pertalozzi's greatest contribution to child-centred education lies in his putting the theory into practice by teaching children himself. It may be said that he took over the functions of teaching from the blind nature and put them in the charge of a sighted teacher.

Summary

Pestalozzi took up the work from where *Rousseau* left but his work was far more practical. His two important books, *Leonard and Gertrude* and *How Gertrude Teaches Her Children,* set forth his main doctrines and educational practices. His important contributions had been in the areas of methodology, child study, motivation and teacher training. *Pestalozzi's* stress that instruction was to proceed from known to unknown and easy to difficult provided experience of actual emotional response of children. These concepts are of great value to the modern educator.

11

Methods of Step by Step Instruction

J.F. Herbart (1776-1841)

J.F. Herbart was a German philosopher and psychologist. He attached a great deal of importance to morality. In this chapter, are identified his aims of education and the methods used to realize the aims. The steps of teaching, he advocated and the development of these steps by his disciples have been examined. Lastly, his influence on educational practices has also been traced.

Background

The first half of the nineteenth century introduced new elements in European thought and practice in education. Whereas in the first half of the nineteenth century, some nations in Europe followed their own line of thought and action, Germany established a national system of education and produced two eminent educationists: *J.F. Herbart* and *F. Froebel*. England articulated her thoughts through the philosophies proposed by people like *Herbert Spencer*. However, France chose to continue with the traditional educational practices.

Life Sketch

Herbart received a good education in classics and philosophy, and later entered the University of Jena at the age of eighteen. There, he got a chance to study *Fitche's* philosophy of idealism. This philosophy did not satisfy him. He took up the tutoring of three children and laid down his theory of education, basing it on the experience of coaching them. Later, he met *Pestalozzi* and was appreciative of his aims and methods. He concluded that *Pestalozzian* ideas applied not only to primary schools but also to education at all levels.

Amongst *Herbart's* works of significance were: *The Application of Psychology to Science of Education, Outlines of Educational Doctrines, The Science of Education,* and *The Book On Psychology*. These titles had been translated from German into English.

Philosophy

Herbart was a realist, but his realism implied that there was a world of real things behind appearance. The nature of the soul was a mystery for him, but he recognized that human beings had some knowledge of the experiences of impressions–mental states–that were made on the soul. Like *John Locke*, he accepted that mind was originally *the Tabula Rasa* (the blank slate). All ideas in the mind were then the product of time and experience.

He considered it the task of a philosopher to strike a balance between specialized and wide knowledge. He, however, appreciated that the skill required to bring about such a balance needed a long personal development and maturity for the philosopher.

Herbart separated psychology from metaphysics and challenged the age-old concept of separate faculties of mind. He advocated more empirical methods to study moral life which earlier had received only speculative treatment. He established relationship between psychology on the one hand and mathematics, medicine and physiology on the other.

Apperception Masses

He thought of mind as "cliques of ideas" (apperception masses), all striving for their appropriate place. According to him, the psychic life consisted of an ebb and flow of "ideas" or "presentation." Human emotions like feelings and willings struggled against other mental happenings to occupy a top place in human consciousness.

He classified ideas into three kinds–similar, contrary, disparate. For example, if one heard a bird sing in the morning and heard the same bird sing in the evening, the song came in the category of a similar idea. However, the song of a bird was different from the baritone. The idea of the song of baritone was contrary to that of the bird. In case of a disparate idea, one could easily conclude that the song of a bird was completely different from a table or a chair. However, the different types of ideas struggled to find their ways into the mind.

Aim of Education

Herbart's aim of education was the development of character, based on sound moral values. Morality, for him, was the foundation as well as the end of education. The implication of his concept of morality was *Aristotlean* or Greek, in that like the Greeks, he also stood for a balance—nothing in excess: balance to be maintained between reason and emotion, between the present and the future, between the demand of God and those of men, between the needs of the individual and those of society. This balance was essential to the production of a good man: that, for him, was the ultimate aim of education. He spelled out five moral ideas. These were: freedom, completeness, good will, right and equity. These ideas constituted morality. "Freedom" meant man's privilege about what was to be done. "Completeness" stood for a type of instruction that was to turn out a broad man, as well as a balanced person. "Good will" was to operate in man's relations with his fellow beings. With respect to "right", men were to respect the rights of others and their property. "Equity" means the rewarding of good behaviour. It was the assimilation of these five moral ideas and the making of these as the part of the value system that contributed towards the production of a good man.

Role of Teachers

In the above five moral ideas, *Herbart* expected teachers to be chiefly concerned with "completeness" or "perfection". But in order to ensure perfection, the teachers were to develop broad interests in the children. He believed that a person with broad interests was most likely to be of good character and noble actions. It was the duty of the teacher to create in the mind of the learner interest for the good life.

He expected the institutions of education to contribute towards the wider interest. He, however, emphasized the point that since interest was related to institution, the teacher had a special responsibility to develop interest. He considered education a life-long and life-like process but instruction was considered a part of education. He cautioned teachers against overdoing their work with respect to character building of the pupils. The overdoing was likely to have crippling effect on the pupils' individuality. In order to help the learner in the formation of character, teachers were to get the learners to accept transcendent values. The criteria for moral values would then be the child's own and not imposed on him by the teachers. To make sure that morality did not remain a myth, he formulated scientific procedures for teachers to measure reasonably well whether they were contributing towards the formation of the child's character.

Methodology

Herbart's methodology was based on psychology, mainly experimental psychology. One of the basic ideas in this psychology was interest. According to him, ideas contended for place in the mind. The contest was a struggle on the part of various interests or experiences. They commanded the attention of the learner.

The recent experiences rose more quickly into consciousness and persisted longer than the older experiences. If the teacher wanted to utilize certain ideas that the child possessed, or build on certain experiences that were part of the child's background, he was to help these ideas and experiences to appear in the child's consciousness. The teacher was to assist the ideas in their struggle for supremacy over the other ideas of the child.

Learners' Interests

The interests of the child were put into a certain frame of reference and certain ideas or habits of action were derived from them. When the child underwent new experiences, these would be fitted into the background of the past experiences and became part of the performed frame of reference. It was the manipulation of interests that was an important part of the educative process. However, as said earlier in this chapter, broad interests were to be measured at an optimum level. Thus, the method was to control the intensity of interest: neither too little, nor too much, but always broad.

In theory, his interests revolved around life itself. But he knew that such broad approach would not help teachers. He, therefore, classified interests into two categories—interests that had to do with the physical world in which the child lived and interests that arose from the social world of the child. He further classified the child's interests into knowledge interests and ethical interests. The knowledge interests dealt with information about the natural and social worlds. The information was interpreted on normative level and attempts were made to identify aesthetic values in it. Ethical information concerned man, society and God.

The Curriculum

Herbart divided the curriculum into two main groups: the historical and the scientific. He considered the historical more important for its humanistic value. Humanities gave the learner sympathy and the sciences provided empirical knowledge. Although he recognized the importance of various fields of knowledge, he also stressed that integration of curriculum was essential to bringing about the desired outcomes that were required of a truly moral man.

The *Herbartian* teacher was expected to relate the new lesson to what the child already knew to help him to retain what had been taught, and to seek to maintain a high level of interest in the learner. Thus, teaching and learning became dynamic processes involving description, analysis and synthesis. Whatever method a teacher employed, it was to be directed at the achievement of good instruction. To aim at such a goal, the teacher was to find the learner's level of maturity and level of experience; otherwise schooling could stand in the way of the learner's growth and development. After the general description of the process of education, are considered his famous steps of instruction.

Steps of Instruction

In his *Science of Education*, *Herbart* used his theories of consciousness, interest, and the laws of association for setting four steps or stages of instruction. These stages were: (i) clearness, (ii) association, (iii) system and (iv) method.

(i) "Clearness" meant that the learner was to see the issue clearly so that he could assimilate new subject.

(ii) The second step of "association" came with the connection of the new ideas to notations already contained in the mind of the pupil.

(iii) The third step "system" was reached through emphasis on clear distinction of the different elements to which the newly associated idea consisted. Additionally, the new idea was to be related to the context and purpose of the lesson.

(iv) The last stage "method" was reached when the student was capable of adding new aspects to the issue in view, and was able to apply his newly acquired knowledge properly to future problems.

However, he did not conceive of the four steps as rigid stages: The steps often overlapped and also depended on different situations in teaching and learning.

His disciples extended his four steps into five and implemented them so fervently as if they were to be the sole answers to the methods of teaching. The five steps were formulated as follows:

(*i*) ***Preparation:*** In this step, an environment was created externally as well as internaly to develop ideas. The subconscious mind was explored to recall ideas, and attention was cultivated.

(*ii*) ***Presentation:*** The lesson was presented to the learners with a lot of suitable illustrations. The lesson was made as concrete as possible.

(*iii*) ***Association:*** This step was important in that in it similarities and differences between old and new ideas were emphasized. The aim was to develop order and consistency in thinking.

(*iv*) ***Generalisation:*** In this step, simplification of facts was done so that their wider meanings were fully understood.

(*v*) ***Application:*** It was recognized that knowledge was for use and was, thus, to become part of human life.

Relevance

We find that *Herbart* made educational psychology an important study. In India, educational psychology is taught in all teacher-training institutions. Furthermore, in most countries, for example in India, even at the J.B.T. level, the elements of psychology are covered. At the B.Ed level, a broader study is made of educational psychology and teaching methods. At the university level, broad as well as deep studies are made and research is undertaken in psychology.

The *Herbartian* steps are, with slight modifications, still used in lesson planning. Even if there is no obvious mention of steps, the spirit behind them—the spirit of systematic teaching—is implicit in lessons, planned by teachers, particularly by teachers in training. Professionally, committed teachers in general all over India try to maximize the learning of pupils through systematic teaching.

The study of sciences and humanities advocated by *Herbart* is very pertinent to Indian education of the future because India wants to develop industrially and at the same time protect itself from the de-humanizing influences of science and technology. General education, sciences, arts, crafts and humanities are being emphasized as important components of new Indian education.

Herbart's aim of education was to turn out a moral man. The Hindu, the Islamic, The Christian institutions and the various governments in India have always made cultivation of moral values as their important concern.

Conclusion

Teachers in training all over the world owe a lot of gratitude to *Herbart* to enable them to teach student-teachers in a methodical manner all the subjects in the domains of arts, sciences, humanities, social sciences and craft.

Summary

During the first half of the nineteenth century in Europe, the systems of education stated taking nationalistic shapes and new thinkers emerged on the educational scene. One of such thinkers was the German philosopher and psychologist, *Herbart*. He said that ideas—similar, contrary, disparate—struggled to find their way into the mind. His aim of education was to produce a moral man who was educated broadly in sciences and humanities. He outlined four steps of teaching which were developed further by his disciples into five steps. The steps emphasized systematic ways of teaching. His views on the importance of educational psychology, broad-based curriculum and morality are still relevant to education in India and other countries.

12

The Pedagogies of Kindergarten: Education of the Total Individual and Society

Fredrich Froebel (1782-1852)

Fredrich Froebel, a German educator, philosopher and scientist was the architect of kindergarten education. His lonely, early childhood experiences coupled with the great love, he had for children, and his deep religious feelings were instrumental in shaping his positive image about children, man in society and the universe in relation to God. He strongly believed in self-discipline, cooperation, creativity, freedom and love. He advocated for the teacher to epitomize those desirable virtues–wisdom, love, warmth, understanding and toierance—which he wanted to inculcate in his students. He was one of the first educational philosophers to introduce the science of psychology in education. His lasting influence has considerably changed and will continue to change and improve contents and practices of education throughout the world.

Life Sketch

Although *Froebel* studied at the University of Jena, and later at Gottingen and Berlin, his early life was one of the most important factors in the evolution of his ideas. His mother died when he was a baby, and he spent a rather lonely childhood, learning what he could from nature, experience and his own personal inclinations.

Throughout his life, *Froebel* continued his self-education. Being a scientist by natural inclination, he embarked on the study of the sciences which had then made rapid strides. Not only was he interested in physics, chemistry, and geology, but also philosophy as well as mathematics engaged his mind. One of the remarkable things about him was that he made sure that he answered his own questions to his utmost satisfactions.

Background

During the period of intellectual ferment that led to and culminated in the nineteenth century revolution, one of the great educational innovations was the introduction of formal education for small children of three or four years of age. This institution was *kindergarten*—a child's garden—taken directly from German and now widely used in English and French-speaking, and other countries.

Kindergarten

A student of *Pestalozzi, Froebel* conceived the idea of the Kindergarten and opened the first school of this type in 1837 in Blankenbury. His educational philosophy, naturally, fell in line with that held by his teacher in Switzerland as well as those held by his predecessors, *Schelling, Comenius* and *Rousseau*. He believed in the natural development of children. Teachers from all over the world attended *Froebel's* school for kindergarten to learn first-hand for themselves this new concept. As a result of this fervour, there was a rapid growth in the establishment of kindergarten schools throughout the world. This was generally attributed to the zeal of the graduates of *Froebel's* school, and to the interest and confidence that he had in his work.

Women's Role

For the first time in the history of educational experiment, women were found playing major roles in the propagation of ideas and in the pioneering of founding schools. This was natural, since women played a greater role in the bringing up and rearing of children. The women of the world owed a great debt to this educational innovator for emancipating them to play their natural, yet not encouraged, roles. Ever since the time of *Froebel*, women have continued to play dominant roles in education of the young. Thus, for instance, in Saxony a "Women's Kindergarten Union" was formed in 1840. In London, *Bertha Rouge*, set up a Kindergarden. *Madame Michaelis* did excellent pioneering work in setting up Kindergarten schools and training teachers for these schools in Croydon and Noting Hill in England. Kindergartens were opened in Manchester by *Adele von Portaugall* and *Bleanore Heerawart. The Baroness Von Marenholts Billow* did excellent propaganda work in Germany, England, France, Italy, and the Netherlands. In America, a *Froebelian* school was opened in 1838 by *Garoline Frankenberg*. A student of *Froebel, W.T. Harris* adopted the kindergarten as part of the educational system of *St. Lous, Missouri* in 1873. *John Dewey* incorporated *Froebelian* principles in the conduct of his University Elementary School.

Influence of Pestalozzi

Froebel lived at a time when Germany was leading the world in philosophical thought. He was naturally gifted as a scholar and as a scientist. As a result of this, his own educational theory was uniquely developed from a combination of observational methods learned from *Pestalozzi* and a study of the ideas of other educators and philosophers. His educational capacities were stirred when he was a teacher of drawing at Frankfurt from 1807 to 1810. There, he tutored three boys. In his autobiography, he summarized the results of that experience with his pupils as a great inspiration to go on experimenting and perfecting a method. He added that the powerful, indefinable stirring and uplifting effect produced by *Pestalozzi* set one's soul on fire for a higher, nobler life.

Views on Philosophy and Education

In developing his philosophy about the world and education, *Froebel* was most likely inspired by his own personal experiences as a child, coupled with a deep love, he had for children. He felt that children frequently lacked security, guidance and love in the home. Thus, education was to start as soon as possible in order to develop warmth and understanding between parents and children. He was opposed to war and regarded it as an enemy of the people, of human culture and education. "How could man progress", he asked, "when he was constantly threatened by destruction?" "How could creativity develop when society emphasized violence? How could family life be strengthened when war killed the best members of society? How could people co-operate and work together for a commonwealth of good if they were at constant war with each other?" These were questions that bothered *Froebel*, as they still bother us today. How can man find happiness in the midst of so many conflicting contrasts? He attempted to find solutions to some of these questions through education, which he suggested was to begin as early in life as possible so as to allow no room for indoctrination or bigotry in the ignorant, innocent, young minds of children.

(i) Religion, God and Man: *Froebel's* educational ideals rested firmly upon a deep faith in religion. He believed that spiritual ideals could not be defined: they could only be experienced. To him, God, as the Absolute Power, included all parts of nature. Man was part of God, and God was part of man. Man was expected to realize that he did not live for himself alone. He also lived for, and with God and his fellow human beings and all other things in the universe. Nothing in this universe, according to him, was without significance. He maintained that God was not a static force, but a living movement that revealed Him in the universe which had achieved a high level of progress. Following the evolutionary theory of the universe, therefore, man like-wise had moved from primitivism to maturity and the attainment of self-consciousness. He was beginning to realize that he was not powerless on the face of this earth. The wind, rain, snow, sun and the other natural elements no longer threatened him, for he could now somehow, sometimes, predict or control them.

(ii) Equilibrium with God: The all-pervading, energetic, living, self-conscious, and eternal and divine unity of God was always present as the law that governed all things: man with God was, therefore, perfectable through a system of proper education. Such education consisted primarily of leading one as a thinking, intelligent being–growing into self-consciousness, to a pure and unsullied, conscious and free representation of the inner law of divine unity with God. Once this inner unity was unfolded through the proper education, *Froebel* maintained that man's consciousness of himself would be fully and freely revealed, and he would attain equilibrium with God, with himself, as well as with his fellow-beings: then he became free and happy. Education was to lead man to knowledge of himself, of mankind, of God and of nature.

(iii) Unity in Diversity: The doctrine of unity in diversity through the maintenance of equilibrium was, perhaps, the most satisfying concept to *Froebel* because it enabled him to reconcile the old, body-mind, physical-spiritual dualism. It also enabled him to accommodate the revelations and discoveries of the new sciences of the physical world. Once this biological analogy with God as the Original Organism–creating an entire changing universe in which man and all else contained in it were part of God Himself–was fully comprehended, the rest of the analogy became straightforward and easy to understand.

(a) Importance of an Individual: Each person as a small, essential, integral entity, contributed to God's purpose insofar as he performed his part very well and fully as a smoothly functioning, balanced unity in cooperation with, and for the benefit of the whole. He saw the world as a machine, which operated in a well organized system. In this case, a missing link, or a malfunctioning part would impair or stop the whole operation. It followed, therefore, that the importance of cooperative effort could not be over stressed. If the strength and variety of mobilized powers of individuals and groups were increased and harmonized in operation, the contribution of the individual to the progress of humanity would be proportionally increased.

(b) Education of Total Individual: According to this functional unity of man's powers and possibilities, the exercise of physical and mental capacities and aptitudes was to be combined in education in order to achieve maximum harmony and freedom in the full realization of human potentialities. Since the individual was the integral part of a unique whole which was God, it, therefore, followed that man himself was also unique. If this was so, we were to educate not merely the mind or body of the child, but the total individual. A one-sided education of the mind or the body was not only incomplete, but might also be harmful to the total productive development of the individual. Furthermore, it conflicted with the idea of harmony within the organism *vis-à-vis* the rest of society and the Divine whole. According this doctrine, it was no longer enough for the human body-mind to be merely a vehicle for the transmission of past ideas, values, and traditions into the future. The basic, historical elements which were worthy of preservation had, of course, to be transmitted through education. But, the past could no longer be allowed to determine the future. It could only influence the trend of human development, because

the future was uncertain and was evolving: perhaps, much faster than man could understand or predict.

(iv) Individual Integration and Social Cohesion: Froebel was very much concerned with the welfare of the individual as he was with that of the group. According to his explanation of individual integration and the social cohesion of human groups, any individual or unity which separated itself from its large unity lost its function and disintegrated into nothingness. In a letter of 1834, he wrote that no community could progress in its development while the individual who was a member of it remained behind. By the same token, the individual who was a member of the whole body could not progress in his development while the community, of which he was a unique part, remained behind. To him, the total development of the individual was as important as societal development, and the two were closely and intricately linked together through group experiences and inter-personal relationships.

According to his biological principle of universal law of creative force or evolution, every unity (physical or mental), whether animal, vegetable, or mineral, had a drive to develop along the levels, fitted to its characteristic lines. Changes through evolution were unknown and unending. Types and species might be the same, but there were individual differences in dexterity due to the environment or divergence of training. All aspects of human life were subject to the same law of development, even though the rate and nature of their development might differ drastically.

The highest and most complex product of this evolutionary process was man who had come to an understanding of his own limitless potentialities. It behoved him, therefore, to devote his superior powers to the deliberate, rational and scientific fostering of the process of civilization.

Basic Principles of Education

***(i) Reconciliation of Contrasts*:** One of the principles was the law of human growth and education, required for the *reconciliation of contrasts*. Man was an active organism that engaged in contrasting or opposing activities–on the one hand were individual interests and resultant activities, and on the other hand were activities with others. Education was, therefore, to prepare one to achieve harmony with these activities. An educated person was happy with himself and with his fellow human beings. The methods by which this could be achieved were learning through cooperative work and play, living together and engaging in individual and group activities, being in contact with nature and the environment and engaging in self-government and discipline.

***(ii) Creative Self Expression*:** The two most important aspects of man were freedom and creativity. Freedom implied the ability to make choices and to avoid evil which was a distortion, or negation of goodness.

Since man was naturally creative, education was to encourage and provide opportunities for him to express this basic, natural talent. The creative self-expression of the child was to be encouraged so as to develop greater life adjustment, and, thus, generate greater contribution to the world. Children needed plenty of constructional material and manipulative, concrete objects to make the lessons more practical, more meaningful and more appealing to their inquisitive minds. Young played with *Froebel's* "gifts", apparatus—solid shapes in the forms of spheres, cubes, cylinders, triangles, sticks etc., and also dancing, singing number games, drawing, and games involving speech were recommended. For older children, the scheme offered such activities as nature study, gardening, building boats, and other useful objects, and group exploration.

(iii) No Evil Nature: Contrary to the views expressed by earlier educational philosophers, *Froebel* believed that the child was not evil by nature. His waywardness was usually due to a lack of vision or misguided values. He was to be taught in such a way that the eternal spark in him would become a living reality. To accomplish this, the teacher was expected to be resourceful, knowledgeable, enthusiastic and optimistic about the child and about the subject mater at all times.

(iv) Developmental Processes: He advocated that education was most effective when it was based on the needs of children. This meant that as nature unfolded in children, potentialities began to appear, they were to be guided and nurtured. It is significant to note here that this nature-nurture axiom in education was also held by such famous teachers as *Socrates, Jesus Christ* and *Gandhi.* Here, *Froebel* skillfully and religiously combined idealism and realism into practical humanism. For all practical purposes, children were not to be forced to learn anything; rather, they were to be guided to see the significance of that learning according to their needs and levels of maturity. A teacher was to attempt to see things from the child's viewpoint, and to organize the learning accordingly. This meant that a teacher was to be "childlike" and not "childish" in his/her teaching behaviour. No doubt, the art of teaching required a thorough knowledge of human development and the psychology of learning.

(v) Moral Values: According to him, moral education and cooperation were to be enforced and strengthened in young children through healthy patterns of socialization in a wholesome environment. Play activities were to be encouraged, not merely because children naturally liked to play, or to exercise the muscles, but also more so to afford them the opportunities to reveal their inner-selves. He was one of the greatest exponents of the fundamental use of play in education, but he envisaged that the activities were to be both guided and progressive. The teacher was to use the play way method to combine work and play into organized, guided, free, productive and continuous development of the child.

(vi) Cultivation of Senses: He believed that to be truly educated, one was to cultivate one's senses, especially hearing and vision. Too many people were indifferent because they were never aware of the beauties around them, and because they did not play creatively and fairly.

(vii) Awareness: Highlighting the importance of awareness, he said that the sum total of education was the cultivation of awareness. The teacher was expected to guide his pupils with patience and affection to become fully aware of themselves–their possibilities, potentialities and weaknesses. The student was to be allowed to discover things for himself, when possible. The teacher was to encourage the child to ask questions, and also guide him to discover things for him because the answers, he found out by his own efforts, had more lasting value and significance to the child than what he heard from others.

(viii) Parents as Teachers: He emphasized the importance of parents as the first teachers of their children. Parents were expected to play a vital role in the education of children, especially during the formative years–from ages one to twelve. They were to care, love, encourage, instruct, construct, play, and work with their children so as to develop in them creative patterns in their mature years. The home and the school were to be linked together through family education. He described those teacher–parents as well as teachers to be the best who taught by examples, communication and love.

(ix) Role of Experience: Since experiences, for *Froebel*, were the best teacher, the curriculum was to develop the foundations of clear perception. Facts were secondary and memorization was to be avoided. We were stirred only when we directly experienced the greatness of life and the universe. One of his contributions lay in his firm belief that education was to fit the individual for full life within the group through emphasis on practical activities. He advocated the view that knowledge was to be useful and related, not absolute and in isolation with real-life experiences. He firmly believed that development of creativity came from within. Therefore, for knowledge to be meaningful and productive, it was to be internalized through practical experience or application.

Influence on Education

The influence of *Froebel* on education in the world has been significant, and will become increasingly so in the future. Many of his principles of education such as learning by doing, the play-way method, child-centred education and parental interest and their involvement in education have long been incorporated into primary school curriculum, although their importance and stress seem to vary. The "creative, self expression", as opposed to memorization of facts, is something that the educational systems have to learn to emphasis as they embark on massive educational programmes for self-sufficiency.

It is unfortunate that many Indians nowadays are merely going to school just for the theoretical information to enable them acquire diplomas and degrees without much regard for creativity, originality, or any useful, practical application of their knowledge; nor are they aware of their social obligations and responsibilities to themselves and to their society. This deplorable trend must be reversed if India were to benefit from its investment in education.

Conclusion

The concept of early childhood or kindergarten education which *Froebel* started some two hundred and fifty years ago is now beginning to be recognized seriously by governments as the countries move slowly toward industrialization. Many mothers, even in the rural areas, are finding it necessary to send their children to school at an earlier age so that they could go and find employment in the stores, construction industries, or in the markets as independent traders. As school enrolment is bound to increase rapidly, more teachers, trained in infant methods, will be needed to care properly for the needs of children.

Summary

There are two types of idealism in the history of education. One type stresses the importance of authority and tradition. It indicates present educational practices for its specialization and scientific contents and liberal approaches. The traditional idealists today want a return to the "Three R's" in elementary education. They believe in a teacher-centred form of education, because they think that the student needs guidance and firmness, especially during adolescent years. The other type of idealism, championed by *Froebel*, advocated a moral representation of education, and the constructive way of life. The dignity and interests of the student were to be safeguarded. No religious or racial prejudices were to be tolerated. The essence of this philosophy was universalism, for it stressed that both education and religion transcended intellectual analysis. Central to this philosophy was the rule of love, and the teacher was to be an example of wisdom, love, warmth, understanding and tolerance. It has been aptly said of *Froebel* that all the best tendencies of modern thought of education culminated in what was said and done by him.

13

Education in Freedom

Maria Montessori (1870-1952)

Progressive, scientific and democratic trends of the twentieth century were represented by some educators who led revolts in educational theory and practice of the past. *Montessori* was one of them and her revolt concerned the liberation of learners and teachers from the old pedagogy which could not justify its continuity. This chapter analyses her principles and methods and traces her influence on education.

Background

The large educational movement of the nineteenth century Europe had some distinctive characteristics which were nationalism, democracy and anticlericalism. National systems of education gradually emerged out of these characteristics. The national systems of education were open to all and provided opportunities for various types of individuals who came to school. With the advent of the new system, the administration of schools was switched over to the people who never were earlier solely responsible for the administration of the school affairs.

As a result of the influence of these characteristics, the educational thought and practice were greatly affected. Outstanding educational leaders and teachers like *Herbart, Froebel* and *Montessori* started translating the democratic principles into the practical school programmes. With the help of these educators, the democratic tendencies began to grow rapidly in the national school systems of Europe.

Many states in Europe began to see the relationship between education and national life and national goals. This was the time when a great need for national education system was also felt in Rome. *Montessori's* role in bringing up a standard national education system at pre-primary and primary school levels in Rome became conspicuous by virtue of the merits of her methods.

Life-sketch

Montessori was born at Chiaravalle, near Ancona in Italy on the 31st August, in 1870. After graduating in medicine from the University of Rome in 1894, the first woman in Italy to do so, she was appointed assistant doctor at the psychiatric clinic of the University of Rome. There, she became interested in the educational problems of mentally-retarded children, and began to teach them. They were taught so efficiently and remarkably that not only did they read and write well but also were able to be presented for examination with normal children of the same age group. The success, they achieved, was attributed to the fact that they had been taught by an improved method.

Between 1896 and 1906, she held a chair in hygiene at a women's college in Rome. At the same time from 1900 to 1907, she lectured in pedagogy at the University of Rome. She was interested in children and continued to pursue the studies in the field of psychology and education.

During 1906-07, she opened the first *Case Dei Bambini* (Children's House), a school for young children in a slum district of Rome. She wanted to apply her method then to the normal children. She got overwhelming success with her new school. It led to the opening of other *Montessori* schools.

So, by the end of 1906, the Director General of Roman Association of Good Building handed over to her the entire organisaiton of the infant schools in the model tenements in Rome. For the next forty years, she travelled very widely and went to Europe, India and the United States. But before she travelled to Europe and other countries of the world, she was very well known in Italy as a woman of great talent, having abundance of knowledge in the art of teaching infants and feeble-minded children. It is, however, worth recording that her concepts of "freedom" for the child was feared by dictators like *Mussolini* in Italy and *Hitler* in Germany, and in both countries, the *Montessorian* schools were discouraged.

Before *Montessori,* two educationists, the *Revs May* and *Seguin,* had contemplated to educate mentally defective children and tried to search for a universal formula which could be applicable to such children in all times. But *Montessori* had a definite success in this direction. She thought that the method, she had discovered, could obviously be applied to children who were at a mental level corresponding somewhat to the stage of development of deficients. Her methods were to be employed in the training of normal infants.

She understood the basic fact that the child under school age generally received a kind of education which, though unsystematic in character, was not completely inconsiderable in amount. But, if such early education was consciously planned and controlled, the results were bound to be remarkable.

The method adopted by her was determined by her training and previous experience. But before discussing her method, let us examine her main principles, she applied in the training of defective children.

Principles: Normal Expansion of Life

One of the principles was that the pupil was to be trained so that he became independent of others regarding the ordinary practices of life. It was an approach to the child's mind at a lower level. It was an appeal to his senses rather than his intellect. This idea was very useful to the physically defective children as it implied training one sense to function more effectively for another. For example: the deaf children would train their feeling sense more by feeling the vibrations of the larynx of the speaker. Thus, predominance was given to the sense of touch to replace the weakness of the sense of hearing.

Another principle was that the educative process was re-formed to suit the stage of mental development of the child. It was adopted to match his interest and was not completely subordinate to the needs of a curriculum. For *Montessori*, education was that experience which helped the normal expansion of life of the child. Therefore, according to her method, it was necessary to present before the child those exercises which corresponded to the need for development, felt by an organism. But if the child's age had carried him past the stage, it would not be possible to achieve in its fullness the development which had missed the proper time. If the child failed to complete the task, the teacher was neither to make him conscious of his error nor to make him repeat the experience. Rather, he was to assume that the task had been offered prematurely and the 'psychological moment' in that particular educative process had not yet come. Then, the teacher was to wait for the symptoms which reflected that the need existed to undertake the task.

Yet, another principle was that there were no prizes in *Montessori* system. The pupils's sense of mastery of a task or exercise was his highest reward. His own development was the only pleasure, he wanted to achieve. In the children's house was presented didactic material, which would make auto-education possible. The children imposed on themselves self-discipline by engaging in the tasks, they liked to perform.

Freedom

Montessori believed in providing perfect freedom to the child. It was a kind of freedom which was in tune with the development of his nature. This freedom or liberty necessitated independence of action. There were forty little beings from ages three to seven in the class. Each one was interested in doing the task of his choice. One liked to do an exercise for the senses; another was helping himself to handle the letters; the third was drawing; and there was the fourth one who was doing an arithmetical exercise. All were busy with a task of their own choice. The environment of the class was so planned that each child was directed by his own self to do an activity, he was interested in. As a result, the most effective kind of discipline was imposed on them by themselves. Such an environment not only provided simple exercises with liberty, but also it made available a means to auto-education which developed within the child the right sort of 'active life'.

Montessori-Method

Montessori practice of the method fell into three classes:

(i) The exercises of practical life,

(ii) The sensory exercises,

(iii) The didactic exercises.

***(i) The Exercises of Practical Life*:** In the 'House of Childhood,' the feeble-minded children were taught to take care of themselves. It was a kind of training in being independent of others. The children learnt how to use little washstand to wash their hands, how to clean their nails, brush their teeth, comb their hair and so on. They learnt the movements about how to dress and undress themselves. All the furniture in the House of Childhood–tables, chairs, etc.—were of such sizes and construction that the pupils could handle them easily. They learnt to move them deftly and without noise. Such movements afforded training in motor adjustment. There were no fixed desks which hampered the movement of children.

She planned certain formal gymnastic exercises in helping the child develop coordinated movements. After observing the spontaneous movements of children, a new set of exercises was devised by her. For example: a wooden spiral stairway, meant to enable children to ascend the stairs, taught them the self-controlled movements. The general outcome of these exercises was to develop in the children a kind of distinguishing grace in their physical bodies.

***(ii) The Sensory Exercises*:** With the help of the experimental psychologists, she drew along scheme of sensory training. She used the experiments on the feebleminded as well as the normal children and found that the results were remarkably welcoming. The normal children liked to repeat exercises for the sake of pleasure, while the deficient children got satisfaction by accomplishing them once. The normal children corrected their own mistakes but the feeble-minded ones were corrected when required.

In providing sensory training, she believed in isolating the senses. For example: blind pupils could be helped to acquire a very fine discriminative ability in the sphere of touch and the deaf ones could know things by developing their sense of observation. A *Montessori* class which provided training in the senses was a kind of psychological laboratory, consisting of a variety of devices to produce different effects.

For perfection of size, a series of wooden cylinders with varying dimensions were provided. For perception of form, geometrical insets in metal or in wood were presented. In order to know the difference in weight, many wooden articles, similar in size but differing in weight, were provided. To develop the sense of touch, a polished surface and a sandpaper surface were given to the children to feel and touch. For the development of colour-sense, a series of coloured wools was presented before them.

In order to reinforce the training in perception of form, the children were required to place wooden shapes into spaces. Geometrical insets of various designs were also provided to fit them into the frames which were made to receive them. Thus, by fitting the insets into the shapes, the children employed not only the visual senses but also the tactual and muscular senses. Through such training, they gradually came to know the forms of various figures, triangles, rectangles etc.

***(iii) The Didactic Exercises*:** These exercises involved the process of writing, reading and number. In the *Montessori* system of didactic exercises, the teaching of writing preceded the teaching of reading. Considering that in normal children the muscular sense was most easily developed in early childhood, she introduced writing first. Reading was a mental task, whereas in writing the child translated sounds into material signs by performing certain movements which were easier.

According to her, writing was not simply copying the words: it was significant writing as it expressed ideas. Before the children started writing, they had acquired sufficient ideas of the forms of letters, cut out in sandpaper and pasted on cards. So, almost by the age of four, they could write and become good in writing in about three months.

When the children had learnt how to write, they were directed to learn reading. Some preparatory exercises to writing, like word-building with sandpaper, were included for pre-reading exercises. She thought that reading demanded inverse process as there was reproduction of the sounds from the symbols and sounds into words. The syllables were properly pronounced and that came only with recognition of the meaning. To her, reading implied the interpretation of an idea from the written signs. The lesson in reading consisted of slips of paper or cards upon which were written clearly the names of objects which were known or which were present before the child. He read them out slowly from the card. His speed of reading was gradually controlled by the teacher until he could read quite fluently. Normal children, trained to read according to *Montessori's* method, could read very well at the age of five.

Her treatment of teaching of number was not accepted with the same zeal as her writing and reading methods had been. It is a common knowledge that the real concept of number starts with the knowledge of counting. Her procedure was based on a comparison of lengths. Various rods, varying in lengths, were provided to the children to know the difference in their lengths. Gradually, with the help of those rods, which were of different colours as well, they also learnt counting and subtraction.

Influence on Education

Montessori's influence on education has been accepted widely. Some of the important elements of her system have opened new dimensions to the modern educators. For example: her method of training in perception of various sorts of forms involved extensive use of motor imagery, and prepared the way for the teaching of writing and other didactic exercises.

The practical exercises which provided sensory training are of direct value as they enable the children to meet the social situations which they encounter everyday. The idea that extensive training of one sense to compensate for the weak sense involved the doctrine of transfer of training has been confirmed by psychologists. Her method necessitated the need of a teacher who possessed training in child psychology and who was capable of applying it to young children. She felt that the broader and richer were the teacher's experiences in the field of experimental psychology, the sooner he would be able to unfold children's real life and interest. The right kind of training to the teacher was revealed to him when he was to intervene in the child's activities and when he was to refrain from intervening. The teacher in *Montessori* system was known as a director or a directoress who was known for his capabilities of directing the activities and who had faith in providing adequate and full freedom to the children. The teacher in her system was, for a greater part, a silent observer and possessed humility. Child-centred education is being appreciated in many countries and the teacher is more of a guide than a little tin-god as in the past.

Her introduction of special devices for sensory training at an early stage is of great significance. Besides introducing these devices, the role of a teacher became more important because of the stress, laid on the training of the individual child.

Influence on India

A close observation of the pre-primary and primary schools in India would reveal that *Montessori* has influenced the classroom and the teacher's role to a great extent. There are pre-primary schools giving *Montessori*-advocated sensory and physical exercises to the children. They greatly enjoy themselves of such activities and exercises. Besides these exercises, 'play' is being recognized as one of the important elements in the child's physical and mental growth. Her didactic exercises, mainly for the training of writing and reading, are prevalent in primary schools today also. Children seem to have been taking interest in such exercises.

For the physical and psychic growth of the child, the professional training of the teacher is being recognised as one of the important aspects of Indian educational programmes. The teacher is provided ample training and knowledge in the field of child psychology, which helps him/her to know the child more thoroughly.

The freedom of the child, though still questioned in many quarters, is gradually being recognized as one of the most important elements in child education. The child is being treated with more compassion and care today than he was treated in the past.

Conclusion

Montessori or Montessori-type schools are found all over the world. Had there been no merit in such schools, these would have petered out because these are expensive to run and require specially trained teachers—both reasons being a reality. The supporters of inclusive education may like to learn from her methods of teaching.

Summary

Montessori was an Italian educator who, after graduating in medicine, dedicated her life to educate the feeble-minded and, later, also the normal children in Italy.

Her method of providing sensory and physical training was of great utility, for it provided motor movements, physical grace and mental maturity.

By her new methods, she has greatly influenced education throughout the world. Her methods contained her devices for sensory training. Her system needed a highly skillful teacher who could provide proper freedom to the pupils in the classroom.

14

Eclectic Tendencies: Instrumentalism and Experimentalism

John Dewey (1859-1952)

In this chapter is discussed the background to education during the twentieth century as many previous movements and tendencies had coveraged on this century to give an eclectic tinge to education. *John Dewey* can be considered as one of the representatives of eclecticism. His major thoughts concerning democracy and education, and instrumentalism and experimentalism have been evaluated and the relevance of his ideas has been identified.

Background

The psychological, sociological and scientific tendencies in education from the past centuries manifested themselves in the twentieth century. A good deal of borrowing took place, but it was not the blind following of the past: it was the intelligent sifting of useful ideas and putting them alongwith new ideas into practice to test their usefulness. Such an eclectic tendency in the twentieth century influenced educators like *Dewey* also. Additionally, something unique was taking place in the democratic institutions of the USA, which further stimulated him to try new ideas in education.

The beginning of the twentieth century witnessed a rich school system in the USA, founded on democratic patterns: both the private and state-owned schools started getting equal popularity. The parents had more confidence as they had more contact with school, and, in turn, schools too gained more parental confidence.

As the educational opportunities were extended to children of all the people without regard to race, creed or colour, there spread a wave for providing equal opportunity for black Americans too. The schools were expected to provide black children with quality learning with no prejudice and racial intolerance.

The school's function, besides intellectual upliftment, was also to bring social solidarity, which could be achieved by providing equal educational opportunities to all children. Such innovations brought about many changes in the American school system, which, by the beginning of the twentieth century, had been moulded into a definite shape. There started an integrated system of schools: it began with primary school and ended with university. Education in America became a big business. The doors of schools were opened for all. Public education witnessed rapid growth. That gave birth to the American teaching tradition, which so far had been influenced by European teaching traditions. The Americans who had studied under the influence of the best pedagogical minds of Europe were now in a position to prepare a generation of American educators. The Americans who were reckoned as leaders in American teaching traditions were *Francis W. Parker* and *Dewey*. If *Parker* was known as the founder of the American educational tradition, *Dewey* was known as one who gave stature to teaching tradition.

Life-Sketch

Dewey was born in Burlington, Vermont in 1859. He completed his early education in public school in Burlington and later on entered the University of Vermont. After his graduation, he became a school teacher. He remained the school master of a county school for about two years. During these years as a school master, his interest in various directions was stimulated greatly and he came back to the University of Vermont to take up higher philosophy. After staying for almost a year at Vermont, he took admission at Johns Hopkins University in Baltimore to pursue graduate courses in philosophy.

When he completed his studies at Johns Hopkins, he took his Ph.D and started teaching at the University of Michigan. From Michigan, he went to the University of Chicago. Later on, he joined Columbia University.

Dewey's academic area was philosophy, but he was more interested in education. When he was at Chicago, he had organized a school called the Laboratory School of the University of Chicago. It was an experimental school—a place where he could outlay his philosophical ideas. Experimenting with children was then thought to be a radical departure from orthodox procedures. Therefore, this new idea caused a great excitement. He led an educational revolution from this school.

Dewey was a prolific and seasoned writer. Even after his retirement, he produced a series of books which showed the extraordinary breath and depth of his interests and capacities. Among his most popular works were: *Art and Education, Creative Intelligence, How We Think, My Pedagogical Creed, The Schools and Society, Experience and Education, The Child and the Curriculum, Democracy and Education, Schools of Tomorrow, Logic and the Theory of Inquiry, From Absolutism to Experimentalism, Reconstruction in Philosophy, Human Nature and Conduct, Experience and Nature, The Quest for Certainty, Individualism, Philosophy and*

*Civilization, The Public and Its Problems, Characters and Events.*A few of these works are discussed below as these pertain to education.

Democracy and Education

Working in the Laboratory School at Chicago, *Dewey* revealed the experimental bent of his thought which continued until his death in 1952. In one of his greatest books, *Democracy and Education*, he drew a different line of philosophical thought and proposed to embark upon the task of developing a better generation. With this idea, he wished to bring to the threshold of the school many new things. He demanded that even the sciences were not to be based on book learning, but were to be learnt by the pupils through actual practice of useful occupations. Agreeing with *Dewey, Will Durant* remarked that the industrialized Europe and America had taught the importance of occupation over books. It was further emphasized that scholastic culture made for snobbishness, but fellowship in occupation made for democracy.

Dewey wanted the school to be a miniature workshop and a miniature community at a time when society was rapidly becoming industrialized. The school was to adopt practices that were to lean less towards the theoretical aspects of teaching. He wanted the schools to bring radical changes by helping the society to climb the ladder of maturity and by maintaining a continuous growth of mind.

Role of Intelligence

Dewey upheld intelligence as the key to shape our fates. If we lacked intelligence, we were just about better than slaves. Goodness was more than simply being obedient. Goodness was a kind of virtue which could be better understood by intelligence. He thought that change was the essence of reality. So human beings were always to be prepared to alter the ways, they normally had been doing things. Man was to pursue his aims rationally and scientifically. Both the ends and the means were to be pursued intelligently. The continual revision of means and ends could help one to reach the best goals in life.

In his work: *How We Think, Dewey* carefully delineated how ideas could be used as instruments in the solution of problems. This he did in five steps:

(i) A felt difficulty or need was to be observed.
(ii) It was to be specifically located and defined.
(iii) Suggestions of possible solutions were to be sought.
(iv) The bearings of the suggestions were to be developed by reasoning.
(v) Further observations and experiments leading to the acceptance or rejection of the proposed suggestions were to be made.

Dewey advocated that thinking was social. Thoughts occurred not only in specific situations but also in a particular cultural/social background. Both the individual and the society influenced each other. When a child was born, he was exposed to customs, manners, conventions, languages and traditional ideas. He was influenced and moulded to fit into the social structure in which he had appeared. Thus, the 'social heredity' rapidly acted on him to bring about changes. Although he was regarded as a naturalist in outlook, he did not accept the role of instinct as it had been claimed by the naturalists. He thought that even the most powerful instincts such as sex and pugancity had been modified to a great extent by social influences and training. He believed that other instincts could also be modified by social influences and proper education. He felt that there was nothing which was impossible; rather it was our training which made it so.

Dewey's unique contribution to educational thought and practice was to highlight the concepts of "instrumentalism" and "experimentalism".

Instrumentalism

Dewey accepted the theory of evolution with less hesitation. Mind as well as body was to him an organ evolved in the struggle for existence from lower forms. He followed *Darwin's* chain of thoughts and accepted his genetic and experimental ideas. *Dewey* was also influenced by the ideas of *William James.*

(i) Instrumentalism meant that concepts and theories were not solutions or answers to the philosophical enigmas, but were instruments which were mental modes of adaptation to reality. These modes carried us from anyone part of experience to any other part, linking things satisfactorily, and enabling us to move forward.

(ii) The intellectual analysis of the different mental acts was controlled by the notion of ends to be attained and the means for attaining them.

(iii) Reality was not a completed system, but in a process of constant change. Nature was fundamentally a process–a correlated series of events.

(iv) Language was the tool *par excellence*, and was the most effective device invented for the purpose of communication and consolidation of meanings. Events were more than mere occurrences; they had implications. Thus, inference and reasoning were possible.

(v) Mind was an organization of vital affairs and exists in connection with some organized body. Thinking was never purely contemplative; it came after something and out of something or for the sake of something. Occasion for thinking was provided when there was some maladjustment between organism and environment.

The material for thinking was anything in the world–anything which presented the problem and suggested modes of dealing with it effectively. Knowledge implies a difference made in things by knowing.

The constructive function of intelligence and thinking was not limited exclusively to making adjustments or adaptations within a particular environmental situation: it was creative. Intelligence as intelligence was forward-looking.

(vi) *Dewey's* philosophy was a constant protest against the divorce of knowledge from action and theory from practice: unnatural separation gave rise to the evils of life.

Dewey was a bold naturalist who declared that man tried to idealize and rationalize the universe at large only when he was unable to master the course of things, which concerned him. Hence, the message was to acquire mastery. He rejected the idea that divinity existed somewhere in the neutral cosmic powers. He also rejected metaphysics which he felt to be an echo and disguise of theology. According to him, the modern era began only when the naturalistic point of view was accepted in all walks of life. Mind and life were to be understood in biological terms as an organ, or an organism, or an environment acted upon and reacting. Mind and life moulded and shaped each other.

He reckoned the brain as an organ of a certain kind of behaviour. Thought was an instrument of readaptation. It was an organ just like limbs and teeth. Ideas were experiments in adjustment. Thought was to be understood as it arose in specific situations.

Experimentalism

Experimentalism was opposed to absolutism and believed that reality was not transcendental: it was well within the human experience. There was no absolute truth: truth was the product of verified knowledge.

Plato stood for government-controlled education for achieving good. The German educator, *J.F. Herbart,* felt that any big change might modify man but it might threaten and destroy him as well. *Dewey* defied both *Plato* and *Herbart*, and said that trial and error, and knowledge and practice were the means of reaching goal. *Dewey* was a kind of experimentalist who would not accept anything until the results were reached by self-discovery. The test of truth lay in the consequence to which it led.

Authoritarianism was replaced by verification of knowledge, using scientific method. A scientific method comprised:

- Definition of the problem
- Critical review of literature
- Comparison with similar phenomena

- Generation of hypotheses
- More observation
- Data analysis
- Simplification of hypotheses
- Unification of hypotheses into a theory
- Testing the theory and predictions
- Reporting the result in clear language

The steps ensured scientific verification of knowledge, although simpler problems might not need to follow them strictly. The quantities of physical objects were determined by intentional operations:

- Knowledge prepared us for further action.
- Nature was interacting and was in a flux. Nature was not to be accepted but controlled.
- In education, experimentalists aimed at developing experimental attitude to test all knowledge. The curriculum was to include scientific, technological and industrial subjects and other subjects were also to be activity-centred. Projects were introduced to challenge the learners to work on them. The skills of exploration, experimentation and co-operation could be incorporated through project method.

Dewey's Pragmatism

In his *Source of a Science Education*, *Dewey* propounded that practice inspired and, thus, educational practices and direct experiments in the field determined educational ends and theories. He rejected *William Jame's* pragmatism that laid stress only on consequences but ignored motives.

Dewey's own pragmatic ideas could be traced from his approach to curriculum. The main hypothesis was that the curriculum consisted of life itself, especially the occupations and associations which served man's main needs.

Herbert Spencer had classified human activities as the biological, the social, political and the cultural. *Dewey* rejected any classification of the activities which constituted human life in order of importance. He maintained that it was impossible to classify human activities for educational purposes. He further reflected that the only ultimate value which could be set up was just the process of living itself.

Dewey, however, maintained that some of intellectual control through significant subject matter was to be maintained to outline the idea of freedom, given in respect of curriculum in the schools. Perhaps, with the contention that human activities could not be classified, he did indicate an order of preference. He felt that the curriculum was to be planned keeping in mind the essentials first and refinements second. The essentials for man's chief needs were food, shelter, clothing, and household and consumable articles. These necessities of life were outlined with the principles having a social quality.

With the pragmatic principles in mind, he emphasized the claim that thinking arose out of practical needs. It was through the action only that knowledge could be acquired and progress made possible.

Dewey's method of attaining knowledge was experimental. So impressed was he with the idea of experimental method that he took it to be the only method of knowledge. He named it experimentalism. He thought that project method was a natural corollary to his teaching. But he maintained that projects were not to be too ambitious and beyond the pupil's capacity to perform. A project was to be a problematic task which arose out of practical needs and the results could be tested by their practical consequences.

Ethical Criterion

For *Plato,* morality was the effective harmony of the whole; for *Jesus*, it was kindness to the weak; for *Nietzsche*, it was the bravery of the strong; for *Swami Vivekananda,* it was the beneficence of the suffering humanity, morality; for *Dewey*, was not the absolute 'good' but a constant process of becoming good. It was not perfection as a final goal but the ever enduring process of perfecting, maturing, and referring which was the aim of living. The bad man was the man who, no mater how good he had been, was beginning to deteriorate and grow less good. The good man was the man who, no matter how morally unworthly, he had been, was moving to become better. Such a conception made one severe in judging himself and humane in judging others.

Dewey's Influence on Education

Dewey, being a twentieth century thinker and philosopher, has greatly influenced educational thinking and practice throughout the world. India is no exception to this. His influence can be traced in the following fields in the Indian educational background.

Diversified courses have been adopted and a wide range of subjects and knowledge is being presented before the pupils to meet their choices. For example: in the National Policy on Education, 1986, the curriculum better represents the necessities of life. The subjects contained under biological, physical and chemical sciences and the subjects representing social sciences reflect *Dewey's* social factors and needs of human beings. A wave of experimental attitude in education in now commonly perceived in all subjects. Knowledge, which used to be laden with theory, is now to be presented through a practical approach which has a more lasting impact on the pupil. The project method is being tried in primary and secondary schools by innovative teachers. The idea to provide the direct experiences in learning has never been so potently felt as it is being recognized today.

Mere lecturing is treated and reckoned as obsolete, and life-situations are taken to be more important for the puplis' experiences in the school world.

Textbooks are being written on activity methods, and other books contain exercises which involve learners in activities and experiences. Education is being recognized as a process of refining and bringing up the generation to the ladder of maturity. School is fast becoming a miniature society wherein the necessary experiences of life are provided. The idea that if a democratic state is the aim of the government, it should also appreciate a democratic form of education. It is being commonly recognized that more freedom be furnished to the pupil in the school to help him exploit his talents and enrich himself and society.

Conclusion

Dewey synthesised the educational wisdom developed from the times of the Greeks when he said that hypotheses tested by experience constituted the nearest approach to knowledge which we had, that science was to become a social pursuit by being applied to the study of all the problems of man and that in order to determine the meaning of an idea, it was required to be put into practice: the consequences constituted the meaning of the idea.

Summary

The beginning of the twentieth century was the beginning of the new era in education. The importance of private schools increased; education was a wide spread phenomenon. More educational opportunities were witnessed in the USA. Racial discrimination was minimized and the coloured population got equal opportunities for learning in schools. In fact, education was heading towards democratic patterns which had not been so recognized before.

Dewey came to the scene when such factors were becoming potent in the American life. *James* wanted pragmatic doctrines to dominate the era, while *Dewey* presented an experimental method. He declared that the experimental procedure was one that reached the heart of things. He stressed that the test of an idea of thinking generally was found in the consequences of the acts to which the ideas led.

In his work, *Democracy and Education*, he laid down educational procedures on democratic patterns. A democratic state was expected to have a democratic form of education.

He accepted the theory of evolution and held the mind and body as organs, evolved in the struggle for existence. He found that thinking was social, and discovered that society could mould man and make him good. He did not accept the idea that divinity lay in the next cosmic powers. Morality, for him, was not the absolute good but it was a constant process of becoming good.

His influence on education has been great. One of the major features was the problem-solving attitude which was to be cultivated in the children. His curriculum was practically-oriented. The curriculum was life itself. It was a kind of experience which prepared men and women for occupations.

He was greatly influenced by experimental approach and upheld that the experimental method was the best way of imparting knowledge.

Dewey's pragmatic/experimental ideas could be traced from his approach to curriculum. The main hypothesis was that the curriculum consisted of life itself, especially the occupations and associations which served man's daily needs:

He felt that the curriculum was to be planned keeping in mind the essentials first and refinements second. The essentials for man's chief needs were food, shelter, clothing, household and consumable articles. These necessities of life were outlined with the principles having a social quality.

15

Educands as Ends

Bertrand Russell (1872-1970)

Bertrand Russell deserves consideration as an educational philosopher, although he is a man of many parts. Such consideration is based on his writings on education and his interest in the discipline of education. He, alongwith his second wife, ran an experimental school. His works on education are overshadowed by his writings on mathematics, logic and philosophy.

Life Sketch

Russell was a British philosopher, logician, essayist and social critic. He is best known for his work in mathematical logic and analytical philosophy. His most influential contributions included his defense of logicism: the view that mathematics was, in some important sense, reducible to formal logic.

He made significant contributions, not just to logic and philosophy, but to a broad range of other subjects, including education, history, political theory and religious studies. In addition, many of his writings on a wide variety of topics in both the sciences and the humanities influenced generations of general readers.

After a life, marked by controversy (including dismissals from Trinity College, Cambridge and City College, New York), *Russell* was awarded the Order of Merit in 1949 and the Noble Prize for Literature in 1950. He was also noted for his many spirited anti-war and anti-nuclear protests. He remained a prominent public figure until his death at the age of 97. Imagine the *wisdom* of authorities who imprisoned a person for disturbing the peace of a locality by his anti-bomb protests because he had been fighting for peace in the world?

Logic

Russell's contributions to logic and the foundations of mathematics included his discovery of "*Russell's Paradox*", his defense of logicism, his development of the theory of types and his refining of the first-order predicate calculus.

He discovered the paradox that bore his name while working on his *Principles of Mathematics.* The paradox arose in connection with the set of all sets that were not member of themselves. Such a set, if it existed, would be a member of itself if and only if it was not a member of itself. The paradox was significant since, using classical logic, all sentences were entailed by a contradiction. His discovery, thus, prompted a large amount of work in logic, set theory, and the philosophy and foundations of mathematics.

He defended logicism. Logicism consisted of two main theses. The first was that all mathematical truths could be translated into logical truths or, in other words, that the vocabulary of mathematics constituted a proper subset of that of logic. The second was that all mathematical proofs could be recast as logical proofs or, in other words, that the theorems of mathematics constituted a proper subset of those of logic. *Russell's* basic idea for defending logicism was that numbers might be identified with classes of classes and that number-theoretic statements might be explained in terms of quantifiers and identity.

As one of the founders of analytic philosophy, *Russell* made significant contributions to a wide variety of areas including metaphysics, epistemology, ethics, and political theory as well as to the history of philosophy, discovering whether, and to what extent, knowledge was possible.

His various contributions were also unified by his views concerning both the centrality of scientific knowledge and the importance of an underlying scientific methodology that was common to both philosophy and science. In the case of philosophy, this methodology expressed itself through his use of logical analysis. In fact, he often claimed that he had more confidence in his methodology than in any particular philosophical conclusion.

He saw that the idealist doctrine of internal relations led to a series of contradictions regarding asymmetrical (and other) relations necessary for mathematics. Thus, he abandoned the idealism that he had encountered as a student at Cambridge, together with his *Kantian* methodology, in favour of a pluralistic realism. As a result, he soon became famous as an advocate of the "new realism" and for his "new philosophy of logic", emphasizing, as it did, the importance of modern logic for philosophical analysis. The underlying themes of this "revolution", including his belief in pluralism, his emphasis upon anti-psychologism, and the importance of science, remained central to his philosophy for the remainder of his life.

Russell's emphasis upon logical analysis also had consequences for his metaphysics. In response to the traditional problem of the external world, he said that since the external world could be known only by inference, he developed distinction between "knowledge by acquaintance and knowledge by description". He then went on to argue that the world itself consisted of a complex of logical atoms (such as "little patches of colour") and their properties. Together they formed the atomic facts which, in turn, were combined to form logically complex objects. What we normally took to be inferred entities (for example, ending physical objects) were then understood to be "logical constructions" from the immediately given entities of sensation, viz. and "sensibilia". It was only these latter entities that were known non-inferentially and with certainty.

According to him, the philosopher's job was to discover a logically ideal language that would exhibit the true nature of the world in such a way that, the speaker would not be misled by the casual surface structure of natural language.

Russell's Social and Political Philosophy

Russell's social influence stemmed from three main sources: his long standing social activism, his many writings on the social and political issues of his day, and his popularization of technical writings in philosophy and the natural sciences.

He was also famous for suggesting that a widespread reliance upon evidence, rather than upon superstition, would have enormous social consequences. He proposed a doctrine which appeared widely paradoxical and subversive. The doctrine in questions was this: that it was undesirable to believe a proposition when there was no ground whatever for supposing it true.

His social activism stretched back at least as far as 1910, when he published his *Anti-Suffragist Anxieties,* and 1916, when he was convicted and fined in connection with anti-war protests during World War-I. Following his conviction, he was also dismissed from his post at Trinity College, Cambridge. Two years later, he was convicted a second time. The result was six months in prison. He also ran unsuccessfully for Parliament (in 1907, 1922, and 1923). He, togetherwith his second wife, founded and operated an experimental school during the late 1920s and the early 1930s. He was best known in many circles as a result of his campaigns against the proliferation of nuclear weapons and against western involvement in the Vietnam War during the 1950s and 1960s.

Although he became the third *Earl Russell* upon the death of his brother in 1931, his radicalism continued to make him a controversial figure well through middle-age. While teaching in the United States in the late 1930s, he was offered a teaching appointment at City College, New York. The appointment was revoked following a large number of public protests and in 1940, judicial decision found him morally unfit to teach at the College.

In 1954, he delivered his famous "Man's Peril" broadcast on the BBC, condemning the bikini H-bomb tests. A year later, together with *Albert*

Einstein, he released the *Russell-Einstein* Manifesto, calling for the curtailment of nuclear weapons. In 1957, he was a prime organizer of the first Pugwash Conference, which brought together a large number of scientists concerned about the nuclear issue. He became the founding president of the Campaign for Nuclear Disarmament in 1958 and was once again imprisoned in 1961—this time in connection with anti-nuclear protests. The media coverage surrounding his conviction only served to enhance his reputation and to further inspire the many idealistic youths who were sympathetic to his anti-war and anti-nuclear protests. Upon being awarded the Noble Prize for Literature in 1950, *Russell* used his acceptance speech to emphasize, once again, themes related to his social activism.

Views on Education

Russell in his book entitled: *On Education:* said that "*we must have conception of the kind of person we wish to produce, before we can have any definite opinion as to the education which we consider best*". Thus, he laid down a complete structure of schooling.

(i) Aims of Education

Russell's aims of education were both individual and social. He wanted to produce individuals who were creative. However, the educated person was also to possess characteristics like intelligence, sensitivity, openness of mind, patience and industriousness. His aims were social in that he would like to provide education to anyone who was keen on learning. Such characteristics provided foundations for a creative character and personality. He was of the opinion that in almost all European countries, the individual was less subject to herd-domination than in America: his inner freedom was greater even where his political freedom was less. A community of men and women possessing vitality, sensitiveness and courage in the highest degree that education could produce would do away with the causes of unhappiness.

(ii) Structure and Curriculum

(a) Education of the child was to start in nursery school like the Kindergarten and *Montessori* schools. Nursery education was to be compulsory and free. Children were to develop the ability of reading and writing.

(b) Geography, history and general knowledge were to be introduced to children after the age of five. By the age of six, moral education was to be nearly complete.

(c) Subjects like science and mathematics started between the age of 12 and 14. Other subjects were physics, chemistry, biology and classical languages (Latin, Greek).

(d) Education between the ages of 14 and 18 years was to comprise classical languages, mathematics and science, and modern humanities.

(e) University education was to be allowed to the bright students, provided they had the will to pursue it. For him, universities existed for two purposes: on the one hand, to train men and women for certain professions; on the other hand, to pursue learning and research without regard to immediate utility—something like the disinterested pursuit of knowledge of *Aristotle*.

(f) Students could study in day or residential schools, as these had their own merit and demerits. Parents were to have a say in selecting schools for their children.

(iii) The Learners

The expectations of learners were high. They were to be regarded as ends. They were to benefit from education at various levels of schooling. They were to participate actively in learning. They were to avail themselves of the opportunities for the development of their individual potentialities in academic, social and physical fields. They were to develop wide ranging interests in political, religious and secular fields. *Russell* recommended sex education for boys and girls.

(iv) The Teachers

(a) Teachers of the nursery schools were to be well-versed in psychology and medicine to cater to the individual differences of the learners. For him, in earlier years, love towards the pupils was most important quality; in the later years, love of the knowledge imparted became increasingly necessary. The teacher was to love his children better than his state or church.

(b) At the second level of education, the teacher was to have sound knowledge of the subject. He was to prepare his lessons well to motivate students to learn. He was to encourage learners to learn independently, exchange ideas and search for the truth.

(c) Teacher was to be free from financial worries, was to get leave for study and undertake research which was directed towards the welfare of the society.

(d) In university teaching, knowledge of skill in pedagogy was not important. What was important was one's subject and keenness about what was being done in it. Research was as important as education. New knowledge was the chief cause of progress. The poet, the painter, the composer or the mathematician was to be occupied in the pursuit of vision, in capturing and giving permanence to something, he had first seen dimly for a moment which he had loved with such ardour that the joys of this world had grown pale by comparison.

(e) He believed that punishment had a certain very minor place in education. Sharp speaking and expression of natural spontaneous indignation were enough. Mild punishments had their utility for dealing with mild offences. Grave faults of character, such as cruelty to animals or humans required their prevention on an *ad hoc* basis. Throughout education, there was to be a sense of intellectual adventure. The world was full of puzzling things which were exciting and delightful but which could be understood by sufficient effort with the help of good teachers.

Relevance of Ideas

Russell gave advice on various aspects of education, tried and tested by other educational thinkers like *Froebel, Montessori* and *Dewey*.

His suggestion to study wide ranging subjects is relevant to curricular content, as narrow specialization in various disciplines is bothering educational thinkers these days.

His devotion to ensure peace in the world was so genuine that no set-backs discouraged him from the right path. What have the war-mongering Europeans, Americans and others achieved by the callous destruction, brought about by the world and regional wars— past and recent?

His view that cnly bright ones were to enter the university seemed to support the class-based ideas: higher education for the upper class.

Some opinions are theoretical as these may be difficult to implement like choice of day and residential schools by parents.

Conclusion

It may be said that with the demise of *Russell*, came to an end the age of philosophers of the twentieth century in the western world. The twenty-first century England has yet to produce a *Russell*.

Summary

Russell wrote on a wide range of subjects—logic, philosophy, education, history, political theory and religious studies. He discovered "*Russell's Paradox*". The Paradox arose in connection with the set of all sets that were not members of themselves. He wrote on social and political issues of his day and was punished for his revolutionary ideas. His aims of education were individual and social. He recommended nursery education and through second level of education only bright children were to join university. Nursery teachers were to be well-versed in psychology and medicine; secondary schools teachers were to have knowledge of the subject; and university teachers were to create knowledge through research. Learners were to be treated as "ends".

16

Pedagogy of the Oppressed

Paulo Freire (1921-1997)

Life sketch

Paulo Freire was born on September 19, 1921 to a middle class family in Recife, Brazil. He became familiar with poverty and hunger during the Great Depression of the 1930s. In 1931, the family moved to the less expensive city of Jaboatao dos Guarapapes, and in 1933 his father died. In school, he ended up four grades behind, and his social life revolved around playing pick up football with other poor children and from them, he learned a great deal. These experiences shaped his concerns for the poor and helped to construct his particular educational view point. He stated that poverty and hunger severely affected his ability to learn. This influenced his decision to dedicate his life to improving the lives of the poor. He said: *"I didn't understand anything because of my hunger. I wasn't dumb. It wasn't lack of interest. My social condition didn't allow me to have an education. Experience showed me once again the relationship between social class and knowledge."* Eventually, his family's misfortunes turned around and their prospects improved.

Freire enrolled at Law School at the University of Recife in 1943. He also studied philosophy, more specifically phenomenology, and the psychology of language. Although admitted to the legal bar, he never actually practised law but instead worked as a teacher in secondary schools, teaching Portuguese. In 1944, he married *Elza Maia Costa Oliveira,* a fellow teacher. The two worked together and had five children.

In 1946, *Freire* was appointed Director of the Department of Education and Culture of the Social Service in the state of Pernambuco. Working primarily among the illiterate poor, he began to embrace a non-orthodox form of what could be considered liberation theology. In Brazil at that time, literacy was a requirement for voting in presidential elections.

In 1961, he was appointed director of the Department of Culture Extension of Recife University, and in 1962 he had the first opportunity for significant application of his theories, when 300 sugarcane workers were taught to read the write in just 45 days. In response to this experiment, the Brasilian government approved the creation of thousands of cultural circles across the country.

In 1964, a military coup put an end to that effort. *Freire* was imprisoned for 70 days as a traitor. After a brief exile in Bolivia, he worked in Chile for five years for the Christian Democratic Agrarian Reform Movement and the Food and Agriculture Organization of the United Nations. In 1967, he published his first book, *Education as the Practice of Freedom.* He followed this with his most famous book, *Pedagogy of the Oppressed,* first published in Portuguese in 1968.

On the strength of reception of his work, *Freire* was offered a visiting professorship as Harvard University in 1969. The next year, *Pedagogy of the Oppressed* was published in both Spanish and English, vastly expanding its reach. Because of political feuds between *Freire*, a Christian socialist, and successive authoritarian military dictatorships, the book wasn't published in Brazil until 1974, when General Ernesto Geisel became the, then, dictator president beginning the process of a slow and controlled political liberation.

After a year in Cambridge, Massachusetts, USA, *Freire* moved to Geneva, Switzerland to work as a special education advisor to the World Council of Churches. During this time, he acted as an advisor on education reform in former Portuguese colonies in Africa, particularly Guinea-Bissau and Mozambique.

In 1979, he was able to return to Brazil, and moved back in 1980. He joined the Worker's Party (PT) in the city of Sao Paulo, and acted as a supervisor for its adult literacy project from 1980 to 1986. When the PT prevailed in the municipal elections in 1988, *Freire* was appointed Secretary of Education for Sao Paulo.

In 1986, his wife *Elza* died. People close to him felt that he had given up after the loss of his wife and worried that he might die. *Freire* was teaching a graduate course, and became reconnected with *Maria Araujo* from Recife. She was a child in the school where he was a principal. Eventually, they fell in love. *Freire* married Maria Araujio, who continued with her own educational work. *Freire* often said that *Nita* saved his life, she was the culmination of the radical love, he sought.

Freire died of heart failure on May 2, 1997 in Sao Paulo.

Contributions

Paulo Freire contributed a philosophy of education that came not only from the more classical approaches stemming from *Plato*, but also from modern Marxist and anti-colonialist thinkers. In fact, in many ways his *Pedagogy of the Oppressed* (1970) may be best read as an extension of, or reply to, *Frantz Fanon's*: *The Wretched of the Earch* (1961), which emphasized the need to provide native populations with an education which was simultaneously new and modern (rather than traditional) and anti-colonial (not simply an extension of the culture of the colonizer).

In *Pedagory of the Oppressed* (1970) (extracts from which are included in this account), *Freire*, making the oppressors-oppressed distinction, differentiated between the two positions in an unjust society, the oppressor and the oppressed. He made no direct reference to his most direct influence for the distinction, which stemmed back, at least, as far as Hegel in 1802, and had since been represented by many authors including *Engels, Marx, Lenin, Gramsci, Simone Well* and others.

Freire championed that education was to allow the oppressed to regain their sense of humanity, in turn, overcoming their condition. Nevertheless, he also acknowledged that in order for this to occur, the oppressed individual had to play a role in their liberation, as he stated:

No pedagogy which is truly liberating can remain distant from the oppressed by treating them as unfortunates and by presenting for their emulation models from among the oppressors. The oppressed must be their own example in the struggle for their redemtion

Likewise, the oppressors were to also be willing to rethink their way of life and to examine their own role in the oppression if true liberation was to occur: *"those who authentically commit themselves to the people must re-examine themselves constantly."*.

Freire believed education to be a political act that could not be divorced from pedagogy. He defined this as a main tenet of critical pedagogy. Teachers and students had to be made aware of the "politics" that surround education. The way students were taught and what they were taught served a political agenda. Teachers, themselves, had political notions, they brought into the classroom. He believed that *"education makes sense because women and men learn that through learning they can make and remake themselves, because women and men are able to take responsibility for themselves as beings capable of knowing– of knowing that they know and knowing that they don't"*.

Teacher-people Relationship

A careful analysis of the teacher-student relationship at any level, inside or outside the school, reveals its fundamentally narrative character. This relationship involves a narrating subject (the teacher) and patient like objects (the students). The contents, whether values or empirical dimensions of reality, tend, in the process of being narrated, to become lifeless and petrified. Education is suffering from narration sickness.

The teacher talks about reality as if it were motionless, static, compartmentalized and predictable. Or else, he expounds on a topic completely alien to the existential experience of the students. His task is to "fill" the students with the contents of his narration—contents which are detached from reality, disconnected from the totality that engendered them and could give them significance. Words are emptied of their concreteness and become a hollow, alienated and alienating verbosity.

The outstanding characteristic of this narrative education, then, is the sonority of words, not their transforming power. Narration (with the teacher as narrator) leads the students to memorize mechanically the narrated account. Worse yet, it turns them into "containers," into "receptacles" to be "filled" by the teachers.

Banking Concept of Education

Education, thus, becomes an act of depositing, in which the students are the depositories and the teacher is the depositor. Instead of communicating, the teacher issues communiques to make deposits which the students patiently receive, memorize, and repeat. This is the "banking" concept of education, in which the scope of action allowed to the students extends only as far as receiving, filing, and storing the deposits.

The banking education maintains and even stimulates the contradiction through the following attitudes and practices, which mirror oppressvie society as a whole:

(1) teacher teaches and the students are taught;
(2) the teacher knows everything and the students know nothing;
(3) the teacher thinks and the students are thought about;
(4) the teacher talks and the students listen-meekly;
(5) the teacher disciplines and the students are disciplined;
(6) the teacher chooses and enforces his choice, and the students comply;
(7) the teacher acts and the students have the illusion of acting through the action of the teacher;
(8) the teacher chooses the programme content, and the students (who were not consulted) adapt to it;
(9) the teacher confuses the authority of knowledge with his or her own professional authority, which she/he sets in opposition to the freedom of the students;
(10) the teacher is the subject of the learning process, while the pupils are mere objects.

It is not surprising that the banking concept of education regards men as adaptable, manageable beings. The more students work at storing the deposits, entrusted to them, the less they develop the critical consciousness which would result from their intervention in the world as transformers of that world. The more completely they accept the passive role imposed on them, the more they tend simply to adapt to the world as it is and to the fragmented view of reality deposited in them.

To resolve the teacher-student contradiction, to exchange the role of depositor, prescriber, domesticator, for the role of student among students would be to undermine the power of oppression and serve the cause of liberation.

Impact in the banking concept is the assumption of a dichotomy between human beings and the world: a person is merely in the world, not with the world or with others; the individual is spectator, not re-creator. In this view, the person is not a conscious being *(corpo consciente)*; he or she is rather the possessor of a consciousness: an empty "mind" passively open to the reception of deposits of reality from the world outside.

The bank-clerk educator does not realize that there is no true security in his hypertrophied role, that one must seek to live with others in solidarity. One can not impose oneself, nor even merely co-exist with one's students. Solidarity requires true communication, and the concept by which such an educator is guided fears and proscribes communication.

Yet only through communication can human life hold meaning. The teacher's thinking is authenticated only by the authenticity of the student's thinking. The teacher can not think for his/her students, nor he/she can impose his/her thought on them. Authentic thinking, thinking that is concerned about reality, does not take place in ivory tower isolation, but only in communication. If it is true that thought has meaning only when generated by action upon the world, the subordination of students to teachers becomes impossible.

Because banking education begins with a false understanding of men and women as objects, it can not promote the development of what *Fromm* calls "biophily", but instead produces its opposite: "necrophily."

While life is characterized by growth in a structured functional manner, the necrophilous person loves all that does not grow, all that is mechanical. The necrophilous person is driven by the desire to transform the organic into the inorganic, to approach life mechanically, as if all living persons were things....Memory, rather than experience; having, rather than being, is what counts. The necrophilous person can relate to an object–a flower or a person—only if he possesses it; hence a threat to his possession is a threat to himself, if he loses possession, he loses contact with the world... . He loves control, and in the act of controlling, he kills life, as Fromm said.

Problem-posing Education

Liberating education consists in acts of cognition, not transfer of information. It is a learning situation in which the cognizable object (far from being the end of the cognitive act) intermediates the cognitive actors —teacher on the one hand and students on the other. Accordingly, the practice of problem-posing education entails at the outset that the teacher-student contradiction to be resolved. Dialogical relations—indispensable to the capacity of cognitive actors to cooperate in perceiving the same cognizable object are otherwise impossible.

Indeed problem-posing education, which breaks with the vertical characteristic of banking education, can fulfil its function of freedom only if it can overcome the above contradiction. Through dialogue, the teacher-of-the-students and the students-of-the teacher cease to exist and a new term emerges: teacher-student with students-teachers. The teacher is no longer merely the-one-who-teaches, but one who is himself taught in dialogue with the students, who, in turn, while being taught, also teaches. They become jointly responsible for a process in which all grow. In this process, arguments based on "authority" are no longer valid: in order to function, authority must be on the side of freedom, not against it. Here, no one teaches another, nor is anyone self-taught. People teach each other, mediated by the world, by the cognizable objects which is banking education are "owned" by the teacher.

Students, as they are increasingly posed with problems relating to themselves in the world and with the world, will feel increasingly challenged and obliged to respond to that challenge. Because they apprehend the challenge as interrelated to other problems within a total context not as a theoretical question, the resulting comprehension tends to be increasingly critical and thus constantly less alienated. Their response to the challenge evokes new challenges, followed by new understandings; and gradually the students come to regard themselves as committed.

Education as the practice of freedom—as opposed to education as the practice of domination—denies that man is obstruct, isolated, independent and unattached to the world; it also denies that the world exists as a reality apart from people. Authentic reflection considers neither abstract man nor the world without people, but people in their relations with the world. In these relations consciousness and world are simultaneous: consciousness neither precedes the world nor follows it.

In problem-posing education, people develop their power to perceive critically the way they exist in the world with which and in which they find themselves; they come to see the world not as a static reality, but as a reality in process, in transformation. Although the dialectical relations of women and men with the world exist independently of how these relations are perceived (or whether or not they are perceived at all), it is also true that the form of action they adopt is, to an extent, a function of how they perceive themselves in the world. Hence, the teacher-student and the students-teachers reflect simultaneously on themselves and the world without dichotomizing this reflection from action, and thus establish an authentic form of thought and action.

Once again, the two educational concepts and practices under analysis come into conflict. Banking education (for obvious reasons) attempts, by mythicizing reality, to conceal certain facts which explain the way human beings exist in the world: problem-posing education sets itself the task of demythecizing. Banking education resists dialogue: problem-posing education regards dialogue as indispensable to the act of cognition which unveils reality. Banking education treats students as objects of assistance; problem-posing education makes them critical thinkers. Banking education inhibits creativity and domesticates (although it can not completely destroy) the intentionality of consciousness by isolating consciousness from the world, thereby denying people their ontological and historical vocation of becoming more fully human. Problem-posing education bases itself on creativity and stimulates true reflection and action upon reality, thereby responding to the vocation of persons as beings only when engaged in inquiry and creative transformation. In sum: banking theory and practice, as immoilizing and fixating forces, fail to acknowledge men and women as historical beings; problem-posing theory and practice take the people's historicity as their starting point.

Education as Lifelong Process

Problem-posing education affirms men and women as beings in the process of becoming—as unfinished, uncompleted beings in and with a likewise unfinished reality. Indeed, in contrast to other animals who are unfinished, but not historical, people know themselves to be unfinished; they are aware of their incompletion. In this incompletion and this awareness lie the very roots of education as an human manifestation. The unfinished character of human beings and the transformational character of reality necessitate that education be an ongoing activity.

Education is, thus, constantly remade in the praxis. In order to be, it must become. Its "duration" (in the *Bergsonian* meaning of the word) is found in the interplay of the opposites—permanence and change. The banking method emphasizes permanence and becomes problem-posing—which accepts neither a "well-behaved" present nor a predetermined future—roots itself in the dynamic present and becomes revolutionary.

Problem-posing education is revolutionary futurity. Hence, it is prophetic (and as such, hopeful). Hence, it corresponds to the historical nature of humankind. Hence, it affirms women and men those who transcend themselves, who move forward and look ahead, for whom immobility more clearly what and who they are so that they can more wisely build the future. Hence, it identifies with the movement which engages people as beings aware of their incompletion—an historical movement which has its point of departure, its subjects and its objective.

The point of departure of the movement lies in the people themselves. But since people do not exist apart from the world, apart from reality, the movement must begin with the human-world relationship. Accordingly, the point of departure must always be with men and women in the "here and now," which constitutes the situation within which they are submerged, from which they emerge, and in which they intervence. Only by starting from this situation—which determined their perception of it—can they begin to move. To do this authentically they must perceive their state not as fated and unalterable, but merely as limiting—and therefore challenging.

Whereas the banking method directly or indirectly reinforces men's fatalistic perception of their situation, the problem-posing method presents this very situation to them as a problem. As the situation becomes the object of their cognition, the native or magical perception which produced their fatalism gives way to perception which is able to perceive itself even as it perceives reality, and can, thus, be critically objective about that reality.

A dependent consciousness of their situation leads people to apprehend that situation as an historical reality, susceptible of transformation. Resignation gives way to the drive for transformation and inquiry, over which men feel themselves to be in control. If people, as historical beings, necessarily engaged with other people in a movement of inquiry, did not control that movement, it would be (and is) a violation of their humanity. Any situation in which some individuals prevent others from engaging in the process of inquiry is one of violence. The means used are not important; to alienate human beings from their own decision-making is to change them into objects.

This movement of inquiry must be directed towards humanization—the people's historical vocation. The pursuit of full humanity, however, can not be carried out in isolation or individualism, but only in fellowship and solidarity; therefore it can not unfold in the antagonistic between oppressors and oppressed. No one can be authentically human while he prevents others from being so. Attempting to be more human, individualistically, leads to having more, egotistically, a form of dehumanization not that it is not fundamental to have in order to be human. Precisely because it is necessary, some men's having must not be allowed to constitute an obstacle to other's having, must not consolidate the power of the former to crush the latter.

Problem-posing education, as a humanist and liberating praxis, posits as fundamental that the people subjected to domination must fight for their emancipation. To that end, it enables teachers and students to become Subjects of the educational process by overcoming authoritarianism and an alienating intellectualism; it also enables people to overcome their false perception of reality. The world—no longer something to be described with deceptive words—becomes the object of that transforming action by men and women which results in their humanization.

Problem-posing education does not, and can not, serve the interests of the oppressor. No oppressive order could permit the oppressed to begin to question: Why? While only a revolutionary society can carry out this education in systematic terms, the revolutionary leaders need not take full power before they can employ the method. In the revolutionary process, the leaders can not utilize the banking method as an interim measure, justified on grounds of expediency, with intention of later behaving in a genuinely revolutionary fashion. They must be revolutionary —that is to say, dialogical—from the outset.

Pedagogy of the Oppossed: Global Impact

Freire's major exponents in North America are *Peter Mc Laren, Donaldo Macedo, Joe L. Kincheloe, Ira Shor, and Henry Giroux*. One of *Mc Laren*'s edited texts, *Paulo Frerire: A Critical Encounter,* expounds upon *Freire's* impact in the field and the Argentinian revolutionary icon *Che Guevara. Freire's* work has also influenced the so-called "radical math" movement in the United States, which emphasizes social justice issues and critical pedagogy as components of mathematical curricula.

In 1991, the *Paulo Freire* institute was established in Sao Paulo to extend and elaborate upon his theories of popular education. The Institute now has projects in many countries and is currently headquartered at UCLA Graduate School of Education and Information Studies where it actively maintains the *Freire* archives. The director is Dr. Carlos Torres, a UCLA professor and author of Freirean books including *A praxis educative de Paulo Freire* (1978). Since the publication of the English edition in 1970, *Pedagogy of the Oppressed* has achieved near-iconic status in America's teacher-training programmes, according to *Sol Stern,* a social commentator, critical of the entry of *Freire*'s Marxist-inspired teachings into the mainstream curriculum. Connections of *Freire's* non-dual theory and pedagogy have also recently been made with eastern philosophical traditions such as the *Advaita Vedanta.*

In 1999 *"PAULO"*, a National Training Organisation named in honour of *Freire,* was established in the United Kingdom. This agency was approved by the, then, Labour Government to represent some 300,000 community-based education practitioners working across the UK. *PAULO* was given formal responsibility for setting the occupational training standards for people working in this field.

The Pedagogy and Theatre of the Oppressed Conference is held each spring, is guided by the theory and practice of these two libratory practitioners. The Conference networks a wide variety of people with interests in *Freire* and *Augusto Boal*–liberatory education and theatre, community organizing, community-based analysis, TIE, race/gender/class/ sexual orientation/geography analysis, performance/performance art, comparative education models, etc.

The *Paulo* and *Nita Freire Project for International Critical Pedagogy* has been founded at Mc Gill University. Here *Joe L. Kincheloe* and *Shirley R. Steinberg* have worked to created a dialogical forum for critical scholars around the world to promote research and re-create a *Freirean* pedagogy in a multinational domain.

In 2012 a group of educators in Western Massachusetts received permission from the state to found the *Paulo Freire Social Justice Charter School* in Holyoke, Massachusetts, which was set to open in September 2013.

At his death, *Freire* was working on a book of ecopedagogy, a platform of work, carried on by many of the *Freire Institutes* and *Freirean Associations* around the world today. It has been influential in helping to develop planetary education projects such as the Earth Charter as well as countless international grassroots campaigns per the spirit of *Freirean* popular education generally.

Evaluation

Shalini Yadava's reflections on the significance of Paulo Freire's philosophy in contemporary times are as follows:

Paulo Freire has made important contributions to contemporary education system. First, his emphasis on dialogue has struck a very strong chord with those concerned with informal education. His method which is a digital or conversational in form rather than a banking method, believes that dialogue involves respect for human persons. Secondly, *Freire's* insistence on situating educational activity in the lived experiences of participants has opened up a series of possibilities for the way informal educators can approach education. His emphasis on critical educational theory or critical pedagogy encourages students to question issues of power —explicitly disparities within social contexts like socio-economic status, race, class, gender, sexual orientation, etc. Facilitating the development of critical literacy promotes the examination and reform of social situations and exposes students to the biases and hidden agendas within texts. Teachers can help to empower students by providing opportunities for them to find their voices. *Freire's* emphasis on diaglouge enables the educators to develop lessons based on the needs and interests of the learners to invite them to take part in a larger community discourse that attempts to solve problems and create alternatives to oppressive situations.

Freire's critique of traditional education that suppresses the oppressed and helps to keep the oppressed in subjection needs to be applied to the Indian educational scenario. There is too much emphasis for narration and memorizing in Indian system to the complete neglect of creative or critical thinking. This methodology needs to be changed completely so that learning becomes a real cognitive activity which leads to meaningful and purposeful transformative action. Although, *Freire* has opened a frontier of liberating education, yet is has to be reinvented according to one's own situations and in one's own words.

Besides educational impact in a country like India, there are vast majority of people who are oppressed. Many are not aware of their rights. Conscientizing them and making them aware about the reality can help them to live a dignified life. In India, *Paulo Freire's* contribution to the empowerment of *dalits*, tribals and women has been substantial. The method followed was one of dialogue and confrontation; dialogue within the circle of the oppressed and confrontation against the oppressor. In the process, the freedom of the oppressed communities was enlarged. *Freire*'s thinking brought some advances and theoretical support for alternative educational methodology. Action researchers, in-service, cognitive apprenticeship, adult literacy have seen new avenues of influencing and pushing social change. In addition, other aspects of education and sociology have been enriched by his contributions, for example: health promotion and occupational safety.

Juma E. Nyirenda of University of Botswana analyses the relevance of *Freire's* contributions to education and development in present day Africa in the following words:

In contemporary Africa, illiteracy rates are very high in many countries, especially in the rural areas. For example, the estimated adult literacy rates for Sub-Saharan Africa for the years 1995 and 2000 are 56.8 percent and 62 percent respectively (UNESCO, 1994). Illiterate people tend to be apathetic and accept do anything to change it. This is reflected, for example, in their behaviour during political elections. Some countries which have recently changed to multi-party politics have complained about the low turn out at elections by illiterate rural people. Zambia is one such example (Nyirenda, 1995). There are several factors that continue to contribute to high illiteracy rates in many countries of Africa. They include high population growth rates, limited capacity of the formal school systems to capture all the school-age population, lack of or inadequate allocation of human, material and financial resources, inadequate training of teachers, and lack of support mechanisms such as rural libraries community learning centres (UNESCO, 1994). Associated with the issue of illiteracy is poverty which is widespread among rural people and urban workers in many countries of Africa. Rural and urban poverty is exacerbated by the economic recession and the effects of World Bank/IMF Structural Adjustment Programmes which have been prescribed for economic growth in many African countries. The effects of the World Bank/IMF prescription for economic growth in Africa have caused greater poverty among the urban workers and rural dwellers alike. They are the most hit of the populations.

These conditions or circumstances provide a context today in which *Freire's* concientization literacy could be applied in order to raise the critical awareness of the rural illiterate people and urban workers so that they can understand why they and their countries are poor and how they can act in order to change the situation for themselves. The *Freire* literacy method seems to have the capacity to attract the participation of many illiterate people in literacy classes since the content of literacy learning will be related to their present social realities and, therefore, be meaningful. To this extent, it can be argued that the literacy method founded on the notions of conscientization and dialogue is relevant to present day Africa. However, for the method to work in these contexts, there would be need to train teams of coordinators (or educators) who should have a new attitude on how dialogue and critical study for conscientization should be elements of the educational process. Such coordinators would need to achieve a sufficient change from their existing potentiality and dialogue. At present, these elements of dialogue and conscientizatoin appear to be absent in our upbringing and education in many countries of Africa. The curriculum and methods of teaching, determined by the elite, still dominate our education systems. Further, the governments in power would need to accept the method and not regard it as subversive.

Conclusion

Freire has done some original thinking on the discipline of education. The western schools of philosophy of education have been challenged in relation to aims, curriculum, learners and teachers.

Summary

Paulo Freire, a Brazilian educationist, was born in 1921 and died in 1997. He studied law, but did not pratise it. He also studied philosophy and psychology of languages. He worked as a teacher in secondary schcols, was the Director of Education and Culture in the state of Pernambuka in Brazil. He was offered a visiting professorship at Harvard University. He also acted as an adviser to the World Council of Churches. He wrote many books. Amongst his books is *Pedagogy of the Opprossed* which highlights his views on education, as it is imparted by the oppressors to the oppressed. This education is 'banking education'. He recomnends education that poses problems, to be jointly solved by the teachers and learners. His ideas are relevant to education in general and the western type of educaton adopted/adapted in the former colonies.

17

Deschooling Society

Ivan Illich (1926-2002)

Life-sketch

Jon Igelmo Zaldivar in "International Journal for Cross Disciplinary Studies vol. I, Issue I, 2011" of Madrid, edited by the author, considered *Ivan Illich* as one of the most influential intellectuals on education of the twentieth century. He was born in Vienna in 1926. In the 1940's, he studied at the Roman Gregorian University, and he became a priest in 1951. Five years later, he travelled to New York in order to keep developing his academic career at Fordham University with *Jacques Maritain* as his mentor. In New York, he got in touch with the Puerto Rican immigrant community, settled in Manhattan. In 1956, with the support of *Joseph Spellman*, cardinal of New York, *Illich* started working as a vice-dean in the University of Puerto Rico. At the age of 30, he was able to speak eight languages: Spanish, Portuguese, English, French, Latin, Italian, German and Croatian.

In the beginning of the 1960s, *Illich* set up two centres in Mexico and Brazil, where he organized seminaries for missioneries, taking part in John XXIII's campaign in an attempt to modernize the Latin American Church. In 1963, together with *Valentina Borremans*, opened a new centre in Cuernavaca, Mexico, named *Centro Intercultrual de Documentation* (CIDOC). In this centre people of different nationalities organized many seminars, dealing with a variety of topics. Some of the most important intellectuals who spent time at the CIDOC and took part in its activities were: *Erich Fromm, Paul Goodman, Peter Berger, John Holt, Paulo Freire, Augusto Salazar Bondy* and *Susan Sontang*.

In the 1960's *Illich* also promoted one of the most transcendental events against Church authorities. Since 1960, he published several articles, criticizing the way in which the Catholic Church took part in the programmes promoted by the United States for Latin America. He presented several texts against the decision made by the Vatican to support a model of progress and development without considering the situation in Latin America and people's needs. Most of these articles were published in the book entitled *The Church Change and Development* (1970). As a

Equal educational opportunity is, indeed, both a desirable and a feasible goal, but to equate this with obligator-schooling is to confuse salvation with the Church. School has become the world religion of a modernized proletariat, and makes futile promises of salvation to the poor of the technological to sequential diplomas not unlike the initiation rituals and heretic promotions of former times. The modern state has assumed the duty of enforcing the judgement of its educators through well-meant truant officers and job requirements, much as did the Spanish kings who enforced the judgements of their theologians through the Inquisition.

Curriculom Considerations

We need a law forbidding discrimination in hiring, voting, or admission to centres of learning, based on previous attendance at some curriculum. This guarantee would not exclude performance tests of competence for a function or role, but would remove the present absurd discrimination in favour of the person who learns a given skill with the largest expenditure of public funds or what is equally likely has been able to obtain a diploma which has no relation to any useful skill or job. Only by protecting the citizen from being disqualified by anything in his career in school can a constitutional disestablishment of school become psychologically effective.

Neither learning nor justice is promoted by schooling because educators insist on packaging instruction with certification. Learning and the assignment of social roles are melted into schooling. Yet to learn means to acquire a new skill or insight, while promotion depends on an opinion which others have formed. Learning frequently is the result of instruction, but selection for a role or category in the job market increasingly depends on mere length of attendance.

Instruction is the choice of circumstances which facilitate learning. Roles are assigned by setting a curriculum of conditions which the candidate must meet if he is to make the grade. School links instruction but not learning to these roles. This is neither reasonable nor liberating. It is not reasonable because it does not link relevant qualities or competencies to roles, but rather the process by which such qualities are supposed to be acquired. It is not liberating or educational because school reserves instruction to those whose every step in learning fits previously approved measures of social control.

Curriculum has always been used to assign social rank. At times it could be prenatal: *karma* ascribes you to a caste and lineage to the aristocracy. Curriculum could take the form of a ritual, of sequential sacred ordinations, or it could consist of a succession of feats in war or hunting, or further advancement could be made to depend on a series of previous princely favours. Universal schooling was meant to detach role assignment from personal life history: it was meant to give everybody an equal change to any office. Even now many people wrongly believe that school ensures the dependence of public trust on relevant learning achievements. However, instead of equalizing chances, the school system has monoplized distribution.

To detach competence from curriculum, inquiries into a man's learning history must be made taboo, like inquiries into his political affiliation, church attendance, lineage, sex habits, or racial background. Laws forbidding discrimination on the basis of prior schooling must be enacted. Laws, forbidding discrimination on the basis of prior schooling must be enacted.

A second major illusion on which the school system rests is that most learning is the result of teaching. Teaching, it is true, may contribute to certain kinds of learning under certain circumstances. But most people acquire most of their knowledge outside school, and in school only insofar as school, in a few rich countries, has become their place of confinement during an increasing part of their lives.

Most learning happens casually, and even most intentional learning is not the result of programmed instruction. Normal children learn their first language casually, although faster if their parents pay attention to them. Most people who learn a second language well do so as a result of odd circumstances and not of sequential teaching. They go to live with their grandparents, they travel, or they fall in love with a foreigner. Fluency in reading is also more often than not a result of such extracurricular activities. Most people who read widely, and with pleasure, merely believe that they learned to do so in school; when challenged, they easily discard this illusion.

But the fact that a great deal of learning even now seems to happen casually and as a by-product of some other activity defined as work or leisure does not mean that planned learning does not benefit from planned instruction and that both do not stand in need of improvement. The strongly motivated student who is faced with the task of acquiring a new and complex skill may benefit greatly from the discipline now associated with the old-fashioned schoolmaster who taught reading, Hebrew, catechism, or multiplication by rote. School has now made this kind of drill teaching rare and disreputable, Yet there are many skills which a motivated student with normal aptitude can master in a matter of a few months if taught in this traditional way. This is as true of codes as of their encipherment; of second and third languages as of reading and writing, and equally of special languages such as algebra, computer programming, chemical analysis, or of manual skills like typing, watchmaking, plumbing, wiring, TV repair; or for that matter dancing, and diving.

In certain cases acceptance into a learning programme aimed at a specific skill might presuppose competence in some other skill, but it should certainly not be made to depend upon the process by which such prerequisite skills were acquired. TV repair presupposes literacy and some math; diving, good swimming; and driving, very little of either.

Progress in learning skills is measurable. The optimum resources in time and materials needed by an average motivated adult can be easily estimated. The cost of teaching a second Western language to a high level of fluency ranges between four and six hundred dollars in the United States, and for an Oriental tongue the time needed for instruction might be doubles. This would still be very little compared with the cost of twelve years or schooling in New York City (a condition for acceptance of a worker into the Sanitation Department) almost fifteen thousand dollars. No doubt not only the teacher but also the printer and the pharmacist protect their trades through the public illusion that training for them is very expensive.

At present, schools pre-empt most educational funds. Drill instruction which costs less than comparable schooling is now a privilege of those rich enough to bypass the schools, and those whom either the army or big business sends through in-service training. In a programme of progressive deschooling of U.S. education, at first the resources available for drill training would be limited. But ultimately there should be no obstacle for anyone at any time of his life to be able to choose instruction among hundreds of definable skills at public expense.

Right now educational credit good at any skill centre could be provided in limited amounts for people of all ages, and not just to the poor. I envisage such credit in the form of an educational passport or an "edu-credit card" provided to each citizen at birth. In order to favour the poor, who probably would not use their yearly grants early in life, a provision could be made that interest accrued to later users of cumulated "entitlements." Such credits would permit most people to acquire the skills most in demand, at their convenience, better, faster, cheaper, and with fewer undesirable side effects than in school.

Skill Teachers

Potential skill teachers are never scare for long because, on the one hand, demand for a skill grows only with its performance within a community and, on the other, a man exercising a skill could also teach it. But, at present, those using skills which are in demand and do require a human teacher are discouraged from sharing these skills with others. This is done either by teachers who monopolize the licences or by unions which protect their trade interests. Skill centres which would be judged by customers on their results, and not on the personnel they employ or the process they use, would open unsuspected working opportunities, frequently even for those who are now considered unemployable. Indeed, there is no reason why such skill centres should not be at the work place itself, with the employer and his work force supplying instruction as well as jobs to those who choose to use their educational credits in this way.

Skill teachers are made scarce by the belief in the value of licenses. Certification constitutes a form of market manipulation and is plausible only to a schooled mind. Most teachers of arts and trades are less skillful, less inventive, and less communicative than the best craftsman and tradesmen. Most high-school teachers of Spanish or French do not speak the language as correctly as their pupils might after half a year of competent drills.

Nature of Learning

The deschooling of society implies a recongnition of the two-faced nature of learning. An insistence on skill drill alone could be a disaster; equal emphasis must be placed on other kinds of learning. But if schools are the wrong places for learning a skill, they are even worse places for getting an education. School does both tasks badly, partly because it does not distinguish between them. School is inefficient in skill instruction especially because it is curricular. In most schools, a programme which is meant to improve one skill is chained always to another irrelevant task. History is tied to advancement in math, and class attendance to the right to use the playground.

Schools are even less efficient in the arrangement of the circumstances which encourage the open-ended, exploratory use of acquired skills, for which I will reserve the term exile, mainly because he refuses to conduct his sessions around words which are preselected by approved educators, rather than those which his discussants bring to the class.

The educational matchmaking among people who have been successfully schooled is a different task; those who do not need such assistance are a minority, even among the readers of serious journals. The majority can not and should not be rallied for discussion around a slogan, a word, or a picture. But the idea remains the same: they should be able to meet around a problem, chosen and defined by their own initiative. Creative, exploratory learning requires peers currently puzzled about the same terms or problems. Large universities make the futile attempt to match them by multiplying their courses, and they generally fail since they are bound to curriculum, course structure, and bureaucratic administration. In schools, including universities, most resources are spent to purchase the time and motivation of a limited number of people to take up predetermined problems in a ritually-defined setting. The most radical alternative to school would be a network or service which gave each man the same opportunity to share his current concern with others motivated by the same concern.

Phenomenology of School

Illich defined *"school" as "age-specific, teacher-related progress requiring full-time attendance at an obligatory curriculum."* But he criticised the school, as for him, *"the school system is a modern concept, as is the childhood it produces."* He continues to say that *"institutional wisdom tells us that children learn in shcool. But this institutional wisdom is itself the product of schools .....*

Role of Teachers

We have learnt most of what we know outside school. Pupils do most of their learning without, and often despite, their teachers.... Everyone learns how to live outside school.... Increasingly educational school demonstrates that children learn most of what teachers preterd to teach from freer groups, from comics, from chawl observations, and alive all from mere participifation in the ritual of school. Teachers, more often than not, obstruct such learning of subject matters as goes on in the school.

Continuing, *Illich* was of the view that under the authoritative eye of the teacher, several orders of value collapse into one. The distinctions between morality, legality and personal worth are blurred and eventually eliminated. Each transgression is made to be felt as a multiple offence. The offender is expected to feel that he has broken a rule, that he has behaved immorally, and that he has let himself down. A pupil who adroitly obtains assistance on an exam is told that he is an outlaw, morally corrupt, and personally worthless.

Institutional Spectrum

In a chapter titled "Institutional spectrum", *Illich* said that school initiates, too, the myth of unending consumption. This modern myth is grounded in the belief that process inevitably produces something of value and, therefore, production necessarily produces demand. School teaches us that instruction produces learning. The existence of schools produces the demand for schooling. Once we have learned to need school, all our activities tend to take the shape of client relationships to other specialized institutions. Once the self-taught man or woman has been discredited, all nonprofessional activity is rendered suspect. In school, we are taught that valuable learning is the result of attendance; that the value of learning increases with the amount of input; and, finally, that this value can be measured and documented by grades and certificates.

In fact, learning is the human activity which least needs manipulation by others. Most learning is not the result of instruction. It is rather the result of unhampered participation in a meaningful setting. Most people learn best by being "with it," yet school makes them identify their personal, cognitive growth with elaborate planning and manipulation.

Once a man or woman has accepted the need for school, he or she is easy prey for other institutions. Once young people have allowed their imaginations to be formed by curricular instruction, they are conditioned to institutional planning of every sort. "Instruction" smothers the horizon of their imaginations. They can not be betrayed, but only short-changed, because they have been taught to substitute expectations for hope. They will no longer be surprised, for good or ill, by other people, because they have been taught what to expect from every other person who has been taught as they were. This is true in the case of another person or in the case of a machine.

According to him, there was also "The Myth of measurement of values."

The Myth of Measurement of Values

The institutionalized values school instills are quantified ones. School inititates young people into a world where everything can be measured, including their imaginations, and, indeed, man himself.

But personal growth is not a measurable entity. It is growth in disciplined dissidence, which can not be measured again by any rod, or any curriculum, nor compared to someone else's achievement. In such learning one can emulate others' only imaginative endeavour, and follow in their footsteps rather than mimic them. The learning I prize is immeasurable re-creation.

School pretends to breakup learning into subject "matters," to build into the pupil a curriculum, made of these prefabricated blocks, and to gauge the result on an international scale. People who submit to the standard of others for the measure of their own personal growth soon apply the same rule to themselves. They no longer have to be put in their place, but put themselves into their assigned slots, squeeze themselves into the niche which they have been taught to seek, and, in the very process, put their fellows into their places, too, until everybody and everything fits.

People who have been schooled down to size let unmeasured experience slip out of their hands. To them, what can not be measured becomes secondary, threatening. They do not have to be robbed of their creativity. Under instruction, they have unlearned to "do" their thing or "be" themselves, and value only what has been made or could be made.

Once people have the idea schooled into them that values can be produced and measured, they tend to accept all kinds of rankings. There is a scale for the development of nations, another for the intelligence of babies, and even progress toward peace can be calculated according to body count. In a schooled world, the road to happiness is paved with a consumer's index.

The Myth of Packaging Values

School sells curriculum–a bundle of goods made according to the same process and having the same structure as other merchandise. Curriculum production for most schools begins with allegedly scientific research, on whose basis educational engineers predict future demand and tools for the assembly line, within the limits set by budgets and taboos.. The distributer-teacher delivers the finished product to the consumer pupil, whose reactions are carefully studied and charged to provide research data for the preparation of the next model, which may be "ungraded," "student-designed," "team-taught," "visually-aided," or "issue-centred."

The result of the curriculum production process looks like any other modern staple. It is a bundle of planned meanings, a package of values, a commodity whose "balanced appeal" makes it marketable to a sufficiently large number to justify the cost of production. Consumer-pupils are taught to make their desires conform to marketable values. Thus, they are made to feel guilty if they do not behave according to the predictions of consumer research by getting the grades and certificates that will place them in the job category, they have been led to expect.

Educators can justify more expensive curricula on the basis of their observation that learning difficulties rise proportionately with the cost of the curriculum. This is an application of *Prarkinson*'s Law that work expands with the resources available to do it. This law can be verified on all levels of schools: for instance, reading difficulties have been a major issue in French schools only since their per capita expenditures have approached U.S. levels of 1950, when reading difficulties became a major issue in U.S. schools.

In fact, healthy students often redouble their resistance to teaching as they find themselves more comprehensively manipulated. This resistance is due not to the authoritarian style of a public school or the seductive style of some free schools, but to the fundamental approach common to all schools—the idea that one person's judgment should determine what and when another person must learn.

The Myth of Self-Perpetuating Progress

Even when accompanied by declining returns in learning, paradoxically, rising per capita instructional costs increase the value of the pupil in his or her own eyes and on the market. At almost any cost, school pushes the pupil up to the level of competitive curricular consumption, into progress to ever higher levels. Expenditures to motivate the students to stay on in school skyrocket as he climbs the pyramid. On higher levels they are disguised as new football stadiums, chapels, or programmes called International Education. If it teaches nothing else, school teaches the value of escalation: the value of the American way of doing things.

School programmes hunger for progressive intake of instruction, but even if the hunger leads to steady absorption, it never yields the joy of knowing something to one's satisfaction. Each subject comes packaged with the instruction to go on consuming one "offering" after another, and last year's wrapping is always obsolete for this year's consumer. The text book racket builds on this demand. Educational reformers promise each new generation the latest and the best, and the public is schooled into demanding what they offer. Both the dropout who is forever reminded of what he missed and the graduate who is made to feel inferior to the new breed of student know exactly where they stand in the ritual of rising deception and continue to support a society which euphemistically calls the widening frustration gap a "revolution of rising expectations".

The Revolutionary Potential of Deschooling

Of course, school is not, by any means, the only modern institution which has as its primary purpose the shaping of man's vision of reality. The hidden curriculum of family life, draft, health care, so-called professionalism, or of the media play an important part in the institutional manipulation of man's world-vision, language, and demands. But school enslaves more profoundly and more systematically, since only school is credited with the principal function of forming critical judgement, and, paradoxically, tries to do so by making learning about oneself, about others, and about nature depend on a prepackaged process. School touched us so intimately that none of us can expect to be liberated from it by something else.

Our options are clear enough. Either we continue to believe that institutionalized learning is a product which justifies unlimited investment or we rediscover that legislation and planning and investment, if they have any place in formal education, should be used mostly to tear down the barriers that now impede opportunities for learning, which can only be a personal activity.

Alienation, in the traditional scheme, was a direct consequence of work's becoming wage-labour which deprived man of the opportunity to create and be recreated. Now schools isolate them while they pretend to be both producers and consumers of their own knowledge, which is conceived of as a commodity put on the market in school. School makes alienation preparatory to life, thus, depriving education of reality and work of creativity. School prepares for the alienating institutionalization of life by teaching the need to be taught. Once this lesson is learned, people lose their incentive to grow in independence; they no longer find relatedness attractive, and close themselves off to the surprises which life offers when it is not predetermined by institutional definition. And school directly or indirectly employs a major portion of the population. School either keeps people for life or makes sure that they will fit into some institution.

In a chapter titled, 'Retualization of Progress, *Illich* examined the role of the university.

Ritualization of Progress

The university graduate has been schooled for selective service among the rich of the world. Whatever his or her claims of solidarity with the Third World, each American college graduate has had an education costing an amount five times greater than the median life income of half of humanity. A Latin American student is introduced to this exclusive fraternity by having at least 350 times as much public money spent on his education as on that of his fellow citizens of median income. With very rare exceptions, the university graduate from a poor country feels more comfortable with his North American and European colleagues than with his nonschooled compatriots, and all students are academically processed to be happy only in the company of yellow consumers of the products of the educational machine.

The modern university confers the privilege of dissent on those who have been tested and classified as potential money-makers or power-holders. No one is given funds for the leisure in which to educate himself or the right to educate others unless at the same time he can also be certified for achievement. Schools select for each successive level those who have, at earlier stages in the game, proved themselves good risks for the established order. Having a monopoly on both the resources for learning and the investiture of social roles, the university coopts the discoverer and the potential dissenter. A degree always leaves its indelible price tag on the curriculum of its consumer. Certified college graduates fit only into a world which puts a price tag on their heads, thereby giving them the power to define the level of expectations in their society. In each country, the amount of consumption by the college graduate sets the standard for all others; if they would be civilized people on or off the job, they will aspire to the style of life of college graduates.

The university, thus, has the effect of imposing consumer standards at work and at home, and it does so in every part of the world and under every political system. The fewer university graduates there are in a country, the more their cultivated demands are taken as models by the rest of the population. The gap between the consumption of the university graduate and that of the average citizen is even wider in Russia, China, and Algeria than in the United States. Cars, airplane trips, and tape recorders confer more visible distinction in a socialist country, where only a degree, and not just money, can procure them.

The ability of the university to fix consumer goals is something new. In many countries, the university acquired this power only in the sixties, as the delusion of equal access to public education began to spread. Before that the university protected an individual's freedom of speech, but did not automatically convert his knowledge into wealth. To be a scholar in the Middle Ages meant to be poor, even a beggar. By virtue of his calling, the medieval scholar Latin learner, became an outsider worthy of the scorn as well as the esteem of peasant and prince, burgher and cleric. To get ahead in the world, the scholastic first had to enter it by joining the civil service, preferably that of the Church. The old university was a liberated zone for discovery and the discussion of ideas both new and old. Masters and students gathered to read the texts of other masters, now long dead, and the living words of the dead masters gave new perspective to the fallacies of the present day. The university was then a community of academic quest and endemic unrest.

In the modern multiversity, this community has fled to the fringes, where it meets in a pad, a professor's office, or the chaplain's quarters. The structural purpose of the modern university has little to do with the traditional quest. Since Guttenberg, the exchange of disciplined, critical inquiry has, for the most part, moved into print. The modern university has forfeited its chance to provide a simple setting for encounters which are both autonomous and anarchic, focused yet unplanned and has chosen.

In a chapter on Institutional Spectrum, *Illich* had something new to say.

Institutional Spectrum: Schools as False Public Utilities

Like highways, schools, at first glance, give the impression of being equally open to all comers. They are, in fact, open only to those who consistently renew their credentials. Just as highways create the impression that their present level of cost per year is necessary if people are to move, so schools are presumed essential for attaining the competence required by a society which uses modern technology. We have exposed speedways as spurious public utilities by noting their dependence on private automobiles. Schools are based upon the equally spurious hypothesis that learning is the result of curricular teaching.

Highways result from a perversion of the desire and need for mobility into the demand for a private car. Schools themselves pervert the natural inclination to grow and learn into the demand for instruction. Demand for manufactured maturity is a far greater abnegation of self-initiated activity than the demand for manufactured goods. Schools are not only to the right of highways and cars; they belong near the extreme of the institutional spectrum occupied by total asylums. By making men abdicate the responsibility for their own growth, school leads many to a kind of spiritual suicide.

Highways are paid for in part by those who use them, since tolls and gasoline taxes are extracted only from drivers. School, on the other hand, is a perfect system of regressive taxation, where the privileged graduates ride on the back of the entire paying public. School puts a head tax on promotion. The underconsumption of highway mileage is not nearly so costly as the underconsumption of schooling. The man who does not own a car in Los Angeles may be almost immobilized, but if he can somehow manage to reach a work place, he can get and hold a job. The school dropout has no alternative route. The value of a man's schooling is a function of the number of years he has completed and of the costliness of the schools, he has attended. The law compels no one to drive, whereas it obliges everyone to go to school.

The analysis of institutions according to their present placement on a left-right continuum enables me to clarify my belief that fundamental social change must begin with a change of consciousness about institutions and to explain why the dimension of a viable future turns on the rejuvenation of institutional style.

Today, for instance, the school systems of Colombia, Britain, the U.S.S.R., and the U.S. resemble each other more closely than U.S. schools of the late 1890's resembled either today's or their contemporaries in Russia. Today, all schools are obligatory, open-ended, and competitive. The same convergence in institutional style affects health care merchandising, personnel administration, and political life. All these institutional processes tend to pile up at the manipulative end of the spectrum.

I believe that a desirable future depends on our deliberately choosing a life of action over a life of consumption, on our engendering a life style which will enable us to be spontaneous, independent, yet related to each other, rather than maintaining a life style which only allows us to make and unmake, produce and consume-a style of life which is merely a way station on the road to the depletion and pollution of the environment. The future depends more upon our choice of institutions which support a life of action than on our developing new ideologies and technologies. We need a set of criteria which will permit us to recognize those institutions which support personal growth rather than addiction, as well as the will to invest our techno-logical resources preferentially in such institutions of growth.

The choice is between two radically opposed institutional types, both of which are exemplified in certain existing institutions, although one type so characterizes the contemporary period as to almost define it. This dominant type I would propose to call the manipulative institution. The other type also exists, but only precariously. The institutions which fit it are humbler and less noticeable; yet I take them as models for a more desirable future. I call them "convivial" and suggest placing them at the left of an institutional spectrum.

it can also be used for the telephone or the postal service, which are primarily accessible to individuals who want to send messages to one another. I wish we had another word to designate such reticular structures for mutual access, a word less degraded by current usage and more suggestive of the fact that any such arrangement includes legal, organizational, and technical aspects. Not having found such a term, I will try to redeem the one which is available, using it as a synonym of "educational web."

What are needed are new networks, readily available to the public and designed to spread equal opportunity for learning and teaching.

Four Networks

The planning of new educational institutions ought not to begin with the administrative goals of a principal or president, or with the teaching goals of a professional educator, or with the learning goals of any hypothetical class of people. It must not start with the question, "What should someone learn?" but with the question, "What kinds of things and people might learners want to be in contact with in order to learn?"

Someone who wants to learn knows that he needs both information and critical response to its use from somebody else. Information can be stored in things and in persons. In a good educational system, access to things ought to be available at the sole bidding of the learner, while access to informants requires, in addition, others consent. Criticism can also come from two directions: from peers or from elders, that is from fellow learners whose immediate interests match mine, or from those who will grant me a share in their superior experience. Peers can be colleagues with whom to raise a question, companions for playful and enjoyable (or arduous) reading or walking, challengers at any type of game. Elders can be consultants on which skill to learn, which method to use, what company to seek at a given moment. They can be guides to the right questions to be raised among peers and to the deficiency of the answers, they arrive at. Most of these resources are plentiful. But they are neither conventionally perceived as educational resources, nor is access to them for learning purposes easy, especially for the poor. We must conceive of new relational structures which are deliberately set up to facilitate access to these resources for the use of anybody who is motivated to seek them for his education. Administrative, technological, and especially legal arrangements are required to set up such web-like structures.

Educational resources are usually labelled according to educators' curricular goals. I propose to do the contrary, to label four different approaches which enable the student to gain access to any educational resource which may help him to define and achieve his own goals:

1. *Reference Services to Educational Objects*–which facilitate access to

things or processes, used for formal learning. Some of these things can be reserved for this purpose, stored in libraries, rental agencies, laboratories, and showrooms like museums and theatres; others can be in daily use in factories, airports, or on farms, but made available to students as apprentices or on off hours.

2. *Skill Exchanges*–which permit persons to list their skills, the conditions under which they are willing to serve as models for others who want to learn these skills, and he addresses at which they can be reached.
3. *Peer-Matching*–a communications network which permits persons to describe the learning activity in which they wish to engage, in the hope of finding a partner for the inquiry.
4. *Reference Services to Educators-at-large*–who can be listed in a directory giving the addresses and self-descriptions of professionals, paraprofessionals, and free-lancers, alongwith conditions of access to their services. Such educators, as we will see, could be chosen by polling or consulting their former clients.

Evaluation: Bob Corbett

Illich longs for a different world than exists today. This world is a much more radically individualist world where fundamental responsibilities fall to the individual. There is an irony here. Much of the tendency toward a more society-dominated world came from people who claimed that radical individualism disadvantaged too many, especially the gigantic underclass, and simply fed class divisions. Thus, many programmes toward government control came from people called in the contemporary sense "liberals," who supposedly want to protect and advance the cause of the underclass. *Illich* believes this has resulted in a disaster which has the following outcomes:

- the poor have even less chance at a fully developed and realized world.
- in the process of "protecting" us, society has taken over much too much of our lives and freedom.
- Society itself has suffered since we have substituted "process" for "subtance" in our quest for objective and fair standards of measurement and in wishing to make up for genuine differences in achievement. These are the sorts of reasons that lead *Illich* to call for a fundamental and radical change of social values. Before I try to clarify these notions and the arguments, he offers for them, let me try to make this picture a bit more vivid. This is extremely difficult to do to people primarily raised in the United States after the mid-1960s. By that time the society was, on *Illich*'s terms "all schooled up,' and most of you will have grown up taking this "all schooled up" society as completely NATURAL and obvious. Not so with me. I was born in 1939 into a St. Louis working class neighborhood. I had finished college before the

1960s when radical changes began to occur. That is, I was an adult, finished with university before "schooling" was the fully dominant world that it is today. While the outside society–outside my working class neighborhood–was changing in this direction ever since the depression, but with more vigour after World War II, the changes were much less noticeable to the working and underclass folks. Thus, I have lived in both these worlds.

- A world in which the dominant watchword was individual responsibility, and in which actual achievement was the measure of success.
- A world in which government guarantee is the dominant watchword and in which PROCESS (following socially prescribed acts) is the dominant measure to open the doors of success.

Summary

Ivan Illich (1926-2002) was once a priest but later became the father of 'deschooled' education. He was of the opinion that universal education through schooling was not feasible. It needed means of alternative institutions, built on the style of present schools. Universal education could neither the delivered by new attitudes of teachers towards their pupils, nor the proliferation of educational hardware and software. The current search for new educational tunnels needed reversal with the search for their institutional inverse: educational webs which heighten the opportunity by learning, sharing and caring. There was a need to 'deschool' just not the institutions, but the ethos of the society.

PART II
INDIAN PHILOSOPHERS

18

Spiritual Absolutism

Samkara

The *Upanishads* are said to be the concluding portions of the *Vedas.* But there are two different tendencies in the *Upanishads:* one tendency affirms the identity of *Brahman,* the individual soul and the world; the other distinguishes them. An eighth century A.D. philosopher—*Samkara*—established spiritual absolutism as the main teaching of the *Upanishads.* His *Karika* is the first exposition of the basic principles of *Advaita* philosophy, the orders of reality, the identity of *Brahman* and *Atma,* the doctrine of appearance, the inapplicability of logical categories as causation to ultimate reality and wisdom as the direct means to *moksha* (freedom).

Major Themes

(i) In the interpretation of texts, *Samkara* claimed not only the authority of the scriptures but also direct experience and intrinsic reasonableness. Only direct experience could bring us into contact with reality as reality was not a metaphysical concept but a spiritual being. It was an object of intuition not influence. Scripture was a record of the experiences of seers.

(ii) He held the *Brahman* as an object of intuition; it was apprehended by immediate experience. It was not an object of preposition or other means of knowledge like inference, analogy, implication and scripture.

(iii) In the experience, everything was felt as the self. The distinction between the knower, the process of knowing and the object known disappeared. There was a feeling of certitude. Rhetorically, *Samkara* asked, *"How can one contest the fact of another possessing the knowledge of Brahman, vouched as it was by his heart's conviction?"*

(iv) The experience was intimate, ineffable and incommunicable. The self alone was witness to it: *atma-saksikani anuttaman*—realization came of the self of pure consciousness, free from all pain. Pain was felt when there was alienation from reality: the pain would disappear if alienation was removed.

(v) *Brahman:*

(a) The famous passage in the *Upanishads, neti neti* (not this, not this), told us that *Brahman* was absolutely nonempirical. It was inapprehensible by logical knowledge. It was pure inwardness of which nonconceptual interpretation was possible. It was indivisible; it was neither external nor conditioned by external causation. Its definition implied transmitting it into an object. It was non-dual *(advaita)*: Ultimate. For *Samkara*, reflection on absolute *Brahman* was possible only through empirical discourse. Spirit beyond subject-object distinction, the unconditioned *Brahman* was conceived of as the subject confronting the subject or the object. We had the interaction between the two which was in cosmic process gradually realizing the values of spirit in its upward ascent from nothingness to the kingdom of God under divine inspiration and influence.

(b) He believed that the ultimate reality was fullness of being *(sat)*. Life became meaningless without the *a priori* notion of being *(astitra-nistha)*. The rise of being could not be explained from non-being. Being was eternal and self-existent. It alone existed for itself. The light of consciousness that illuminated the universe was *Brahman.*

(c) Ultimate reality was not wholly unknown to us, for it was our very self. *Atman* was not the subject but was the basis of the subject-object distinction. *Atman* existed for itself, everything else had "being" in and through the self.

(d) *Brahman* was "being" *(sat),* consciousness *(hit)* and "bliss" *(ananda)*. The universe lived on a fraction of the supreme bliss. *Brahman* was the supreme bliss. Knowledge was the essence of *Brahman* and not an attribute which qualified *Brahman.*

(vi) *The Status of the World:*

(a) *Samkara* did not assert the absolute oneness of *Brahman* and the world but only their difference.

(b) The world was not independent of *Brahman* who was both *Isvara* and *Jiva* (the cosmic Lord and the individual ego). *Isvara* was associated with cosmic *maya* while the individual was associated with *Avidya* (ignorance). God was material as well as the efficient cause of the universe. The existence of the world was less than that of *Brahman.* The world had empirical existence which was quite different from the eternal being of *Brahman* and absolute non-being.

controlled: there was full concentration. At this stage, the 'I' lost its identity and got absorbed into *Brahman.* So to say, the learners passed from physical stage through intellectual stage to spiritual stage. There were children of superior category, who studied the *Vedas;* the average learnt devotion; and the inferior devoted themselves to *Karma.*

(iii) The Teachers

The idealist philosophy in the western world started with the Greek philosophers like Socrates and Plato. The Greeks stood for good life for learners as well as their teachers. Although the words that teacher was a co-worker with God in perfecting man were that of a philosopher—*H.H. Horne*—of the modern times, these were close to the highest expectation of teacher in the *Advaita* doctrine. The *Maths* were the centres of learning and the teachers were *Shankaracharyas* or *Jagat Gurus.* They were teachers and preachers not only for their own *Maths,* but also they spread scholarship to the entire world. They were scholars of high order and their messages were received by learners with attention, seriousness and devotion. They were thorough in the *Brahman Gyan.* It was this saturation with spiritual knowledge that enabled them to prepare the learners to lead a virtuous life, master the art and science of *Vandantic* knowledge and ultimately be one with *Brahman.*

Europe had monks in their monasteries who were scholars. The Buddhist monks were erudite in their discipline of Buddhism. The monks in *Samkara's Maths* were given to an austere life, devotion to learning and teaching and endeavouring not only to attain salvation themselves, but also prepare their scholars for the *Moksha.*

(iv) The Curriculum

Samkara divided Reality into three categories (a) Reflection, (b) Practical and (c) Spiritual.

(a) Reflection was illustrated by the example of the mirage in that a rope appeared to be a serpent in the partial darkness or in a shadow. But, when light was shown, the mirage disappeared.
(b) The practical category included the recognition of and behaviour with the material environment.
(c) The transitory satisfaction with material world was discovered to be unreal, when the highest stage of spiritualism was reached.

The courses of reading and the methods of teaching depended on the category of the learner. The superior types of learners were exposed to universal knowledge that consisted of real and unreal. The power of discernment of the learner then recognized the differences between unreal and real—shadow and substance, mirage and reality. The teacher enabled the learner to understand the differences and recognize the superiority of the *Brahman.* The conclusion that the *Brahman* was the ultimate reality was not reached dogmatically but logically. The soul was different from and superior to body, mind and intelligence—individually and collectively. Through reasoning was reached the stage of *Brahman.*

The second category of learner—the average—was inducted into devotional curriculum. In it, through prayers and devotion, the learner endeavoured to merge the "Self" into the "Ideal". This self-realization was brought about by the process of surrender before the Ideal.

The third category of learners—the inferior ones—were given the opportunity to fast, to be charitable, to practise abstinence and purify themselves so that they also ascended the stage of self-realization and prepared for the journey to attain salvation.

Idealists in the western world attached great importance to subjects like literature, history, art, music, poetry, religion, metaphysics, ethics, geography, mathematics and science. But in the *Advaita* School, arts and humanities were given the pride of place in the curriculum and sciences and vocational subjects were assigned a low status.

Influence

(i) *Samkara* put the *Upanishads* philosophy of *Advaita Vedant* into practice by establishing four centres of learning *(Maths)*. One *Math* was at Badri Nath with accent on *Atharva Veda.* The area of its work and influence covered the northern states. In the southern states was established the Shringeri *Math* to encourage the gospel of *Yajur Veda.* The eastern part of India was served by the gospel of *Rig Veda.* In the western part of India was Sharda *Math* to preach the gospel of *Sam Veda.*

(ii) His views were straightforward development of the doctrines of the *Upanishads* and the *Brahma-sutra.* There was no influence of Buddhism on him.

(iii) He rejected the views of all the current rival schools, including Buddhism and Jainism.

Limitations

(i) In order to establish the supremacy of the *Upanishads,* the *Brhma-Sutra* and the *Bhagvad Gita, Samkara* rejected the views of other rival schools, leaving lacunea which his followers did not find easy to fill. As a consequence, many new schools came into existence and offered their own interpretation of the *Upanishads.*

(ii) Questions were raised on *Samkara's* interpretation relating to how the world, which was *Maya,* caused at all? Why *Brahman* did issue forth the inanimate world? What was the role of *Maya?*

(iii) It was not clear how the three categories of learners—superior, average, inferior—were identified and then educated in somewhat segregated groups. If the aim of life was to cross all hurdles and be one with *Brahman,* what scope was there for the inferior category of learners to reach this sublime stage?

(iv) The *Advaita* school of philosophy was backward looking, even when the claim that all knowledge and wisdom were available in the *Vedas* could be justified. To expect the entire humanity to live in the *Maths* was somewhat unconvincing and unrealistic.

(v) Other religions of the world also had their holy books, which provided moral and spiritual guidance. To claim that the Hindu philosophy was so universal that it could show the path to the people of all religions might not be acceptable to people of other religions and beliefs.

Conclusion

When the great Indian classics merely decorated the shelves of the libraries, or were dismissed as myths, or even as superstitions, there arose great people like *Samkura* to focus on the ancient wisdom with a view to highlighting its importance as guide to action in life.

Summary

In the eighth century A.D., a philosopher like *Samkara* established "spiritual absolutism" as the main teaching of the *Upanishds.* For him, reality was not metaphysical, but spiritual. The *Brahman* was an object of intuition. Knowledge was the essence of the *Brahman.* He upheld the law of *Karma. Samkara's* aims of education were individual and social. *Maths* were the seats of learning. Learners were the *Brahman.* Teachers were *Jagat Gurus.* Samkara divided Reality into three: reflection, practical and spiritual.

19

Vidya is Endless

Guru Nanak (1469-1539)

Sikh religion had been founded conjointly by the great teachers or *gurus:* the line began with *Guru Nanak* and ended with *Guru Gobind Singh* (1666-1908). Sikh Philosophy is contained in the religious-poetic compositions *(Gurbani)* of *Guru Nanak.* The philosophy and religious thoughts, contained in the *Gurubani,* are the result of revelation and not of formal logic.

Life Sketch

How great men are born in ordinary households is true in case of *Nanak* also, for he was born in a village called Talwandi, on the river Ravi. The village was renamed as Nankana Sahib, now in Pakistan.

Nanak started talking about God when he was only five years old. In the present times, *Sathya Sai Baba* spoke of God very early in his life. At school, *Nanak* advised his companions to join him not in ordinary games but in those in which there was presence of God. Once he said to his teacher, *"to love Him is the end of knowledge and to forget Him is to forget the Trutn, even though one may carry a cartload of books"*. The teacher was astonished and submitted to *Nanak.* The traditional schooling came to an end for *Nanak.*

He was married at the age of fourteen years and got two sons. But the family life made little difference to his meditations. His sister took him to Sultanpur Lodhi, near Kapurthala and he was appointed in the *Modikhana* (government store for provisions). He worked honestly. He was so charitable that he distributed his earnings amongst the poor and needy and he named this transaction as *Sacha Sauda.*

Nanak left the service in 1496, and in the company of two disciples–*Bala*, a Hindu and *Mardana*, a Muslim–he set out to preach his message of love, selfless service, honest living and faith in God. He travelled far and wide to holy places of the Hindus, the Buddhists, the Jains and the Muslims.

In the last phase of his life, he settled at Kartarpur in the Punjab with his family. There, he held prayers and religious discussions. His message to people was that they could earn their living honestly and yet worship

God. They needed not to run away to solitary places to seek God. *Nanak* lived an ideal life and passed away on 22nd September 1539.

Principles of Life

Nanak exhorted his followers to observe five principles in life:

(i) *Nam* (singing praises of God);
(ii) *Dan* (charity for all or the needy);
(iii) *Ashnan* (daily bath to keep the body clean);
(iv) *Seva* (service to humanity), and
(v) *Simran* (constant prayers for the deliverance of the soul). *Guru Granth Sahib* contains his 974 hymns.

General Philosophy

Philosophical thoughts of *Nanak* are enshrined in his *Banis.*

(i) Concept of God: *Bani "Japji"* gave *Nanak's* concept of God. God was Absolute One, True Name, Eternal Reality, and Creator of all things. He was without fear and enemity. He was beyond birth and death and was not subject to time. He was formless, imminent in his Creation and was known by the *Guru's* grace. God was Supreme Truth, Supreme Consciousness, Supreme Intelligence, Beauty, Bliss and Grace. He was Immortal, Unborn and Self-Existent. He was *Hari, Ram, Gopal, Allah, Khudha* and *Sahib.* He Himself was the Creator, Sustainer, Destroyer and Recreator. He was Omnipresent, Omnipotent and Omniscent. He was incomprehensible and indescribable.

(ii) Man: For *Nanak,* man was the supreme creation of God. He had some understanding of this universe and its creator. He was a creature of unlimited potentialities. The purpose of man's life was to seek God and unite with Him. God-centred men *(Gurumukhs)* would raise themselves from ordinary men and women to the level of supermen *(Braham Gyani).* The path of contemplation and illumination led to the highest stage of self-realization. An ideal man was to be truthful, fearless, pure, generous, gracious and sweet, and was to have love for all and malice towards none.

(iii) Religion: *Nanak* believed that there was only one religion in the universe, i.e., unity of mankind and God. Religion was indivisible. He wrote: *"I see here neither a Hindu nor a Muslim, only a man".* Furthermore, he said that there were three cardinal principles of religion.

These were:

(a) To earn one's living by honest labour – *Kirt Kama*
(b) To share one's earning with poor – *Vond Chhakna*
(c) To meditate the name of God – *Nam Japna*

The implication was that honesty was basic to how we lived our life and then whatever we earned, irrespective of the quantity and value, we shared it with the poor. Only then the singing of glory of God was meaningful from this world to the other worldliness.

(iv) Nature: In *Nanak's* words Nature was *Duniya, Jagat, Qudrat and Jahan. Duniya* is a urdu word, meaning the world, Jagat is a Hindi word, meaning the world, Qudrat is a Urdu word meaning nature, and Jahan is again a Urdu word meaning universe or cosmos. In his *Bani, Asa- Di-Var,* he said that Nature was all form *(Sarb-Akar),* all knowledge *(Sarb-Vichar)* and all love *(Sarb Piar).* It was God Who had created Nature out of His name, *Hukam* (order) and Self and made it His abode, temple and manifestation.

Philosophy of Life

Nanak laid emphasis on three aspects of life and nature:

(i) to establish a living relation of harmony and oneness of God, man and nature;
(ii) to develop *Nam* character;
(iii) to work constructively with continuity, disinterestedness and optimism for establishment of God's kingdom on earth which meant evolution of Divine *Hukam* (order) in life, individually and collectively. *Nanak's* philosophy to establish God's kingdom on earth was not a Utopian dream, but a vision. To make the vision a reality, he suggested:
  (a) God's will and creative joy;
  (b) His grace and action;
  (c) His praise and its beautiful expression;
  (d) Evolution and enlightenment of His *Sabad* (command);
  (e) His contemplation and service;
  (f) His truth and *Nam* (name), practised with spiritual music and wisdom;
  (g) Austerity and optimistic enthusiasm; and
  (h) Religion and *Karamyoga* (noble deeds) with sincere faith and devotion.

Teachings

Nanak's teachings were based on four fundamental principles:

(i) Absolute Purity;
(ii) Absolute Love;
(iii) Absolute Honesty; and
(iv) Absolute Unselfishness.

The key word is "absolute", which, though used as an adjective could stand for a noun also. As an adjective, it means total, but as a noun it means a principle which is valid at all times and in all circumstances.

Philosophy of Education

Nanak's philosophy of education was closely linked with his philosophy of life and this characteristic, he would like to develop in an educated man. He used the word, *Vidya,* for education. His use was somewhat like the concept of a life-long education as he said that *Vidya* knew no limits and it was endless. In *Raga Aga Sabad* 25, he said that "*Vidya Vichari Ta Parupkari*"" the more we thought of education, the more the good would be done.

An educated man was God-centred; he had the garland of *Ram Nam* round his neck; he established the kingdom of God in his life by raising the flag of *Nam* in his mind; he won victory over lust, anger, greed, infatuation and ego. He was a saint-soldier and a sincere comrade of God, man and nature. He regarded his life as the veritable shrine of God. He was full of virtues of discipline, justice, austerity, research, optimism, courtesy, creative service and *Nam* contemplation, and his personality or his powers of body, mind, soul and spirit were fully developed and divinised.

(i) Aims of Education: *Nanak's* aims of education can be easily identified in his conception of an educated man. His aims were individual as well as social. These were to prepare a learner for living a pious life through spiritual development for the betterment of society.

(a) Individual aims: Nanak considered the aim for an individual to be the complete development—physical, spiritual, intellectual and social. The four fundamentals of his teaching—purity, love, honesty, unselfishness—guided the development of God-gifted body of the learner. Spiritual development was crucial to the harmonious development of personality in that, according to him, the aim of human life was to achieve union with God. Education was to prepare man for salvation *(Mukti),* art of life *(jugti) and* joy or bliss of life *(Bhagti).* Education was to alleviate course of alienation between man and God. The ultimate aim of education was self-realization. He wanted education to inculcate virtues like:

- truth, contentment and reflection.
- compassion, righteousness and charity.
- faith, tolerance and restraint.
- forgiveness, humility and service.
- love, knowledge and work.

Through character development, education was to contribute further towards the harmonious development of personality in that the person became *Gurmukh* and *Sachiara.* It seems that the intellectual development takes place as a result of the mental debate in which a person rejects the shadow in favour of a substance: which is God.

(b) Social Aims: Nanak was an example of how to live life as a household person to fulfil his obligations and yet preach and practise virtues that led to self-realisation and unity with God. The following quotations throw sufficient light that he wanted education to prepare

learners for successful life in the society and work for its betterment: *We could get an honourable seat in the court of God, only when we practised disinterested service in the world. And thus won glory and joy of life—Adi Granth. He was really an educated man who did good to others—Adi Granth.* To put his social aims into practice, he emphasized the ideal of social service by sharing one's earning with the needy, doing manual labour and providing free community meals. *Jodh Singh*, a philosopher, was of the opinion that it was *Nanak* who used the concept of *Hindustan* as an integrated country when he complained to God against *Babar's* reign of terror.

(ii) The Institutions of Learning: In Nanak's conception of institutions of learning, we could identify two types of institutions—existing one and the ideal ones. In the existing ones, the curriculum required subjects relating to spiritualism in addition to traditional subjects. The ideal institutions were to be organized with spiritualism as the basis and other subjects were to be of secondary importance.

(iii) The Learners: There were tremendous responsibilities on the learners. They were expected to develop as individuals—physically, spiritually, intellectually and socially. Their spiritual development was most demanding of discipline. As social beings, they prepared themselves to be good house-holders, charitable bread-winners and self-disciplined persons.

(iv) The Teachers: In the western philosophy of idealism, a teacher is glorified to the extent of assigning him the role of a co-worker with God in perfecting man. *Nanak* examined the role of a teacher as missionary: he did not teach for money, but was dedicated to the cause of mastering and communicating knowledge, guiding his pupils and working for the welfare of society at large. Teacher was a friend, guide and philosopher: teacher was a friend in that he dealt with pupils gently and sweetly. He solved the problems for them and guided them to solve problems. He motivated them to understand the intimate relationship between man, nature, society and God.

Nanak used *Guru* for a teacher, *Wahe Guru* for an ideal teacher and *Sat Guru* for a real *Guru.* Guru is highly regarded. *Nanak* said:

"Without the Guru, there can be no Bhakti (worship), no love,
Without the Guru; there is no access to the company of the saints."

"Without the Guru, one blindly engages in futile endeavour, but with the Guru, one's mind is purified, for its filth is purged with the world"

–Adi Granth

The teacher was to know his subject. He was to be enlightened, creative, content, excellent communicator, graceful, sweet, humble, sympathetic, devoted and humane. He was to be God-centred and awaken divine intelligence in his pupils.

(v) The Curriculum

(a) *Nanak's* curriculum was so wide ranging that one wondered whether it was possible to implement it. As God had created the universe and He had expressed Himself in it, it was our duty to study the universe. He assigned top place to curriculum that developed spirit. This was to be carried out through philosophy of *Nam.* Thus, philosophy and ethics were to be the heart-core of subjects. Humanities and sciences were also recommended.

(b) In pedagogy, *Nanak* gave top place to reflection. He said, *"Not through studying, but through understanding, the Lord's secret is found"—Adi Granth.* Further, he stressed the need of reflection thus: *"he who reflects upon his self is the knower of God".*

(c) Difficult concepts were to be taught by illustrating from nature—fire, water, agriculture, tree, air, animal and bird life, and flora and fauna.

(d) He recommended scientific methods in which hypocracy, superstitions and blind faith had no place. He used, and recommended, observation and demonstration methods in which observation was followed by collection of data, analysis of data and generalization.

(e) He also used deductive, inductive, dialectic and pragmatic logical methods.

(f) Many other methods like project method, story telling method, travelling method, discussion method, activity method, mass drill and recitation, persuasion, correlation and so on were used to make teaching and preaching effective.

(vi) Impact: The impact of *Nanak's* philosophy and educational ideas has been great.

(a) What educationists and education planners are advocating and implementing in the present times, *Nanak* thought about such progressive ideas almost six centuries ago: for example, his idea about the provision of education for all. We have planned it, but it is yet to be fully and effectively achieved. National Policy on Education, 1986 with its amendments is more of a road map: we have to tread along it to reach the destination-education for all.

(b) He sweetly blended the individual aims of self-realization with social aims of betterment of society. Naturalist *Rousseau* was anti-society, pragmatist *Dewey* was anti-individual, but *Nanak,* many centuries ago, realized the importance of the individual as well as many individuals, constituting society.

(c) We are trying to find unity in diversity, even in the twenty-first century. *Nanak* showed us the way how to come to terms with ourselves, with nature, with society and with God. Religion, caste and socio-economic positions were no barriers to achieving self-realization and betterment of the society. How many humanists can we find who have preached and practised the fatherhood of God, motherhood of Nature and brotherhood of mankind—and with great success, as *Nanak* did.

(d) Thinking of democratic and secular education and education for world peace about six centuries ago was the work of a man of vision, courage, conviction and hope. His impact is felt by mankind more because a man spoke to the other man— not an angel or a god-head to a man.

Limitations

To trace limitations in *Nanak's* philosophy and educational ideas will be an attempt at hair-splitting. Perhaps the only limitation, if at all, we can call it a limitation, is the comprehensive nature of his views, which may be difficult to implement.

Conclusion

Greatness of *Nanak* lies in his being a theoretician as well as a practitioner of the philosophy of life and education. He lived like a human being but worked like an angel. The philosophy of Sikhism has done away with skepticism and intellectual uncertainties. It has asserted faith. concentration, and realization of truth and the final emancipation of the soul as cardinal principles. For these, *Nanak's* contributions are well recognized by people who are free from ego-centrism, who appreciate greatness and who look backward so that they can move forward more carefully and more successfully.

Summary

Guru Nanak revealed *Gurbani* along with other *Gurus.* He laid down principles of life. His general philosophy is in the *Banis*. His aims of education were individual and social. Teacher was a *guru*. He recommended wide ranging subjects and methods of teaching. He stood for education for all. He lived like a human being and worked like an angel.

20

Temporal and Spiritual Knowledge

Swami Dayananda (1824-1883)

Life-Sketch

Swami Dayananda founded the *Arya-Samaj* in 1875 to turn Hinduism into a combatant and proselytizing faith with a view to preventing conversions and recovering the Hindus who had been converted into other faiths. In this chapter are presented his philosophy and views on education. He was born in Gujarat in 1824. His original name was *Mool Shankar*. He studied Sanskrit at the age of five and by the time, he was fourteen, he had memorized several parts of the *Vedas* and also mastered Sanskrit grammar. The forms of temple worship of his time dissatisfied him and when he was twenty one, he ran away from home and become a *sanyasi*. He practised *Yoga* and studied *Vedanta* philosophy. In 1862, he found a *guru* who exhorted him to fight against the falsehood of *Puranic* Hinduism and restore the true teachings of the *Vedas*. In 1863, he and his *guru* visited many places in northern India. In 1875, *Dayananda* established the *Arya-Smaj* in Bombay. Until his death in 1883, he organized the branches of the *Smaj* and translated the *Vedas* into Hindi.

Philosophy

Dayananda's philosophy was based on the *Vedas* and *Vedic* literature. Thus, it was not a new philosophy, although he interpreted the *Vedas* truly so that the messages from them could regenerate the society.

(i) The Metaphysical Position: God and Soul: His metaphysical position was that of the *Vedas* and, thus, he believed in the existence of God, Who was Universal Spirit, Personification of Existence, Knowledge and Bliss (*Sat, Chit* and *Ananda*). Other attributes of God were that he was the creator, sustainer and discoverer of the universe. He was immortal, infinite, absolute, formless and pervading. The soul was also eternal and immortal, and it transmigrated. However, its capacity for knowledge was limited, and because of its ignorance, the soul was in the bondage of the world where it was subjected to pain and suffering. Its salvation lay throught the worship of God, by doing righteous deeds and by associating with virtuous persons.

For him, heaven and hell were not separate worlds. Heaven was the enjoyment of happiness and hell was the undergoing of suffering on this very earth.

He recognized the attributes of God, somewhat the same way as these had been recognized by Hinduism, Christianity and Islam, but his idea of heaven and hell differed from the ideas of those religions. That heaven and hell were not geographical territories but conditions of mind, motivating human action—for good or for bad—was a revolutionary idea.

(ii) Epistemology: The western world had identified empiricism, intuitionism, relevation, authoritarianism and rationalism as instruments of knowledge. *Dayananda*, on the basis of *Nyaya Shastra* identified five sources of knowledge which were more wide-ranging as would be clear from the following list:

(a) The *Vedas* and the nature of God,
(b) Law of nature,
(c) The practice and teachings of the pious and learned men (*Aptas*),
(d) The purity and conviction of one's own soul, and
(e) eight kinds of evidences like –
- direct
- cognizance
- inference
- analogy
- testimony
- history
- deduction
- possibility
- non-existence or negation

(iii) Axiology: The western schools of philosophy had presented ethics, aesthetics, religion, and education etc. as the realms of values. *Dayananda* presented an ethical code of conduct based on the *Vedas* but it had a universal appeal as could be seen in the areas of code of conduct:

(a) Ahimsa – Non infliction of pain
(b) Satya – Practice of truth
(c) Astya – Non-stealing
(d) Asang – Non-attachment
(e) Hri – Modesty
(f) Asanchaya – Want of storing for the future
(g) Astikya – Faith in religion
(h) Brahmrcharya – Abstinence
(i) Maun – Silence
(j) Sthariya – Steadiness
(k) Kshama – Forgiveness
(l) Abhaya – Fearlessness

Views on Education

Dayananda was a supporter of education for all men and women but they were to be educated according to the vocation, they were to follow, particularly women. Knowledge of grammar, *Dharma* (religion), medical science and mathematics etc. was for all. Women were to be trained in home management, and in reproducing, bringing up and instruction of their children. *Brahmin* and *Kshatriya* women were to acquire all kinds of knowledge, but *Shudra* women were to learn the art of cooking and *Vaishya* women were to learn some trade and practical arts. He was against co-education. He suggested that the boys' schools were to be at least four miles away from those of the girls. Boys and girls were to be free from eight kinds of sensuous approaches. These approaches were: (a) Looking at a person of the opposite sex with lustful eyes; (b) Intimately talking about them; (c) Playing with them; (d) Associating with them; (e) Indulging in sexual thoughts (f) Reading or talking of libidinous subjects; (g) Embracing them; and (f) Having sexual intercourse with them.

Such strictures on sexual behaviour, perhaps, could save boys and girls from HIV/AIDS, and teen pragnancies, prevalent all over the country and the world these days.

(i) Aims of Education: In his *Satyartha Prakasha*, *Dayananda* attached great importance to knowledge, but he defined education in a broad sense in that it eliminated ignorance and prepared for happiness by increasing knowledge, developing culture, character, morality, good conduct, and spirituality—and ultimately it prepared people for liberation or salvation.

From the point of view of the western schools of philosophy, *Dayananda's* aims of education were close to the idealistic stand in which mind, soul and thoughts were considered real and the essence of human life was spiritual. Furthermore, God existed and the universe was created by Him. Values of life were eternal. The aim of education was to enable learners to achieve self-realization through moral, spiritual and cultural development. Idealists commended simple living and high thinking.

(ii) Institutions of Learning: In the western schools of philosophy, the role and importance of institutions of learning had varied. A naturalist like *Rousseau* wanted only a tutor; *Pestalozzi* ran a school for learning in a free atmosphere; *Froebel's* kindergarten became a hub of educational activities for children; and *Montessori* encouraged auto education in the schools. For idealists, school introduced children to their culture and it was the value-realizing institution. For a pragamatist like *Dewey*, school supplied the volume of learning, each new generation needed; it made the heritage of the past function fruitfully in the present and it enabled learners to master language.

For *Dayananda*, schools were to be like the *Gurukuls* of the *Vedic* times. These were to be sufficient in number to cater to the needs of students who were to come from all homes, even to be called compulsorily. To start with, *Gurukuls* came up at Hardwar, Dehradun, Baroda, Aligarh, and other colleges and schools were established. Now there is a network of institutions—not *Gurukuls* alone—particularly in the northern parts of the country, providing modern education also.

(iii) Learners: In naturalism learner was free to learn the way, he liked. In idealism, the learner was treated as a spiritual being—finite person, growing, when properly educated, into an infinite person. Pragmatism treated learners as biological, sociological and psychological beings.

For *Dayananda*, learners were to lead a noble, simple and virtuous life. They were expected to lead a celibate life *(Brahmacharya)*, and live like a member of teacher's family. They were to accept strict discipline, including acceptance of punishment, for deviant behaviour from his teacher.

***(iv) Teachers*:** In the western schools of philosophy, a naturalist teacher operated from behind the scene and did not interfere with the activities of the learner. An idealist teacher guided, directed, suggested and controlled the learner. A pragamatist teacher was an organizer of the environment for the learner to experiment and discover.

Dayananda's teacher was expected to be knowledgeable of the *Vedas,* their literature and other religious texts. He was to establish an intimate relationship with his pupils. He was to lead a virtuous life. Celibacy (*Brahmcharya*) was much desired in a teacher. He was to be a strict disciplinarian and was not to hesitate punishing errant students, although he accepted his pupils as members of his family.

(v) Curriculum: Generally speaking in the western schools of philosophy, for naturalists Nature itself was the wide book to learn from. The idealists emphasized the study of ethics, religion, arts, music, philosophy and humanities. The pragmatists advocated practical and utilitarian subjects—scientific and sociological—hygiene, physiology home science, sociology, geography, history and agriculture.

Dayananda's curriculam included *Panini's* phonetics, grammar, *Nighantu* and *Nirkuta* (*Vedic* vocabulary and philology), *Chhandograntha* (prosody), *Manu Smriti*, *Ramayana* and *Mahabharta*, six *Shashtras* of Indian philosophy and ten *Upanishads*, four *Vedas* and four *Brahmanas,* four *Upvedas* and *Jyotisha Shahstra* comprising arithematic, algebra, geometry, geography, geology and astronomy.

He was against foreign languages as a media of instruction. A sound system of education was to encourage students own languages and Sanskrit was to be given a pride of place in the curriculum.

He stood for the consideration of general education with religious education and professional training in order to produce a complete personality.

He supported the *Gurukula* methods of teaching which included (a) advising and lecture methods (b) concentration method, (c) introspective method, (d) practical method and (e) introspection. In these methods, (a), (b), (c), (d) and are being followed in modern methods of teaching, but (e) introspection is rare. In the western schools of philosophy, naturalists emphasized play-way method, pragmatists stood for experimental method and idealists were close to the methods of *Dayananda* except for their absence of introspective method. In relation to discipline, naturalists advocated uncontrolled freedom, pragmatists supported social discipline and idealists wanted self-discipline, but *Dayananda* was of the view that parents and teachers were to enforce strict discipline, including punishment to the erring children.

Dayananda's Influence

Dayananda's influence was great in so far as the revival of interest in the *Vedas* was concerned. He also stood for universal and compulsory education, an idea that is being implemented after many years.

As said early in this account, his ideas on education were put in practice in institutions like *Gurukuls* at Hardwar, Brindaban, Baroda and Sansi and many Anglo Vedic Colleges and later schools and colleges of high standing in many parts of India.

Although he suggested different type of additional curriculum that suited the men and women of different castes, in the contemporary scenario such ideas are being considered derogatory, and equality of educational opportunities is being encouraged through constitutional provisions and social policies.

That in this age of materialism, a need is being felt for the restoration of faith in God and Supreme Truth in the form of *Sat*, *Chit* and *Anand*, his position is not only relevant but a must for the school system.

Conclusion

Dayananda did attempt to protect the Hindu values from the Christian and Islamic influences, but the dynamics of acculturation stand for building bridges rather than barriers. Influences are mutual: we cannot avoid them.

Summary

Dayananda's philosophy was based on the *Vedas* and *Vedic* literature. He believed in the existence of God. He restated the attributes of God as being immortal, eternal, infinite, absolute, formless etc. He highlighted five sources of knowledge. He delineated twelve codes of conduct. He championed the cause of universal and compulsory education for men and women, but wanted additional subjects according to the caste and station of vocation in life. Learners were expected to lead a disciplined life and teachers and parents were to enforce discipline, even by administering punishment. Some of his ideas influenced educational thinking but those which were caste-based are not suitable to the modern times.

21

Education in Natural Environment

Rabindra Nath Tagore (1861-1941)

Perhaps, as a reaction to the dullness of the western type of education in India and lack of interest in legal studies in England, and yet displaying great interest in self-study and writing, and in giving a practical shape to the hidden creativity in man make *Tagore* a unique person. He was not educated formally and yet it might he said with justification that he was widely educated in the letter and spirit of what an educated man is expected to be.

Life Sketch

Tagore was born on 6th of May in 1861 in an educated, well-to-do and respectable family. His father coached him in Sanskrit, Indian philosophy and astronomy. For higher education, he was sent to Bengal Academy. He found the courses of reading uninspiring and left the Academy. However, he was sent to England to read law. It seemed whether it was British type of education in India or British education in England, Tagore found these dull. He returned home without a degree in law.

He applied himself to self-study, started writing articles for Bengali magazines and later wrote stories and novels. By his creative genius and ceaseless efforts, he became a versatile genius—poet, writer, dramatist, painter and philosopher. He translated his *Gitanjali* into English. He was honoured with noble prize for literature. Calcutta and many other universities honoured him with doctorate degrees. He travelled to the USA, Japan and Europe. The world mourned his death in 1941.

Shanti Niketan and Vishwa Bharti

The father of R.N. Tagore—Devindra Nath Tagore—established an institution at a place which was called *Shanti Niketan*, about two miles from Bholpur in Bengal. The son set up a school there in 1901. By 1921, it had developed into *Vishwa Bharti*. In *Tagore*'s words the institution was to: *(i)* teach different cultures of the East, especially those that originated in India or were found within her shores; *(ii)* establish the institute of rural reconstruction in order to lay the foundation of happy and contented human life in the villages; and *(iii)* seek to establish a living relationship between the East and the West. Furthermore, it was to promote individual would promote welfare, not only of his own country, but also of the world at large.

(v) *Complete Development:* The various aspects of development—physical, mental, spiritual and social—culminated in the production of a harmonious personality. Such a personality would shun discrimination between man and man within our own culture and the cultures of the world. Society was a means of self-realisation. Consciousness of the universe was an essential condition in realization of the self. Thus, he harmonised the individual aims with social aims.

(2) The Institutions of Learning: There appears to be a contradiction in *Tagore*'s views on the formal institutions of learning and Nature being the school without walls when we take into account his *Shanti Niketan* which had all the requirements of a formal institution of learning. Tagore's own thinking was not static and dogmatic. He established *Vishwa Bharti* at *Shanti Niketan* as an institution at which the best of the Indian culture, traditions, philosophy, sciences, arts, technical education and crafts were to be taught to students from within and outside the country: the walls were not for dividing but these were to make learning convenient. The serenity of the environment was to be like that of Nature. Even Nature had barriers for man to cross. How man and Nature could cross barriers and build bridges was proved by *Tagore* at *Shanti Niketan.*

(3) The Learners: In *Tagore's* philosophy of education, child was expected to enjoy full freedom; he was given opportunities for self-expression; and he was motivated to obtain knowledge from original sources. He even de-emphasized education for a vocation. Instead of becoming farmers, craftsmen or clerks, they were to become complete human beings. Naturalist *Rousseau* advocated that child was born free but society was likely to spoil him. So, he was to be given negative education. *Pestalozzi* brought the concept of teacher as a gardener; *Froebel* created a kindergarten; and *Montessori* recommended and practised auto-education.

Tagore also treated the learner as born good. Education was to enrich his goodness both on the lap of mother and within the natural institution like *Vishwa Bharti*. Whereas *Rousseau* had somewhat of a blind spot for female education, *Tagore* was a great protagonist of women education at par with education of men.

(4) The Teachers: Teacher in *Tagore's* philosophy of education had a human face—he was not a tin-god, not a gardener and not even a supervisor. He was expected to handle children with love and sympathy. He encouraged them to engage themselves in constructive and creative activities. It appeared that Nature was a reality which the learner was to seek, and its description, interpretation and narration were the books. The original source was more important than its secondary sources. Even within the school, the emphasis was to be on child-centred activities. The teacher was to encourage class participation through question-answer, discussion and activity methods. If we examine his advice that *"teaching while walking is the best method of education,"* the arm-chair type of teacher may have to take his class on the "constitutional" trips to ensure better health and effective learning!

(5) The Curriculum: In case of *Tagore*, curriculum—formal or informal—was to aim at the complete development of human personality. Also, the total experiences of the learners in and out of the school were steps forward to accept the concept of curriculum being the activities under the guidance of school. The children learnt by interacting with each other, with teachers, with books and with Nature.

In the institutional setting, the subjects at *Vishwa Bharti* were traditional like history, geography, nature study, agriculture, horticulture, gardening, field study, laboratory work, creations, arts, sculpture, vocational, professional and technical subjects. The range of subjects was such that there were liberal studies as well as vocational training.

To supplement the curricular experiences, co-curricular activities like dancing, singing, designing, painting, knitting, rowing, cutting etc., were also available. The aesthetic appetite of the learners was also satisfied by various cultural activities.

As *Tagore's* education was predominantly individualistic and learner-centred, the strategies of teaching included discussions, question-answer methods, activity-based methods, particularly physical exercises.

Impact

The impact of *Tagore's* educational ideas was great: *Vishwa Bharti* became a unique institution. Here, the eastern and western knowledge and wisdom influenced learners who were the embodiments of harmoniously developed personalities.

He put into practice what he had preached—returning to nature and creating natural environment in the institutions of learning.

He had run away from books in the institutional setting, yet he recommended these at *Vishwa Bharti*—not as the sole source of learning but a component with Nature in the learning process.

Limitations

There were contradictions in his views. for example, de-emphasizing books and recommending subjects without which it was not possible to study these at the higher level.

His philosophy was not a coherent one. It was somewhat eclectic in nature and, as such, carries the weaknesses of eclecticism.

Conclusion

The multi-dimensional personality of *Tagore* left its mark on the educational, literary and cultural life of India. That many institutions like *Vishwa Bharti* did not spring up in the country or abroad simply means that the expectations of establishing such institutions were too high to make the required move in that direction.

Summary

R.N. Tagore ran away from school-based education, first in India and later in England, but he undertook self-study and writing. Aims of his education were individual and social. The learner was to be developed physically, mentally, spiritually and socially. *Vishwa Bharti* became a model for institutions of learning. The learners were free to express themselves and be motivated to glean knowledge from various sources. Teacher was to love children and encourage them to benefit from education. Curriculum was vast and varied. Because of the hard requirements to establish a *Vishwa Bharti*, many such institutions have not come into being.

22

Man-Making Education

Swami Vivekananda (1863-1902)

Amongst the philosophers in the spiritual realm, stands *Swami Vivekananda* as a towering figure. Not only did he recapitulate the ancient Indian wisdom but also interpreted it for the benefit of all mankind.

Life Sketch

Swami Vivekananda was born in 1863 in Calcutta. His name was *Narendra Nath Dutta*. The atmosphere of the family was religious and he was inducted in religious ceremonies. He was an intelligent person and studied literature, history and Indian philosophical traditions. Later on, he studied the western literature and philosophy. His headmaster introduced him to *Swami Ramakrishan Paramhansa* who impressed the young boy. After a stay of six years, he was initiated into saintly order and was known as *Vivekananda*. He established *Ramakrishna Mission* in 1896 and preached in Asia, Europe and the USA. He died in 1902.

Major Themes

Some of the major themes related to:

(1) universal religion
(2) intellect and religion
(3) *Ahimsa*
(4) fear
(5) evolution
(6) *Karma* and
(7) views on education

(1) Universal Religion: The beginning of the twentieth century, with surging tides of atheism, agnosticism and materialism made many people think that the cause of religion was lost for ever. *Vivekananda* defended religion from the point of view of Hinduism, Christianity, Islam and other religions. Defending religion from the Hindu point of view, he quoted the *Gita*–Krishna said in the *Gita: "I am the self-existent in the heart of all beings... He, who sees all beings in the self, and the self in all beings, hates none."* Harmony on earth was the heart of the matter and was of cosmic significance. Illustrating from the Christian angle, he quoted the

Christ, who had suggested: *"He that is without sin amongst you, let him first cast a stone"*. *Christ* wanted that we were to love even our enemies. Supporting Islamic faith as inclusive universal religion, he quoted from the *Quran which says* that:

There is not person but a warner has gone among them.
And every nation had a messenger,
And every nation had a guide,
And certainly we raised in every nation a messenger saying serve *Allah* and shun the devil.
To every nation we appointed acts of devotion which they observe.
For everyone of you did we appoint a law and a way!

Vivekananda's faith in one universal religion was supported by a scholar like professor *Arnold Toynbee* who expressed his personal belief that: the four higher religions that were alive in the age in which he was living were four variations on a single theme and that, if all the four components of this heavenly music of the spheres could be available on each simultaneously and with equal clarity to one pair of human ears, the happy hearer would find himself listening not to a discord, but to a harmony.

Universal religion did not imply the conversion of all to one religion or starting a new religion. It simply meant that there was one God. He might be called by different names by people of different religions and those speaking different languages. It is worth recording that if there is one God, he could not have given different messages to the prophets, saints, sages and inspired souls—particularly, messages that are antagonistic to one another in their contents or their intentions.

(2) Intellect and Religion: In the times, when the concept of high intelligence quotient (I.Q.) was in fashion, it could be said that intellect could think, analyse, synthesise, solve problems and, thus, approach the issue of religion also as an intellectual exercise. But *Vivekananda* was against such a concept. He was of the view that religion belonged to the super sensuous and not to the sense plane. It was beyond all reasoning and was not on the plane of intellect. It was a vision, an inspiration, a plunge into the unknown and unknowable, making the unknowable more than known, for it could never be "known". Similar views on the role of intellect in religion were expressed by *Samkara* when he said that the pure truth of *Atman* (the soul) buried under *Maya* (illusion) and the effect of *Maya* could be reached by meditation, contemplation and other spiritual disciplines such as one who knew *Brahman* (absolute soul) might prescribe but never by subtle arguments. It appeared that both *Samkara* and *Vivekananda* drew sustenance from the *Vedas* in which soul was treated divine, held in bondage of matter.

One was to break this bond and gain *Mukti* (freedom)–freedom from imperfection, misery and death. *Vivekananda* believed that the bondage could only be broken through mercy of God, and this mercy came on the pure. It was the pure and the stainless that saw God.

(3) Role of Ahimsa: *Vivekananda* treated *Ahimsa* (non-violence—no injury to others) as the most important trait in a person. He wanted *Ahimsa* not only to human beings, but also to the lower animals (but not to the extent of protecting vermin on the bodies as some monks used to do). For him, the test of *Ahimsa* was absence of jealousy. *Mahatma Gandhi* made *Ahimsa* not only an individual attribute but also social and political weapon which he successfully used against social discrimination in South Africa, political slavery of the British Colonial government in subjugated India and religious and caste discrimination in free India.

(4) Fear: Physiologists and psychologists treated fear as a basic human emotion with anger and love being the other two emotions. But *Vivekananda's* views on fear were different. For him:

> *When man has been himself as one with the infinite being of the universe, when all separateness has ceased, when all men, all women, all angels, all gods, all animals, all plants, the whole universe has been melted into that Oneness, then all fear disappears. He who in this world of man sees that One; he who in this world of shadow catches that Reality, unto him belongs peace, unto none else.*

It is, perhaps, possible to control fear, but its physiological basis may be difficult to control. For example: a loud explosion will startle all, the degree of impact may vary–from, perhaps, a shriek by some, through trembling by others, and a mild sensation of fear in a few. May be, a person in deep meditation will not hear the loud noise.

(5) Evolution: *Vivekananda* did not agree with the theory of evolution in which sexual selection and survival of the fittest had been highlighted. He was of the opinion that competitions for life or sex gratification were only momentary, unnecessary, extraneous efforts, caused by ignorance. Even when all competition had ceased, then perfect nature behind would make us go forward until every one became perfect. But that boundless freedom had to be worked through the virtuous life.

He rejected *Hegel's* dialectics of thesis, anti-thesis and synthesis phenomenon, also upheld by *Marx. Vivekananda* argued as to how the finite could become infinite in that the position of these philosophers was that the infinite was trying to express itself in this universe and that there would come a time when the infinite would succeed in doing so. *Engles* borrowed *Hegelian* illustration of the grain of barley germinating and dying but producing a plant which was the negation of the grain. Plant grew, producing stalk, at the end of which were produced grains of barley.

As soon as these ripened, the stalk died and was, in turn, negated. The original grain of barley was multiplied tenfold—change negating a given state. *Vivekananda* treated the grain and the plant as one in finer and grosser form. The seed had to work for some time beneath the soil. It broke into pieces, degenerated: and regeneration came out of that degeneration. The historical evolution followed the breathe-in, breathe-out, rise and fall pattern.

(6) Karma: Believing in *Karma* and reincarnation, *Vivekananda* permitted a man to enjoy the desire for power and everything else before coming to the state of calmness, serenity and self surrender. The *Karmic* theory dispensed with the possibilities of any chance or accidental. Element in human life emphasised the essentially causal character of all existence. Belief in rebirth was to engender a universal love because all living things and creatures in the course of their numberless lives and our own had been our beloved parents, children, brothers, sisters and friends. The virtue of our creed encouraged all those which arose from the universal love, tolerance, forbearance, charity, kindness and compassion.

Views on Education

Vivekananda's views on education are contained in his *Man Making Education.* He considered universal education to be essential to equipping people to understand themselves, society and nature. The following paragraph expressed the quintessence of his man- making education.

> *The ideal of all education, all training should be man-making. Education is not the amount of information that is put into your brain and runs riot there undigested, all your life. We must have life-building, man-making, character-making assimilation of ideas. If you have assimilated five ideas and made them your life and character, you have more education than any man who has got by heart a whole library. If education is identical with information, the libraries are the greatest sages in the world and encyclopedias are the Rishis.*

Furthermore, he looked upon religion as the innermost core of education. He was of the opinion that we wanted western science coupled with *Vedanta*: every improvement in India required first of all an upheaval in religion as the Indian mind was first religious, then any thing else. The national ideals of India were renunciation and service. Spiritual ideas were to come first; then were to follow the socialistic or political ideas. After preaching spiritual knowledge, alongwith it would come that secular knowledge and every other knowledge. Any attempt to get secular knowledge without religion would never have a hold on the people.

He considered education to be the *"manifestation of divine perfection already existing in man."* He wanted that education by which character was formed, strength of mind was increased and the intellect was expanded, enabling one to stand on one's own feet.

An analysis of *Vivekananda's* views on man-making education shows that he has briefly stated what our holy texts have already said and there is a good deal of agreement with some Indian philosophers and philosophers of the western world, as is shown below:

Indian Thoughts on Education

(1) The *Rig Veda* expected education to make a man self-reliant and selfless.

(2) The *Upanishads* considered the end product of education to be salvation.

(3) The *Vedantic* view was that education was to quicken, vivify, and kindle the urge of spirituality inherent in every mind.

(4) For *Shankracharya* education was realization of the self.

(5) According to *A. Ghosh*, education helped the growing soul to draw out that was in it.

(6) For *Tagore*, education was to give us inner light, love and truth and make one's life in harmony with all existence.

(7) *Gandhiji's* view was that education was to draw out the best in child and man—body, mind and spirit.

(8) The culmination of Indian thought and action was reached in University Education Commission Report (1948-49). The Report said that education, according to the Indian traditions, was not merely a means of earning neither a living nor it was only nursery of thought or a school for citizenship. It was initiation into the life of spirit, training for human souls in the pursuit of truth and practice of virtue. It was a second birth–*divinity* and *janma*.

Western Thoughts on Education

(1) As far as the western philosophers were concerned, for *Plato*, education was the capacity to feel pleasure and pain at the right moment. It developed in the body and the soul of the pupil all the beauty and all the perfection of which he was capable.

(2) *Aristotle's* education aimed at the creation of a sound mind in a sound body.

(3) *Pestalozzi* considered education as natural, harmonious progressive development of man's innate powers.

(4) For *Froebel,* education was the process through which the child made internal external.

(5) *Nunn* laid emphasis on the complete development of individuality so that he made an original contribution to human life according to the best of his capacity.

(6) For *Dewey*, education was the development of all those capacities

in the individual which would enable him to control his environment and fulfil his possibilities.

(7) *Horne* thought of education as the process of man's reciprocal adjustment to nature, to his fellows, and to the ultimate nature of the cosmos.

Scope of Man-Making Education

Vivekananda's man-making education included the following concepts:

(1) Education was individual as well as social.
(2) It was spiritual in nature.
(3) It was both learner-centred and teacher-centred.
(4) It was purposive.
(5) It was theoretical as well as practical in nature, but more of practical.
(6) It was science as well as art.
(7) It was formal, informal and non formal.

(1) Individual and Social Aims

(i) For *Vivekanand,* all knowledge that the world had ever received came from the mind; infinite library of the universe was in man's mind. The external world was only the suggestion, the occasion which set one to study one's mind. The falling of the apple gave suggestion to *Newton* and he studied his own mind. He rearranged all the previous limits of thought in his mind and discovered a new link among them which he called the law of gravitation.

(ii) The Christian philosopher, *St. Augustine*, also said that the knowledge was within the learner. Teacher showed the light to illuminate it to bring it out to some extent. *Froebel* came close to *Vivekananda* as the former also believed that child developed his nature the same way as the plant did its own. As against such views, a philosopher like *John Locke* treated child's mind to be like a blank sheet, the (*Tabla Rasa)* on which senses, perceptions and experiences wrote the knowledge.

(iii) *Vivekananda*, however, believed that the advancement of a nation depended on education. It was education that emancipated the poor masses and they developed their individuality as free people.

(2) Spiritual Aims

(i) One of *Vivekananda's* aims of education was to teach religious and moral education. It was essential to countering the evil influences of materialism. He said that if we were to give "secular education", we had to follow the plan, laid down by our ancestors: that was to bring all the ideals slowly down among the masses by raising them slowly up, raising them to equality. But secular knowledge was to be imparted through religion. Students were expected to worship saints to follow their ideals—*Rama, Krishna and Mahavir. Rama* and *Krishna* were particularly chosen as models. The aim of religious education was to harmonise science with religion, to develop qualities like patriotism, service, sacrifice, virility, self-confidence, love of humanity and truthfulness. For him, truth was God as truth was power; it was knowledge, and it was light-giving.

(ii) Although he preached universal religion, yet for India, he recommended the *Gita,* the *Upanishads* and the *Vedas* as the most important scriptures for study. By implication, the religious works of other religions—the *Bible* and the *Quran*—were appropriate studies for the followers of Christianity and Islam respectively. In the western world, an idealist philosopher like *Herman Horne* considered truth, beauty and goodness as the spiritual ideas of the race and education was to aim at equipping the child to adjust himself to those realities. The Roman Catholic realists aimed at the production of a supernatural man who thought, judged and acted constantly in accordance with right reasons, illumined by the supernatural light of the example and teaching of the *Christ. Froebel's* educational ideals rested firmly on a deep faith in religion. For him, man was part of God and God was part of man. Education led man to a knowledge of himself, of mankind, of God and of Nature.

(iii) In India, *Aurobindo Ghosh* defined education as a true building or living evolution of the powers of the mind and spirit of human being. *Paramahansa Yogananda* emphasized on *Kriya Yoga,* which mainly meant certain techniques of meditation, the practice of which led to realization of God. To live education, the *Kriya Yogi* mastered his body and mind and achieved victory over his "last enemy": death.

(3) Learner-centred and Teacher-centred Education

(i) *Vivekananda* believed that knowledge resided within the individual, the same way as soul resided in us. The knowledge was with the soul. The learner set about the process of self-development. So to say, he started educating himself through his perception and thought. Education required concentration which could only be done individually. External advice or pressure on the learner could achieve little, if he was not self-motivated to concentrate on a task. *Vivekananda* expected the learners to practise *Brahmacharya* (chastity) for developing the power of concentration. The sex drive was converted into a spiritual force. Here again, the practice was feasible at the individual level and might be difficult to be institutionalized. He exhorted one to go into one's own and get the *Upnishads* out of one's ownself until inner teacher opened: all outside teaching was in vain.

(ii) But, teachers too had a role to play. They were to have thorough

understanding of the needs of learners. These needs were determined in terms of the tendencies, inherent in children, and not according to what the parents or teachers thought. As he was an advocate of vocational education, some one like a teacher or an instructor could facilitate the training in agriculture and industry. The teacher was also to provide suitable environment for the learners to derive maximum benefit from it in self-development. He expected teacher to be a philosopher, friend and guide, helping the learners to go forward in their own ways.

(iii) There was a time when, for lack of communication tools, teacher was the only source of knowledge. Then books came and knowledge became teacher-centred as well as pupil-centred, with teacher still dominating. With more inventions, the media and the computers, the balance went in favour of child-centredness. The present position is that we have teachers of subjects, teachers of children and teacher technicians. *Vivekananda's* high expectations of teachers are still relevant to our times.

(4) Education is Purposive

(i) Vivekananda's man-making education was for physical, moral, spiritual, vocational and social development, both for men and women.

(ii) He wanted learners to be physically strong and encourage fitness in others. The strong body gave power, and power was happiness. He went to the extent of saying that it was more important for the young man to play football than to study the *Gita.* The aim of moral education was to develop character. It was through character that one would be able to develop faith in one's own self and promote universal brotherhood. The kind teacher would bring up learners who would also be kind to everything and everyone. Kindness was a moral weapon against evil deeds.

(iii) The ultimate aim of education was spiritual—to study the *Vedanta, Upnishads, Puranas,* religion and philosophy so that one realized the Divinity; the knowledge of *Brahma* was the ultimate goal of man. Education was for building spiritual brotherhood.

(iv) Vocational development was part of developing a harmonious personality. A person who could not stand on his own feet was useless. Thus, training in agriculture and industry would enable people to earn their living, neither by exploiting others nor by amassing wealth. Women were to be educated to be like *Sita,* or *Ahilya Bai* or *Mira Bai* or *Rani of Jhansi*—fearless, brave, perfect.

(v) As far as social development was concerned, the purpose of education was mass emancipation. It was through education that the gems of spirituality in the holy books would be brought to the

common man through the medium of mother tongue. His desire to establish national system of education, universalism and spiritual brotherhood were social in nature.

(5) Theoretical and Practical

(i) *Vivekananda's* man-making education was theoretical as well as practical in that some of his ideas relating to soul, spiritual divinity and knowledge residing within the individual were theoretical, as there was a lot of metaphysics and epistemology involved in such ideas. Very few people had the experience of the supernatural world. But there were many concepts which could be put into practice.

(ii) Education according to the needs of children, education for all, national system of education and women education could be, and had been, put into practice in India and elsewhere.

(iii) Celibacy and renunciation were ideal, but only a few men and women had subjected themselves to such ways of life.

(iv) Practical nature of education was reflected in his ideas when he recommended vocational education to learners: home science for girls and carpenter agriculture and industry for boys.

(6) Science and Art

(i) *Vivekananda* wanted to harmonise western science with *Vedanta* as such harmony would inspire man to use the resources of science for peaceful purposes and the progress of mankind.

(ii) He observed that art was an indispensable part of life. Art was a part of religion. However, it was through science and art that education equipped individuals to find unity in diversity.

(7) Formal, Informal, Non-formal

Vivekananda's man-making education was formal, informal and non-formal.

(i) It was formal in the sense that it could be imparted at school or in a religious place or in a library. The environment could be controlled. Teachers supervised and guided.

(ii) Education was informal as it could also be imparted through mass media. It was life long.

(iii) His education was non-formal in the sense that it could be imparted through correspondence courses, mass media, seminars and workshops. Educand was motivated for receiving further education.

Conclusion

Vivekananda was one the greatest religious minds of the nineteenth century. When the western world was busy sorting out matters relating to theism and atheism, agnosticism and skepticism, science and religion, he clarified the *Vedanta* Hindu philosophy which earlier had been dismissed by the western philosophers as an assortment of superstitions. His impact on the USA was great but it was greater on the rest of the world, including India. As is evident from the presentation above, his views on man-making education have the sublimity, breadth and profundity.

Summary

Swami Vivekananda said that if one believed that all beings were in the self and the self was in all beings, then one would hate none. Religion was beyond all reasoning. *Ahimsa* was not only for human beings but also for lower animals. The *Karamic* theory dispensed with possibilities of any chance. Evolution followed breathe-in and breathe-out pattern. We were to have man-making, character-building and life-making education. Education was a devine perfection He drew the attention of the world to the greatness of India's philosophy and religion.

23

Education Is Indivisible

Mahatma Gandhi (1869-1948)

In the history of societies have appeared men with exceptional abilities. Some of such able persons have made the best use of their endowments, inspite of the adverse circumstances, they faced; others resigned to the forces, they found too strong to fight against. Yet, a few did not have the motivation to make their expected contributions. *Mahatma Gandhi* came in the category of those who were conscious that they were born with a mission. He showed a great motivation to realize the aims, set for the societal good. He, with the "weapon" of non-violence, fought against racism in South Africa, colonialism in British India and casteism in free India. He was a colossus who strode the Indian socio-political life for almost half a century: surprisingly, the sound of his 'thuds' reverberated, not only in India, but also all over the world.

He achieved a great deal during his lifetime, but more important was his legacy. In terms of philosophical positions in diverse fields—political, social, economic, educational—he has left behind a rich legacy for the Indians in particular and the world in general. If the inheritors were serious to benefit from this legacy, they were not likely to regret the experiences.

Life Sketch

Gandhiji's full name was *Mohan Dass Karam Chand Gandhi*. He was born on 2nd October, 1869 at Porbandar, Kathiawar in Gujarat in a well-to-do and respectable family. His father was a *Diwan* of Rajkot and mother was a kind-hearted person. He was married to *Kasturba*, when he was only 13 years old.

After passing his matriculation examination, he was sent by ship to England to study law. He passed law examination in 1891 and returned to India. After practising law for a short time in India, he left for South Africa as a legal adviser in 1893. There, he fought the White Government in a non-violent way for its inhuman treatment of subjects of Indian origin. He returned to India in 1915 and started non-violent struggle against the British colonialism in India.

Gandhiji established *Sabarmati Ashram* at Ahmedabad with a view to uplifting the *Harijans,* established village industries, started social reforms and launched creative programmes for national uplift. It was in 1921 that he started the non-violent civil disobedience movement against the British Colonial Government in India. The Indian National Congress also passed a resolution to demand complete independence. The British Government realized the gravity of the situation and "*Gandhi-Irwin* Pact" was the outcome. He went to England for a Round Table Conference, but there was no positive outcome. He was arrested in 1942 and put in prison. On his release, he gave a call for "Quit India" to the Colonial Government, which tried to crush the movement. The rise of Indian National Army under the leadership of *Netaji Subhash Chandra Bose*, the troubles in the Navy, and mass movements for independence all combined to force the British Government to grant independence to India on 15th August, 1947. There was partition of India into India and Pakistan. The country suffered the agony of communal riots, for the control of which *Gandhiji* tried his best. He was shot dead on 30th January 1948. The irony of the situation was that a person who preached and practised non-violence died a violent death. But death does not seal the voice of all departed souls: some like *Gandhiji* continue living through their words, deeds and actions.

Before going into details about *Gandhiji's* philosophy of education, it is important to examine him as a philosopher.

Gandhiji as a Philosopher

We have simplified the definition of philosophy to mean that it is a search for meaning in life. In this context, *Gandhiji* was a profound philosopher. His metaphysical, epistemological and axiological positions were clear and interrelated. His metaphysical position was that reality is monistic. He believed in the absolute oneness of God and humanity—many bodies but one soul. God, for him, was "life, truth, light." He was love. He was the supreme. Only God was real, the world was an illusion. His epistemological position was that knowledge was drawn out of the learners by a competent teacher who also motivated them through experiments and activities. But ultimately the theories of knowledge were to ensure merger of the finite being into the infinite. The value system was to form pure character to ensure self-realization for the individual and the society.

If we examine *Gandhiji's* philosophy in relation to God and man *vis-à-vis* the ancient and modern European and American philosophers, we find some of his philosophical positions akin to them, but we can also identify some uniqueness in his philosophy.

Let us examine the philosophy of the western world, beginning with the Greek philosophy. Somewhat in a different vein from *Gandhiji, Socrates* acknowledged the supremacy of God as the owner of human life. For *Plato*, God was not a bodily thing—all things had their being from God and from something immortal. The "Forms" identified by *Aristotle* pointed to something beyond the human sense-related experiences.

For a Christian theologian and philosopher like *St. Augustine*, God was something above the soul. His philosophical ideas ran through the middle ages. In later centuries, when questions had arisen about the contradiction between faith and reason, *St. Thomas Aquinas* had attempted to solve the problem by advocating that faith and reason could not contradict each other because such a contradiction would reflect on God, Who was the First Principle of all and the first principles of reason were equally derived. While defining the nature of the intellect, *St. Thomas* said that in order to see God, there was needed some intellect, capable of seeing God.

The modern European philosophy had also taken philosophical positions akin to those taken by *Gandhiji*. *Rene Descartes* said that philosophy was concerned with God, soul and immortality. As a founder of rationalism, he, however, tried to seek proofs for inferring the existence of God from our idea of Him. Yet, another rationalist, *Benedict Spinoza,* differed from *Descartes* and held that no proof was needed for the existence of God. God and Nature were only two different words, meaning the same substance. Religion and science were, therefore, compatible—particular things including human minds, while being in themselves mere potentialities, were actualized in the essential existence or eternity of God.

The resultant empiricism had, by and large, emphasized human experience. However, a philosopher like *Immanuel Kant's* "thing-in-itself" came close to the *Brahman* of the *Vedantists.* The intellectual life of the nineteenth century was such that it had led a revolt against traditional systems of thoughts in philosophy, politics and economics. When we move from the European thinking to the American philosophy, we discover pragmatists like *William James, Charles Peirce* and *John Dewey* subjecting reality and truth to mean the object of our fixed beliefs about which after prolonged inquiry, consensus of opinion had been secured and truth happened to be merely a quality of these beliefs. Man, through his action, could create the world's salvation. There appears to be a marked tendency in pragmatism to assign too much power to society to control its environment—natural and human.

The Wardha Scheme

Like many educational thinkers of the world, *Gandhiji* was not a teacher in the professional sense of the term. He did not teach in a classroom or a school. He had, however, contributed a great deal to the theory and practice of education in India. According to him, education was indivisible, for it harmonised man's problems as an individual with the society, his biological issues with his ethical and his physiological motivations with his spiritual motivations.

Although references to education are found in many of *Gandhiji's* writings, two books–*Shiksha ki Samaasya (The* Problem of Education) and *Sachchi Shiksha* (True Education)—form the foundations of his theory and practice of education. The objectives of education were realized through the "Wardha Scheme". *Gandhiji's* philosophical positions were practised through the "Basic Education– *Nai Talim*."

Basic education was to meet the needs of the rural and poor urban children whose parents could not afford to send them to government schools. Moreover, taking children away from their homes would have deprived parents of their assistance in various farming and other occupations. Basic education was self-supporting. Away from education for white-collar jobs, *Gandhiji* expected learners to appreciate dignity of labour. Basic education *was* to build a *Sarvodaya Society,* a welfare society, something like the so called *Ram Raj* or the Marxist concept of classless and stateless society–without distinction of caste, creed, sex or socio-economic factors. *Gandhiji* said that basic education would provide a healthy and moral basis of relationship between the city and the village and thus go a long way towards eradicating some of the worst evils of the present social insecurity and poisoned relationship between the classes. It was to place the destiny of the masses in their own hands. Basic education was a non-violent education.

Philosophy of Education

Gandhiji's philosophy of education was deep, broad and viable: deep for its idealism, broad for its realism and viable for its pragmatism.

(1) The Aims

Gandhiji wrote that, *"Education was not an aim in itself but, rather, an instrument and that type of education could be called real education which helped us in building of sound character"*. We notice that the theme of building of a sound character had also been highlighted by philosophers and educationists of other ages and countries. *Socrates* equated knowledge with virtue. The education, training and service which *Plato* had stipulated for the philosopher-kings contributed to character building. For *Aristotle,* there were two kinds of "virtues"—intellectual and moral, the former resulting from teaching and the latter from habit. By forming good habits, we found pleasure in performing good actions. The Roman educationist–*Quintillion*—aimed at producing an eloquent speaker, but basically, he was to be a man of character. The Christian philosophy laid emphasis on spiritual and moral development. *Erasmus,* the champion of humanism during the renaissance period, also aimed at the moral development of the learners. The Christian reformists had laid a great emphasis on spiritual and ethical development.

A pragmatist like *William James* had advocated a doctrine to make people virtuous and happy. Existentialists, however, considered it important to assist a feeling, suffering, and rejoicing, free person fashion an essence for him. Moral development might take place when individuals confronted their situations and created meaning out of "nothingness".

If we translate *Gandhi's* philosophy into practical principles, we find him advocating that education was to be woven round a suitable craft. The craft was to meet the expenses of the teachers' salaries. The concept of self-supporting education was not mainly for economic independence of the pupils or the school; it emphasized the dignity of labour. The concept of dignity of labour had also been emphasized by the Christian philosophers. In modern times, a pragmatist like *John Dewey* also supported the economic aspects of education and further highlighted the importance of *"their scientific content and their social value."*

It is pertinent to note that the idea of self-supporting education could not be divorced from the ideological background of non-violence. *Gandhiji* had conceived of non-violence as the panacea of all evils. True education could only be imparted through non-violence. But education was not merely an individual acquisition; it had its social dimensions too in that it was an education for citizenship. A minimum of education was considered essential to exercising of rights and duties, citizenship and fulfilling one's obligations by rendering useful service to the society—*"as a member of an organized civilized community."*

(2) The Institutions of Learning

A naturalist like *Herbert Spencer* had found a basis for school in nature. Thus, school was expected to prepare learners for "complete living". But emphasis was also placed on individual development.

For the idealists, education existed as an institution of human society because of spiritual necessity, and not of natural necessity alone. School was considered important for education so that individual children could be given birth as men. School was an agent of the society and a value-realising institution. The idealists also attached importance to home and religious institutions as moulding places for the learners.

The realists treat education as a social institution and school as a "forging place of men." *John Wild* considered school to be an important place wherein the man's inherited tendencies were determined and directed. Among the basic rights, he considered the right to education as *"the most precious and the most in need of realisation"*. *Harry Broudy's* argument in favour of school as a central place to realise the aims of education was based on his realistic assumption about knowledge which was treated to be belonging to a profession and was no more the possession of all the people than was the science of medicine.

The pragmatists had really glorified school. School supplied the volume of learning to each new generation. School could be simpler than the complex society, thus facilitating learning. They, however, emphasized the point that children were not likely to get a balanced representative acquaintance with society unless the spirit and approach of their schools were democratic.

Gandhiji, though an original thinker, was modest in recognizing the influences on him of writers like *Tolstory* and *Ruskin.* Perhaps, similarities between him and others western educational thinkers were merely coincidental.

In *Gandhiji's* scheme of education—"Wardha Scheme" or Basic National Education–the school played a dominant role. School was mandated to impart true compulsory education and have craft as the centre of education so that school became self-supporting. All other subjects were to be taught at school through the crafts.

(3) The Learners

A naturalist like *Herbert Spencer* treated the human child neither naturally good nor morally depraved: he was a bit of both. Furthermore, the child could not be made good by education as it was administered by human adults who could not guarantee an unadulterated success–perhaps because of their own imperfections.

The idealists treated the pupil as a "self", a spiritual being. *H.H. Horne* sumed up the conception of pupil as a finite person whose real origin was deity, whose nature was freedom, and whose destination was immorality.

A realist like *Harry Broudy* described the pupils' growth in terms of principles or stages like appetitive, self-determination, self-realisation and self-integration which comprised the essence of the human self. It was after passing through these stages that a pupil acquired a dynamic personality.

Dewey's conception of the pupil was that although he was unique, he was a part of the life process in which biological, psychological an sociological forces constituted an overflowing stream.

Gandhiji's concept of the learner was that he was to accept the soul force which was more potent than the strength of members. This soul force came through self-discipline and self-purification. Furthermore, he found no distinction between the inner progress and the service of society–service was the same as *Yajna.* He was a practical person in that his expectations of the learners were based on the reality of the situation in India. He wanted boys and girls taught together. The learner was to know the why and the wherefore of every process. Generally speaking, he would not compel the child to learn: interest was to be the basis of learning. At the stage of late adolescence, the young man and woman were to receive education according to his or her desires and circumstances.

His role expectations of the learner contained the best that was available in the educational wisdom of the western and eastern worlds.

(4) The Teacher

The naturalists considered teacher to be an important functionary, as he was the one who provided the sustained protection and guidance to the learner for a long time. The teacher, however, was to understand the natural rhythms of development while guiding the learners. But at the same time, the teacher was to realize his own limitations in aiming at producing a perfect personality.

The idealists glorified the teacher. *Horne* considered the teacher as the personification of reality for the child. He was to be an expert in his teaching subject and knowledgeable about the children. He was always to be learning. In short, he was to be a co-worker with God in perfecting man.

The role of the teacher in realism was summed up by *Harry Broudy* who considered the science of education as a body of knowledge which belonged to a profession and was no more the possession of all the people than was the science of medicine.

The pragmatists stipulated a new role for the teacher. He was expected to plan for learning activities which placed higher demands upon the use of his intelligence. He was a member of the learning group and was also to arrange the conditions which provided the subject matter and content for experiences that satisfied these needs and developed these capacities. According to *Dewey,* in the process of learning which fully employed experience, the teacher lost the position of an external boss or a dictator, but took on that of leader of group activities.

Gandhiji realized that there was lack of the requisite type of teachers to translate his "Wardha Scheme" of education into a success. He expected teachers to be imbued with the spirit of service and self-sacrifice. He, thus, advocated for better conditions of service for teachers to prevent the drainage of talent to other lucrative professions. Improving the conditions of service for teachers was considered crucial to the success of the Wardha Scheme. *Gandhiji* lived a simple life and expected teachers to emulate him and, thus, to manage within the modest salaries. It was felt that his views on the salary of teachers made it merely a pittance.

(5) The Curriculum

The naturalist, *Herbert Spencer,* considered "complete living" as the general aim of education. He attached importance to science as knowledge capable of realizing the aim of complete living. However, he also advocated psychology for a good upbringing, sociology for citizenship, and sculpture, painting, music, drama and poetry for enjoyment.

The idealists had prescribed physical, biological and social sciences, fine arts and practical arts, including history and government. It was expected that knowledge would become ideas and ideas would become "ideals". In terms of methods of teaching, self- activity of the learner and his imitation of men of inspiring greatness and genius were recommended.

A realist like *Harry Broudy* treated curriculum as the means of forming desirable habits by mastering organized subject matter in the fields of natural sciences, social sciences, social philosophy and the classics. However, the Communist realists emphasized polytechnical education and socialization of the learner in the Marxist-Leninist ideology. Like *Broudy,* they also expected the learner to master the exact knowledge.

The position of the pragmatists was represented by *Dewey*. He laid down elementary school curriculum elaborately from manual arts through social sciences to communication skills. The secondary school curriculum was envisaged to be the broadening and deepening of what had been learnt in the elementary school. He recommended the problem and project methods of teaching, for these methods were considered pupil-centred.

In the Wardha Scheme, Gandhiji advocated free and compulsory education. To make education at such a large scale a success, he laid down curriculum that suited the rural India. He made "craft" as the centre of education. The *Zakir Hussain Committee* elaborated on the concept of productive work and said that it was for the exploitation of education purpose of the resources, implicit in craft work so as to inspire the method of teaching other subjects. The craft was to be learnt systematically and scientifically. The economic aspect of the scheme was to avoid unemployment but equally important were the cultural and educational aspects of the objectives. The idea of self-supporting education was nurtured by *Gandhiji's* philosophy of non-violence. The products of the scheme were to be socialized in such a way that, in addition to being self-supporting, they helped in the elimination of class and communal hatred, and all forms of exploitation.

The important question of the medium of instruction was answered boldly by *Gandhiji.* The medium of instruction was to be the "mother-tongue" of the learners. He supported his position by presenting cogent linguistic, cultural, ethical and aesthetic reasons in recommending the mother-tongue as the medium of instruction.

The Wardha Scheme also emphasized the idea of citizenship with a view to understanding the rights and duties, rendering useful service to the civil community and realizing the sense of personal worth and dignity in a changing India. Closely connected with the ideal of citizenship was the idea of a co-operative community in which the motive of social service dominated all the activities of children during the plastic years of childhood and youth. The *Zakir Hussain Committee* prepared the main outline of the "correlated" programme of work for the duration of seven years: the syllabus contained the basic crafts, the mother-tongue, and mathematics, social studies, general science, drawing, music and Hindustani. The epistemological position was that knowledge came through experience. But the experience was morality-based as it resulted in an attitude of non-violence.

Evaluation

Gandhiji's standing in India had been so tall that the possibilities of accepting all what he had said and written had always existed. Yet, some critics pointed out that the Wardha Scheme was more of a sentimental venture rather than something containing a real merit. However, a close examination of the scheme was convining in that it was based on sound psychological, pedagogical and philosophical principles.

Doubts were also expressed about the feasibility of teaching every subject by means of '*Takli*' or any other basic craft as far as possible. 'Correlation' was the heart of the matter. Various subjects were to be learnt by correlating them to the craft. *Gandhiji*, though he emphasized crafts, also recommended other processes to supplement knowledge.

Critics made reference to the lack of requisite type of teachers to implement the scheme. By changing the orientation of teachers through training and by improving their conditions of service, it was observed that, by and large, teachers had been working with zeal and effectiveness.

The lopsided approach to education in the Wardha Scheme was pointed out in that the secondary and higher aspects and levels of education were ignored. It was true that *Gandhiji* concentrated his effects on the primary schooling, but it was not done with any contempt for higher education. In fact, he expected university education to be enriched by the provision of better libraries, laboratories and research institutions. Otherwise also, it was with a firm foundation of education at the primary level that the deserving learners could climb up the educational ladder to the second level of education and from there to the university level.

Lastly, it was feared that the craft-based scheme was likely to set the clock of scientific civilization back. He planned the scheme for lacs of villages in India. In such villages, practising the traditional crafts was common; through the Wardha Scheme, additional subjects were also to be taught by means of the correlation method. Teaching the modem technology at whatever rudimentary stage was not possible, at least, in the beginning of the scheme. The self-supporting aspect of the scheme was to minimize the drift of rural youth to the cities in search of jobs. The non- availability of jobs and the aimless life of the unemployed had resulted in social ills.

It was *Gandhiji's* belief that through the Basic Education, it was possible to do away with casteism and rehabilitate the *Harijans,* emancipate women, and save the country from the social ills by introducing prohibition.

The Wardha Scheme received support of the educationists and statesmen. The Government of India appointed the *Kher Committee* and it made viable recommendations for implementing the scheme which had made a good start, but suffered some set-back in certain provinces. Ultimately the scheme started becoming popular. After independence in 1947, the scheme received more support.

Although contemporary India had been trying to catch up with the technologically advanced countries of the world, the scheme still had a place in the educational system. The rural India needed the scheme, although improvements could have been made in it.

Conclusion

Gandhiji is a philosopher who has offered the best of wisdom of the past and has also contributed his unique ideas to the educational philosophy. We could have, however, continued examining and even modifying his philosophy of education so that it did not become a dogma. But an irony of the situation was that, first, the Indian Education Commission and later the National Policy on Education, by and large, ignored the scheme. The question that could have been answered was whether we really had reached a stage when we could forget *Gandhiji's* contributions?

Summary

Gandhiji believed in the absolute oneness of God and humanity. He designed the Wardha scheme of education. His views on education are found in his *Shiksha ki Samasya* and *Sachi Siksha.* His aim of education was to build a sound character. School played an important role in education of the learners. The learners were expected to accept the soul force. The teachers were expected to be self-sacrificing. *Gandhiji's* curriculum was craft-centred. All other subjects were to be correlated to the craft. The medium of instruction was to be the mother tongue of the learners.

24

Integral Education

Aurobindo Ghose (1872-1950)

The common feature in the philosophical views of Indian thinkers was that none of them could run away from the spiritualism which is the basis of our culture. *Aurobindo Ghose's* "integral education" is also saturated with spiritualism.

Life Sketch

Sri Aurobindo was born on 15th August, 1872, as *Aurobindo Akroyd.* His father was District Surgeon of Rangapur, Bengal and mother was the daughter of *Rajnarayan Basu*, a Brahmo religious and social reformer. His father had studied medicine at Kings College, Aberdeen and had lived in Britain. He had wanted his children to get European education, which they did. *Aurobindo* was first tutored at home in England, then at St. Paul's School in London and later at Cambridge University. He was a brilliant student of classics (Latin and Greek) and wrote poetry. He passed written papers of ICS, but chose to drop the practical of horse riding.

Political Stand

He joined state service of Baroda, taught French and English, became Vice Principal, learnt Sanskrit and other Indian languages, but was more interested in joining those working for the freedom of India. He visited Calcutta and got in touch with the revolutionaries. *Bankim Chatterji, Swami Vivekananda* and *Tilak* influenced him. He was arrested in connection with Alipore Bomb case but was released. He wrote poetry and articles on political issues for *Bandematram*. In April, 1910, he retired from politics and went to Pondicherry for philosophical and spiritual pursuits.

Politics to Spirituality

He concentrated on Yoga for four years, and then in 1914, launched a 64-page monthly review called *Arya*. The serialized publication included *The Life Divine, The Synthesis of Yoga, Essays on the Gita, The Secret of the Veda, The Upanishads, The Renaissance in India, War and Self-determination, The Human Cycle, The Ideal of Human Unity, The Future of Poetry etc.*

The Mother

The "Mother," as she was called by *Aurobindo*, was his close spiritual collaborater. She was born in Paris to Turkish and Egyptian parents on 21st February, 1878 and was named *Mira Alfassa*. She was later involved in the cultural and spiritual life of Paris. She came to Pondichery on 28th March, 1914 and finally settled there in 1920. *Aurobindo* considered her his spiritual equal and collaborator. *Aurobindo* retired into seclusion in 1976 and she planned, built and ran the growing *Ashram*. She also supervised *Aurobindo* International Centre of Education. *Aurobindo* died on 5th December, 1950.

Philosophy

Aurobindo's philosophical achievement was to introduce the concept of evolution into the *Vedantic* thought. *Samkhya* did propose such notion countries ago, but *Aurobindo* rejected the materialistic tendencies of both *Samkhya* and *Darwin, and* proposed that spirit also evolved with the matter: evolution of matter resulted from evolution of spirit.

For *Aurobindo*, world was not a *Maya* (illusion) and renunciation was not the only way out. For him, it was possible not only to transcend human nature but also to transform it and live in the world as a free and evolved, human being, with a new consciousness and new nature. Such nature could spontaneously perceive truth of things and proceed in all matters on the basis of inner oneness, love and light. He called the new consciousness as the Supermind, the active principle present in the transcendent *Sachindananda* as well as the roots of evolution: a unitary level of which our individual minds and bodies were minuscule subdivisions.

Evolutionary Philosophy

According to *Aurobindo*, the human kind was not the last rung in the evolutionary scale: it could evolve spiritually beyond its current limitations to a state of spiritual and supramental existence, a "divine life on earth", characterized by a spiritualized, superamental, trust-consciousness-oriented humanity.

Process of Creation and Evolution

Aurobindo spoke of two central movements in the process of creation: (1) involution of consciousness from an original omnipresent Reality, manifesting a universe of forms, including matter, (2) an evolution of those material forms in creation of upward life, mind, and spirit, reconnecting to their spiritual source.

(1) *Involution:* Involution was the process by which the energy of creation emerged from a timeless, spaceless, ineffable and immutable reality. The reality extended thought to Being/Existence

(*Sat*), Consciousness that generated a force (*Chit*); and Bliss (*Ananda*) –self enjoyment in existing and being conscious. Through the action of Supermind (Truth Consciousness), the Force (*chit*) of *Sat-chit-ananda* was divided into knowledge and will, eventually formulating into an invisible Energy that was to become the source of creation. Out of that Energy, through its own wilful self-absorption of consciousness, the Universe began as Inconscient material existence.

(2) *Evolution:* Evolution was the process of conscious existence which emerged out of the Inconscient. Initially, it emerged gradually in the stages of matter, life and mind: matter evolved from simple to complex forms. Finally, mind emerged in life and evolved from rudimentary to higher forms of thought and reason. Humanity represented the stage of development of mind in complex material forms of life. But evolution worked beyond to higher levels of a spiritual and supramental consciousness. The higher evolution was a dual movement; inward away from the surface consciousness and into the depths, culminating in the realization of the Psychic Being (Mind, Intuitive Mind and Overmind), ultimately culminating in the final stage of supramentalisation. Particular individuals had attained the higher levels of consciousness, but these were to emerge in a new species on earth to be united in consciousness with *Sachhidananda*.

The Omnipresent Reality (Brahman)

Aurobindo considered the truth of existence as an omnipresent Reality that both transcended the manifested universe and was inherent in it. The reality (*Brahman*) was an absolute in that it was not limited by any mental conception or duality–personal or interpersonal, existent or non existent, formless or manifested in a form, timeless or extended in time, spaceless or extended in space: it was simultaneously all of these, but was bound by none of them. *Brahman* was the deepest and secret reality of humans' life and it was united through the yoga that humans' life was united with their essential Reality.

Triple Transformation of the Individual

Man, according to *Aurobindo,* was born as an ignorant, divided, conflicting being, the product of mother, not knowing anything about reality. Man was to embark on a process of self discovery of his divine nature through triple transformation: psychic transformation, spiritual transformation, superamental transformation.

In psychic transformation, man saw the oneness and unity of creation and the harmony of all opposites, experienced in life. In spiritual transformation, man's mind expanded and he experienced knowledge through light, intuition and revelation, culminating in superamental perception. Light entered from the heights and began to transmute various parts of his being.

The Evolving Soul (Psychic Being)

Aurobindo emphasised on finding and living in the psychic being (i.e. an Evolving Soul) within which was the essence of our individual being. By foregoing into the deepest parts of our being, we came upon a personal evolving soul to overcome the limits of consciousness of the individual human. From there, we perceived our true nature and essence, became more aware of our surrounding, brought timelesseness with time and evoked the powers of the Infinite into this finite existence. When we plunged within and touched evolving soul, it became easy to move up in consciousness above mind to spiritual mind of illumination, intuition, revelation and (supramental) truth consciousness. The psychic was itself evolving: The connection to the evolving soul was, thus, the key to the evolution, from this the human side as from there we overcame the inherent ignorance, division, dualities, and suffering of man, enabling him to fulfil his human aspiration of God, freedom, joy and immortality.

Suffering

According to *Aurobindo,* pain was a smaller element than joy in life. Pleasure was our normal state and pain was abnormal. We felt pain more intensely because it was abnormal. Pain helped break down our resistance to the truth and eroded the hold of the ego. If suffering were to come, one was to accept it calmly.

The Goal

Reviewing the goals of life, *Aurobindo* said that the Christans sought Heaven, the Buddhists sought *Nirvana* and the Hindus sought *Moksha* (liberation from the cycle of life and death). But these were other worldly goals: the goal was not the attaintment of heaven in after life, but a perfect life here on earth. Man was not a mind, a life and a body but a soul, incarnated for divine fulfillment on earth. The goal was to live from within, from the soul centre. A person who lived in the Spirit was one with all.

As will he seen, there is a marked influence of the spiritual ideas of *Aurobindo* on his philosophy of education.

Philosophy of Education

In *Aurobindo's* words: *"the true basis of education is the study of the human mind–infant, adolescent and adult"*. Such education was termed as Integral Education. The education of a human being was to begin at birth and continue throughout his life.

(1) The Aims of Education

According to the Mother's writings, education to be complete was to correspond to the five principal activities of the human being–(i) the physical, (ii) the mental, (iii) the psychic and the spiritual and (iv) the vital. Education was to begin at birth and continue throughout life.

(*i*) *Physical Education*: Physical culture was an important component of integral education. In *Aurobindo's* yoga philosophy, the physical body was meant to be made fully conscious and awakened to its identity as a material form of divine consciousness, translating its eternity to immortality. As part of the integral education, physical education was a preparation of the physical consciousness, enhancing in inner capacities for health, longevity, coordination, harmony, endeavour, stamina, capacity for intensity of experience and the direct intuitive skill of a working physical instrument. To put the theory into practice at the *Aurobindo ashram*, exercises, group activities and sports were mandatory at all levels of education—even continued voluntarily into advanced age. Physical exercises destroyed an independent consciousness of the body. Choice was made of colisthenics, long distance running and the individual activity alongwith coordinated group activities of a variety of forms.

(*ii*) *Mental Education:* A true mental education prepared man for higher life and had five principal phases, normally one after another. These were:

(*a*) Development of the power of concentration, the capacity of attention.

(*b*) Development of the capacities of expansion, widening, complexity and richness.

(*c*) Organisation of one's ideas around a central idea, a higher ideal or a supremely luminous idea, that was to serve as a guide in life.

(*d*) Through control, rejection of undesirable thoughts, to become able to think only what one wanted and when one wanted.

(*e*) Development of mental silence, perfect calm and a more and more total receptivity to inspirations coming from the higher regions of the being.

(*iii*) *Psychic Education and Spiritual Education:* As an important part of integral education, psychic education tackles the problem of the true motive of existence –the purpose of life on earth, the discovery to which life was to lead and the result of that discovery: the consecration of the individual to his eternal principle. The discovery was associated with mystic feeling, a religious life, for religions concerned themselves with mystic life. However, the mystic notion of God might be replaced by the more philosophical notion of truth, yet the discovery remained essentially the same, but the road leading to it might be taken by the most intransigent positivist, for mental notions and ideas had only a very secondary importance in preparing one for the psychopathic life. The important thing was to live the experience that carried with it its own reality and force.

It was through the psychic presence that the truth of an individual being came into contact with him and the circumstance of his life. Psychic education was to be practised for the purpose of obtaining mastery and becoming conscious of the psychic presence.

The starting point was to seek in oneself that which was independent of the body and the circumstances of his life. One was to find in the depths of one's being that which carried in it a sense of universality, limitless expression and unbroken continuity. But the path to such realization was long and difficult. The mind was incapable of judging spiritual things.

(*iv*) *Vital Education:* The vital education was the education given so that the learners are physically healthy, mentally alert and spiritually dedicated. In the physical development, the development of senses was vital: sense of sight, hearing, smell, taste and touch. To these was added the cultivation of discrimination and the aesthetic senses. The learner was to be taught to appreciate beautiful, lofty, healthy and noble things in nature and human creation. Their refinement would bring nobility and generosity to the learner.

The other aspect of vital education was the development and transformation of character through coercion, suppression, abstinence and asceticism which eliminated the possibilities of the intervention, help and collaboration of the vital. The child was to observe, note his reactions and impulses and their causes to become a discerning witness of his desires, movement of violence and passion and domination and the background of vanity. In addition to developing the power of observation, the will for progress and perfection was also to grow. Method of setting an example was more effective than other methods. Persistent efforts were to continue acquiring mental and spiritual education also. Education was to foster the growth of the integral consciousness in every pupil and bring back to legitimate of the spirit over a matter fully developed and utilized. All the systems of yoga combined and converged on the path to supermind.

> According to *Raina, Aurobindo*: *was sovereignly aware of the variation in the concept of man, his life and destiny of the nation and of humanity and the life of human race, which get reflected in the respective philosophies of education and developed his scheme of integral education, rooted in the developing soul of India to her future need, to the greatness of her coming self-creation, to her eternal spirit.*

One had to gain full knowledge of one's character and the acquire control over one's movements in order to achieve perfect mastery and the transformation of all the elements that love to be transformed.

(2) The Institutions of Learning

To put his ideas of integral education into practice, *Aurobindo*, on the 6th of January, 1952, inaugurated *Sri Aurobindo International University, Centre*: later in 1959, its name was changed to *Sri Aurobindo International Centre of Education*. The objectives of the institution of learning were to evolve and realize a system of integral education.

The Centre consisted of sections from kindergarten till higher courses (graduate level). The system of learning and teaching was flexible. A science student with right attitude could qualify himself more than a graduate. Average performance of the student was considered, and if a student excelled in a particular subject, he could be promoted to a higher class in that subject.

(3) The Pupils

The children, before they entered school, were expected to be brought up carefully by the family, particularly the mother. The parents were to be models worth imitation. Parents were not to scold their children without good reason. If the child did something wrong, he was to confess the wrong and was to be forgiven; there was not to be a lingering fear between the child and the parent. The child was not to be forced to eat food which he/she found distasteful. The body knew instinctively what was good and what was harmful to it, provided the child was taught to distinguish between needs and desires. Children were to be taught to respect health.

(4) The Teachers

The first characteristic of the teacher was to have cultivated a disciplined life so that he/she taught learners more by precept than the words. As one of the principles of integral education was that, *"nothing can be taught,"* so the role of the teacher was that of a mentor, helping the students to learn how to acquire knowledge for himself or herself. The source of knowledge was "within the students." The teacher was to help the students to perfect their instruments of knowledge to raise it to the surface. Something similar to *Aurobindo's* concept of "knowledge within" was also postulated by the Christian philosopher, *St. Augustine* in the fourth and fifth centuries A.D. as against *Locke's* concept of the *Tabula Rasa* much later.

(5) The Curriculum

If we analyse the curriculum of International University Centre, we find that the curriculum met the needs of students in diverse fields like arts, sciences, humanities, and professional courses like engineering, aesthetics, crafts, physical education, and the yoga. The concept of integral education was to integrate all knowledge for the development of an integral social personality of the learners.

Great importance was attached to the learning of one's own language as such a system prepared one to master other languages.

Manas or mind, the sixth sense of Indian psychology, received the images of things translated into sight, sound, smell, taste and touch (sensations). The six senses were trained by the child himself under the teachers' direction to the perfect accuracy.

Conclusion

Aurobindo, an explorer and adventure in consciousness, a visionary of evolution, wrote that we one could write about his life because it had not been on the surface for man to see. *McDermott* felt that *"interpreting the life of a great spiritual personality is always a treacherous enterprise, and the life of Sri Aurobindo is peculiarly inscrutable."* It is true that the spiritual experience is so personal, so mirage-like, so overwhelming that even the experiencing person finds it difficult to describe. In relation to education, *Aurobindo's* integral education showed the pathway to spiritual experience—not by renunciation of the every day life but by living it, by experiencing it.

Summary

Sri Aurobindo was educated in England and taught briefly in India. He joined the revolutionary forces, fighting against British rule. But he turned to spiritually from politics and settled at Pondichery. He was joined by a women, called the "mother" who continued his good work. He advocated the evolutionary philosophy in which human mind was also evolving. Man was transformed psychically, spiritually and supermentally. He introduced the concept of integral education and put it into practice at the International University Centre. Knowledge was within the learner and the teacher was to develop it. He attended a great importance to wide-ranging curriculum and assigned pride of place to the mother longue of the learner in the process of education.

25

Education for Exaltation of Ego

Mohammad Iqbal (1873-1938)

One would have thought that *Mohammad Iqbal's* name should have been included in an anthology of Urdu poetry but, as the following brief phiolsophical account in this chapter shows, that his poetry also contained his sublime as well as profound views on philosophy.

Life-sketch

Moḥammad Iqbal was born in Sialkot (now in Pakistan) in February, 1873. He got his MA. Degree in Philosophy from Lahore, Honours Degree in philosophy from Cambridge and Doctorate from Munich. He was called to the Bar in London, but his main interest was in writing poetry and, thus, he did not take his practice seriously. He knew well languages like Urdu, Persian, Arabic, English and German, and had the working knowledge of many ancient and modern languages. He used Urdu and Persian as the main languages to express the profundity, sublimity and breadth of his poetry.

He taught philosophy and literature in a college at Lahore and after a few years gave up teaching and started the law practice until the fag end of his life. He was also elected a member of the Punjab Legislative Assembly of undivided India for a term and President of the All India Muslim League for a year. He was honoured with honorary degrees and knighted for his fame in poetry. His first philosophical poem was *Asrari Khudi* (the Secrets of the Self) and second was *Ramuzi Bekhudi* (the Secrets of Selflessness) He wrote mainly in Persian and Urdu but used English also equally effectively to express his thoughts. He died in April 1938.

Philosophy

Iqbal was influenced by the philosophical thoughts of the West and East, but there was also a marked influence of Islam on him. His conception of the universe was that it was designed to serve as the theatre of man's growing and manifold activities. It was not predetermined; it was not a finished product; and it was capable of infinite growth and development. His interpretation of the *Quran* was that it awoke in the man a higher consciousness of his manifold relations with God and the Universe. For him, it was not God Who changed the conditions of men but men by means of what was in themselves. About the mind, he said, that the wealth of mind once secured was never lost.

Man

Iqbal had faith in man as the roof and crown of all creations of God. Man was the only creature who was an active participant in the creative activity of his Maker. He was to use the resources of his knowledge and the power it gave him for the enrichment of human life. According to him, *"No form of activity was so powerful, so inspiring and so beautiful as the spirit of man."* A good man led a creative life, applied his intelligence to exploit the forces of nature, subordinated his life to God, tried for self-realisation, did not compromise with evil, developed his power by contact with his environment and was courageous, tolerant and proud. But man also had his two fold ego: (1) efficient ego which corresponded to the material world and (2) appreciative ego which was spiritual existence, experienced in meditation.

Religion

For *Iqbal*, religion in its highest manifestations was neither dogma, nor priesthood, nor ritual alone in preparing a person *"for the burden of the great responsibility which the advancement of modern science necessarily involves and restores to him that attitude of faith which makes him capable of winning personality here and retaining it hereafter"*: it was a dynamic inspiration for the whole of life. Prayer was a normal vital art by which the little island of our personality suddenly discovered its situation in the larger whole of life. It was an expression of man's inner yearning for a response in the careful silence of the universe. Prayer was a fruitful communion between the inner self and God.

Political Vision

Iqbal stood for equality, liberty and fraternity, but he was a true nationalist also, because he sang a song in praise of India so to say: that it was the best country in the world (*Sare Johan Se Achha Hindustan Hamara*). It showed his patriotism.

Educational Philosophy

Iqbal's educational philosophy was derived from his general philosophical concepts about human life, nature, society and God.

(1) The Aims of Education

There was a great stress on the development of individuality *(Khudi)* as *Iqbal* called it. But social, intellectual, cultural and moral aspects of development were no less important.

(i) Development of Individuality: In his view, *"The power of individuality makes a grain of mustard grow into a mountain."* This

hyperbolic link from his poetry typified the importance, he attached to development of individuality. It was education that was to bring the inner strength and richness, provide abiding values and refine and spiritualise lower forms of desire. According to him, man was both creator and creative. Children were to be given opportunities for free expression to develop creativity.

(ii) *Social Development:* Social development implied the ability of the creative children to adjust with the society. They were to appreciate the cultural values of the society and adhere to them. The educands were to develop patriotism and the individual was to be moral but the morality arose out of a willing cooperation of the free egos. However, some people may misinterpret the following statement: *"China and Arabia are ours, so is Hindustan. We are Muslims and the whole world is our native land."*

(iii) *Intellectual Development:* For *Iqbal,* man sought knowledge constantly in Nature, which yearning was not against spiritual development: knowledge of Nature was the knowledge of God's behaviour. In Nature, man sought a kind of intimacy with the absolute Ego and that was only other form of worship. All search for knowledge was essentially an act of prayer, and that the scientific observation of Nature was a kind of an act of prayer. If knowledge was passive and mixed with no sense of passion, no thrill of self fulfillment, it was like the knowledge which the book-worm acquired by eating away the written pages. In his words, *"In all knowledge there is an element of passion and the object of knowledge gains or looses in objectivity with the rise and the fall in the intensity of passion. This is more real to us which stirs the entire fabric of our personality."* Search for knowledge does enhance the intellectual development of the learners.

(iv) *Cultural Development: Iqbal* considered one's own cultural heritage important because the person was to feed on it. An educated person was to be able to understand, appreciate, assimilate as well as critically assess the culture, and within the range of his capacities, help in its reconstruction. But the learner was also to be receptive to the best cultural inputs from outside. He, perhaps, appreciated the process of acculturation, which could not be avoided in the cross flow of ideas and practices from other cultures. Learners required freedom to find sources of information in their own special cultural patterns.

(v) *Moral Development:* He recognized the important role of knowledge in human life, but he also pointed the dangers of over-intellectualism. Thus, he identified the role of knowledge as doubting and questioning, probing and enquiring which led to adventure and quest. Science and technology, the product of knowledge, needed to be supplemented by intuition. Direct perception by the heart enabled human beings to apprehend and associate directly with reality in its wholeness. Education was to provide opportunities for social and moral experiences.

Iqbal's aims of education were close to the western school of idealism which also emphasized spiritual, moral and cultural development to produce a complete man, but he also emphasized bookish knowledge. For him, the universe was not a predetermined and finished product, but capable of infinite growth. God was absolute Ego and man's ego proceeded from Him. Man was the best creation of God. Religion was a dynamic inspiration for the whole of life. The aim of education was to develop a learner's individuality through his physical, social, moral and cultural development.

(2) The Institutions of learning

Iqbal had high expectations of the institutions of learning. The institutions were to make provisions for facilitating the implementation of a broad-based curriculum—arts, sciences, morality and religion. The infrastructure called for libraries and qualified teachers.

(3) The Pupils

The pupils of both sexes were expected to be the type who would be willing to gain from an education which struck a balance between the material and the spiritual, intellectual and intuitive, and activity-centred and contemplative. He had great reverence for women and wanted to ensure a respectable place for them in society. Thus, he stood for equal opportunities in education for them. As he advocated complete freedom for them, the learners were expected to cultivate self-discipline. *Iqbal*, however, stood for complete freedom of the child.

(4) The Teachers

Iqbal had high expectations of teachers. They were to be well qualified to teach a variety of subjects but they were also to be exemplary in their moral conduct. Although they were to teach moral and spiritual values to their students, they were to be the role models to be effective teachers. They were to use a variety of techniques of teaching.

In the western philosophy, the idealists directed and guided the learner, and the teacher practised regulated freedom in the class, and encouraged self-discipline.

(5) The Curriculum

Iqbal's curriculum was broad-based. He recommended sciences, morality and religion, history, cultural heritage political science, economics, Persian etc. He also outlined the main philosophy behind the subjects.

Sciences, particularly physics and chemistry, were instruments for the preservation of life. But these were to be taught with controlled faith in ethical principles. Moral and religious education was to help man to understand and appreciate modern social, political, scientific or philosophical problems. History was important to understand the past in the true understanding of the present. He considered Urdu and Persian-teaching essential to educating the Muslim children. But many Hindus also mastered Persian and particularly Urdu.

As *Iqbal* had been a teacher at a college, he had some feel of the school system also. Thus, he suggested principles and techniques of teaching. For example:

(i) He advocated the principle of freedom for the learner who was to carry on experimenting in the environment. The activities were to be creative. Intellectual freedom promoted unlimited advances in knowledge.

(ii) The second principle related to experience. Man learnt through the first hand knowledge, even by making mistakes, but learning from them. Error was an indispensable factor in the building up of an experience.

(iii) The third principle, he laid down, concerned activity which interested the learner and ensured learning.

(iv) The fourth principle of direct contact meant that the teacher was to develop the power of observation and train the senses of the learners so that they learnt about the actual and concept object.

(v) The fifth principle was of variety which meant that the teacher was to divide the lesson into different units so that the variety could help the learner to focus on the variegated units. The variety could be introduced by making the learners memorise and recite poems and teacher was to tell stories.

(vi) The sixth principle concerned the development of discernment by giving the learners opportunities to judge persons, objects and opinions–not casually but logically.

(vii) The seventh principle of moral development was for the teachers to teach moral values, but more by being models of morality.

In the western world, idealists emphasized ethics, humanities, religion, art, music and philosophy and realist supported sciences. But *Iqbal* was eclectic in his approach to curriculum. He placed equal emphasis on arts, sciences and humanities, thereby surpassing idealists, realists and pragmatists. In terms of methods of teaching, idealists used text book methods and realists and pragmatists attached importance to experimentation, but he integrated various methods so that effective teaching-learning took place.

Relevance of Iqbal's Ideas

In the secular approach to education, as we have in India, teaching of ethics is acceptable, but teaching religion in a multi religious society would be impracticable—and may even be undesirable. However, *Iqbal's* view to empower the learners with knowledge, skills, competencies and attitudes so that they became useful, cultured and productive citizens is relevant to the present day situation in India.

His advocacy of a wide-based curriculum and variety of teaching principles and methods is worth taking note of by the teacher-trainers.

Generally speaking, he was a great poet and philosopher and influenced people in India and abroad. Through education he wanted to produce poetry with intelligence, tolerance, ccurage, love and dedication to higher values of life.

Conclusion

Lovers of Urdu poetry still remember *Iqbal* and rightly, but at the same time nobody can deny his deep thoughts about man, nature and God. Without the help of intuition, the intellect cannot reach the core of being. So that man is in tune with the Infinitely Creative 'Plan', *Iqbal's* writings have that enthusiasm to equate poetry with philosophy and vice-versa.

Summary

Iqbal was educated in India, England and Germany. He started practising law but his main interest was in Urdu poetry. He was honoured for his poetry and philosophy. He had full faith in God and His creation, the man. He was a person of patriotism. Education for him was the development of the full man with physical, social, intellectual, moral and cultural characteristies. He stood for imparting a broad-based curriculum in schools with motivated learners and trained teachers.

26

Education by Example and Precept

*Bhagat Phool Singh (1888-1942)**

Life Sketch

Bhagat Phool Singh was born on 24th February 1885 at Mahra village in Rohtak District (now Sonepat) of Haryana state. He was named *Harphool*. His parents were poor. His father, *Baber Singh*, sold his house to pay for the debits of a money-lender who had sued him. The father built a small house nearby.

Hide and Seek with Studies

When *Harphool* was eight years old, he was sent to a nearby school at Juan village. He worked hard and passed classes I, II, and III, standing first or second. He was admired by his teacher.

But later, he fell in the bad company of some boys of the village and started playing truant. The teacher brought the matter to the notice of *Baber Singh* who was surprised at his son's behaviour. When the father inquired of the son, the latter tried to make excuses, but ultimately when he saw the anger on his father's countenance, he responded that he would not go to school at all. His father's advice to him to go to school fell on deaf ears. Later, *Harphool* relented and decided to go to school, but paid no attention to his studies. During the examination, the teacher detected that *Harphool* was deliberately answering questions wrongly and he reported the matter to *Baber Singh.* He advised his son to mend his ways and to study, but his efforts and those of the other members of the family were in vain. He was then subjected to hard work and was provided with scanty clothes and no shoes. He was put to get sugarcane crushed by *Kohlu* (oxen-driven sugar mill). There happened to be an incident in the neighbourhood in which a father had been punishing his son for some reason and *Baber* in the presence of *Harphool* told his other son, *Mansa Ram*, that *Harphool* had to go to school otherwise he would receive the same harsh treatment. Fearful of his father and brother and of the punishment as was being given to the son of the other person, and on the advice of his mother, he started going to school and passed fourth class creditably.

---

*Dr. Sandeep Berwal

Later, he was sent to *Mehrouli School* where he passed fifth and sixth classes and entered seventh class when he was fifteen years old.

He passed eight class with flying colours from *Kharkhoda Middle School*.

Job as a Patwari

After passing the middle school, *Harphool* was trained as a temporary *patwari* (revenue clerk), and in 1904 started working at *Seenkh Pathari* village in district Karnal. In 1907, he become a regular *patwari* and was posted to *Urlane* village which was inhabited by Muslim Rajputs. When he was 20 years old, he was married to *Dhoop Kaur* of *Khanda* village in Rohtak district.

Contact with Arya Smaj

A *patwari* named *Preet Singh*, based at *Israna* village, was a famous person of Arya Smaj. He used to attend a *satsang* (religious congregation) at Panipat every month. *Phool Singh* and *Preet Singh* were friends. Once they met at Panipat for three months on official duties. *Preet Singh* presented a booklet containing devotional songs of the Smaj. *Phool Singh* sang the songs melodiously and started attending the *satsang* and motivated his friends for the *satsang*. He even paid the expenses of his friends and took them with him to famous Gurukul Kangri, Haridwar to attend a function. Once there, he heard *Mahatma Munshi Ram* (*Swami Shradananda*) saying: *"It is difficult to be born as a human being. They repent who waste their life in enjoyment and show off. Do noble deeds and keep off ignoble deeds. The main mission of Arya Smaj is to be beneficient to the world. Lead the bewildered people to the right path."* These words made a deep impression on *Harphool* who decided to devote some of his time to preach the messages of *Arya Smaj*. Once he had gone to attend a function of the *Smaj* at Panipat where he came across *Pandit* (*Swamy*) *Brahmananda*. Accepting *Phool Singh*'s request to accept him as his disciple, the *Swamy* presented him with a *Yogyapaveet* (sacred thread) and the *patwari* became the member of *Arya Smaj*.

Devotion to Spread Vedic Religion

Whenever *Phool Singh* was free from his duty as a *patwari*, he would assemble people and invite scholars, saints, sages and singers of devotional songs to give spiritually-elevating messages. He advised villagers to keep themselves and their surroundings clean: cleanliness was his theme. He helped those in misery as a duty-bound person.

Establishment of Girls Gurukul at Khanpur Kalan

In 1925, Haryana province suffered from a drought. Animals had no fodder and human beings suffered from lack of food. Moreover, as the *Bhagat* spent more time in social service, he lacked time to mobilize funds for the boys' *Gurukul* at *Bhonsla*. Yet, he considered education of the girls as very important and put forward a suggestion for a *Gurukula* for girls before the management committee which opposed the suggestion. But the *Bhagat* persisted in his efforts and asked for land from the residents of *Khanpur Kalan*. They donated thirteen bighas of land and the *Gurukula* started in 1936. As people did not consider education of the girls necessary, the *Bhagat* went from house to house to collect girls and seventeen small girls were brought. Donations were sought and obtained to buy books under the direction of *Bhagat's* daughter, *Shubhasni,* and one *Abhimanyu*. The institution started making progress. It was the time of drought. The supporters of the two *Gurukulas* became restive and wanted to leave the organizations. They blamed the *Bhagat* for spending too much time in *panchayats*. But he told them that social services was also important, yet many left. However, a person called *Sarup Lal* of *Anbali* village devoted his life to the service of the *Gurukula*. Similarly, *Seth Jugal Kishore* denoted hundreds of rupees. *Chaudhari Chotu Ram* also helped finanancially and in other ways. Many other people donated money. Thinking beyond the mandane present was the *Bhagat's* vision for the future and gradually the financial situation improved.

Graduates of Gurukula

If was in 1932 that three *Brahmcharis* completed their education after twelve years and awarded the qualification of *Vidya Prabhakar*. Nearly, fifteen thousand people had gathered to watch the ceremony which was addressed by *Chaudhari Chhotu Ram*. He gave his advice in these words:

> *Dear graduates! You have been educated in the benign care of Mahatma Phool Singh. His life will influence you. You are aware of his aspirations and keen desires. I request you to respect his wish and work accordingly. The rural Haryana is backward in education and is poor. Bad customs are entrenched in the life of the people. People have been unsuccessful in getting rid of conservatism. If you can rid society of the evils, you will be doing a noble deed. I congratulate you and wish you success in you life.*

The *Bhagat* also addressed the graduates and asked them to rid the society of mutual enemity in Haryana. He also advised them to lead a noble life and spread the Vedic knowledge, and congratulated them. He rededicated himself to the service of the *Gurukula* and motivated others to serve the temple of learning. *Bhagat's* advice to the new graduates was inspiring and practicable.

The Bhagat's Philosophy

Like *Swamy Dayanand's* philosophy, *Bhagat Phool Singh's* philosophy could be gleaned from his actions in life and his sayings. His metaphysical position was his faith in God Who was all-pervading. All that happened in human life was according to His will. In order to obtain salvation, man was to perform righteous deeds.

Aims of Education

The *Bhagat's* aims of education were not different from the aims of the *Gurukuls*, and particularly those practised by *Swamy Dayananda*. The physical development of the learner took place through hard manual work, simple food and abstinence from sex. The entire climate of the *Gurukula* was encouraging to imbibing moral values. The social development was ensured by interactions with the fellow learners and teachers, and by associatiing with outside people in religious festivals and meetings. The emotional development took place by controlling anger and fear, and by sublimation of the sexual urges. In the development of culture, the Vedic literature played an important role. The confusion created by exposure of learners to the western and Islamic values was clarified by the study of the Vedic and Sankrit literature. The aim was developing persons imbued with Indian culture and ethos.

The Pupils

The pupils at *Bhainswal Kalan* were boys and at *Khanpur* were girls. They were to lead a celibate life and devote all their time to learning and to prayers. But they were to lead a disciplined life and even punishment could be given to erring pupils. They led simple, virtuous and noble life. Boys and girls were to be taught in separate institutions. The students were expected to keep in control the sensualities—in thought, word and action.

The Teachers

The teachers were expected to be knowledgeable and skillful. They were to transform their pupils into spiritual entities. They were to treat pupils as their own children. They led a noble, virtuous and simple life. The *Bhagat*, however, appreciated the inability of some of the teachers to render free service when they quit the services in times of hardship like droughts and famines.

The Curriculum

The curriculum was broad-based, with emphasis on the Vedic literature. The scope of such literature was comprehensive in that the medical science, government, music, mechanical arts, arithmetic, algebra, geometry, geography, geology and astronomy were expected to the taught, probably on the availability of teachers. Various methods like advice, lecture, self-study, introspection, reasoning, concentration and learning in real life situations were used.

Conclusion

Bhagat Phool Singh deserves being considered as a great educator not only for his efforts to establish the *gurukuls,* but also for the strength of his character which is worth emulating.

Summary

Bhagat Phool Singh was born on 24th Feb, 1885 and was assisnated on 14th August, 1942. He started as a good student, wavered in his attitude to studies for sometime and again got interested in studies and passed class eight. He became a *patwari*. Later, he was influenced by the *Arya Smaj* and he started *Gurukuls*—one for boys at *Bhonsle Kalan* and another for girls at *Khanpur Kalan*. The institution at *Khanpur* is now a Women's University. He fasted many times. His contribution to education was the *gurukuls*.

27

Learning: Varities of Experience

Sarvepalli Radhakrishnan (1888-1975)

Biography and Context

Early Years (1888-1904)

Rather little detail is known of *Radhakrishnan's* earliest childhood and education. *Radhakrishnan* rarely spoke about his personal life, and what he did reveal came to us after several decades of reflection. He was born in Tirutani, Andhra Pradesh into a brahmin family, in religious orientation. Predominantly Hindu, Tirutani was a temple town and popular pilgrimage centre and his family was active participants in the devotional activities there. The implicit acceptance of *Sankara's Advaita* by the *smarta* tradition is good evidence to suggest that an *advaitic* framework was an important, though latent, feature of his early philosophical and religious sensibilities.

In 1896, *Radhakrishnan* was sent to school in the nearby pilgrimage centre of Tirupati, a town with a distinctively cosmopolitan flavour, drawing *bhaktas* from all parts of India. For four years, he attended the Hermannsburg Evangelical Lutheran Missionary school. It was there that the young *Radhakrishnan* first encountered non-Hindu missionaries and 19th century Christian theology with its impulse toward personal religious experience. The theology taught in the missionary school may have found resonance with the highly devotional activities connected with the nearby *Tirumala* temple, activities that he undoubtedly would have witnessed taking place outside the school. The shared emphasis on personal religious experience might have suggested to him a common link between the religion of the missionaries and the religion practised at the nearby Tirumala temple.

Between 1900 and 1904, Radhakrishnan attended Elizabeth Rodman Voorhees College in *Vellore*, a school run by the American Arcot Mission of the Reformed Church in America. The mandate of the Mission was to preach the gospel, to publish vernacular tracts, and to educate the "heathen" masses. It was here, as Robert Minor points out, that *Radhakrishnan* was "*introduced to the Dutch Reform Theology, which emphasized a righteous God, unconditional grace, and which criticized Hinduism as intellectually incoherent and ethically unsound.*" At the same time, the Mission demonstrated an active concern for education, health care, and social uplift through its participation in famine relief, the establishment of hospitals, and education for all irrespective of social status. Such activities were not inconsistent with the mandate of the Mission as they often served as incentives for conversion. In was in this atmosphere that he encountered what would have appeared to him as crippling assaults on his Hindu sensibilities. He also would have witnessed the positive contributions of the social programmes undertaken by the Mission in the name of propagation of the Christian gospel.

Thus, *Radhakrishnan* inherited from his upbringing a tacit acceptance of *Sankara's Advaita Vedanta* and an awareness of the centrality of devotional practices associated with the *smarta* tradition. His experiences at Tirupati brought him into contact with Lutheran Christian missionaries whose theological emphasis on personal religious experience may have suggested to him a common ground between Christianity and his own religious heritage. In Vellore, the presence of a systematic social gospel was intimately bound up with the religion of those who sought to censure his cultural norms and religious worldview.

Radhakrishnan was married to Sivakamuamma in 1904 while living in Vellore. The couple had six children: five daughters and a son.

It was in this historical and hermatic contexts and with these experiences informing his worldview that *Radhakrishnan* encountered a resurgent Hinduism. Specifically, he encountered the writings of *Swami Vivekananda* and *V.D. Savarker*'s *'The First War of Indian Independence'*. The Theosophical Society was also active in the South Arcot area at this time. The Teosophists not only applauded the ancient wisdom they claimed to have found in India, but were persistent advocates of a philosophical, spiritual, and scientific meeting of East and West. Moreover, the Society's role in the Indian nationalist movement was evidenced by *Annie Besant*'s involvement with the Indian National Congress. While *Radhakrishnan* does not speak of the Theosophists presence at this time, it is unlikely that he would have been unfamiliar with their views.

What *Vivekananda*, *Savarkar*, and Theosophy did bring to *Radhakrishnan* was a sense of cultural self-confidence and self-reliance. However, the affirmation he received from this resurgence of Hinduism did not push him to study philosophy nor to interpret his own religion. It was only after his experiences at Madras Christian College that he began to put down in writing his own understanding of Hinduism.

Madras Christian College (1904-1908)

In 1904, Radhakrishnan entered Madras Christian College. At this time his academic sensibilities lay with the physical sciences, and before beginning his MA degree in 1906, his interest appeared to have been law.

Two key influences on him at Madras Christian College left an indelible stamp on his sensibilities. First, it was here that he was trained in European philosophy. He was introduced to the philosophies of *Berkeley, Leibniz, Locke, Spinoza, Kant, Mill, Spencer, Fichte, Hegel, Aristotle,* and *Plato* among others. *Radhakrishnan* was also introduced to the philosophical methods and theological views of his MA supervisor and most influential non-Indian mentor, Professor A.G. Hogg. Religious value judgements gave knowledge which was different from, though not necessarily opposed to, theoretical knowledge. This distinction led to the conclusion that doctrines and scriptures were records of personal insights and were therefore necessary for religious, and specifically Christian, faith. This distinction left its mark on his philosophical and religious thinking and resonated throughout his writing.

A second key factor shaping his sensibilities during this time was that it was at Madaras Christian College that he encountered intense religious polemic in an academic setting. He later recalled: "*The challenge of Christian critics impelled me to make a study of Hinduism and find out what is living and what is dead in it... I prepared a thesis on the Ethics of the Vedanta, which was intended to be a reply to the charge that the Vedanta system had no room for ethics.*"

Early Teaching and Writing (1908-1912)

Upon the completion of his MA degree in 1908, *Radhakrishnan* found himself both at financial and professional crossroads. His obligations to his family precluded him from applying for a scholarship to study in Britain and he struggled without success to find work in Madras. The following year, with the assistance of *William Skinner* at Madras Christian College, he was able to secure what was intended to be a temporary teaching position at Presidency College in Madras.

At Presidency College, *Radhakrishnan* lectured on a variety of topics in psychology as well as in European philosophy. As a junior assistant professor, logic, epistemology and ethical theory were his stock areas of instruction. At the College, he also learnt Sanskrit.

During these years, *Radhakrishnan* was anxious to have his work published, not only by Indian presses but also in European journals. The Guardian Press in Madras published his MA thesis, and scarcely revised portions of this work appeared in *Modern Review* and *The Madras Christian College Magazine.* While his efforts met with success in other Indian journals, it was not until his article "*The Ethics of the Bhagavadgita and Kant*" appeared in *The International Journal of Ethics* in 1911 that he broke through to a substantial Western audience. As well, his edited lecture notes on psychology were published under the title *Essentials of Psychology.*

The War, Tagore, and Mysore (1914-1920)

By 1914, *Radhakrishnan*'s reputation as a scholar was beginning to grow. However, the security of a permanent academic post in Madras eluded him. For three months in 1916, he was posted to *Anantapur*, Andhra Pradesh, and in 1917 he was transferred yet again, this time to *Rajahmundry*. Only after spending a year in *Rajahmundry* did he find some degree of professional security upon his acceptance of a position in philosophy at *Mysore* University. This hiatus in his occupational angst was short lived. His most prestigious Indian academic appointment to the George V Chair in Philosophy at Calcutta University in February of 1921 took him out of South India for the first time only two and a half years later.

Between 1914 and 1920, he continued to publish. He authored eighteen articles, ten of which were published in prominent Western journals such as *The International Journal of Ethics, The Monist, and Mind.* Throughout these articles, he took it upon himself to refine and expand upon his interpretation of Hinduism.

There was strong polemical tenor to many of these articles. He was no longer content simply to define and defend *Vedanta*. Instead, he sought to confront directly not only *Vedanta*'s Western competitors, but what he saw as the Western philosophical enterprise and the Western ethos in general.

His polemical sensibilities during these years were heightened in no small part by the political turmoil both on the Indian as well as on the world stage. His articles and books during this period reflected his desire to offer a sustainable philosophical response to the unfolding discontent, he encountered. World War One and its aftermath, and in particular the events in Amritsar in the spring of 1919, further exacerbated his patience with what he saw as an irrational, dogmatic, and despotic West. *The Reign of Religion in Contemporary Philosophy 1920* was indicative of his heightened polemical sensibilities during this period.

A more positive factor in his life during these years was his reading of *Rabindranath Tagore*, the Bengali poet. He joined the rest of the English-speaking world in 1912 in reading *Tagore*'s translated works. Though the two had never met at that time, *Tagore* would become perhaps *Radhakrishnan*'s most influential Indian mentor. *Tagore*'s poetry and prose resonated with *Radhakrishnan*. He appreciated *Tagore*'s emphasis on aesthetics as well as his appeal to intuition. From 1914 on both of these notion–aesthetics and intuition–begin to find their place in *Radhakrishnan*'s own interpretations of experience, the epistemological category for his philosophical and religious proclivities. Over the next five decades, he repeatedly appealed to *Tagore*'s writing to support his own philosophical ideals.

Calcutta and the George V Chair (1921-1931)

In 1921, *Radhakrishnan* took up the prestigious George V Chair in Philosophy at Calcutta University. As honoured, though hesitant, heir to *Brajendranath Seal*, his appointment to the Chair was not without its dissenters who sought a fellow Bengali for the position. In Calcutta, he was for the first time out of his South Indian element–geographically, culturally and linguistically.

However, the isolation Radhakrishnan experienced during his early years in Calcutta allowed him to work on his two volume Indian Philosophy, the first of which he began while in Mysore and published in 1923 and the second followed four years later. Throughout the 1920s, his reputation as a scholar continued to grow both in India and abroad. He was invited to Oxford to give the 1926 Upton Lectures, published in 1927 as *The Hindu View of Life,* and in 1929 Radhakrishnan delivered the *Hibbert Lectures,* later published under the title *An Idealist View of Life.* The later of these two views is his most sustained, non-commercial work. *An Idealist View of Life* is frequently seen as his mature work and has undoubtedly received the bulk of scholarly attention on him.

With the publication of *An Idealist View of Life*, *Radhakrishnan* had come into his own philosophically. In his mind, he had identified the "religious" problem, reviewed the alternatives, and posited a solution. An unreflective dogmatism could not be remedied by escaping from "experiential religious" which is the true basis of all religions. Rather, a recognition of the creative potency of integral experience tempered by a critical scientific attitude was, he believed, the only viable corrective to dogmatic claims of exclusivity founded on external, second-hand authority. Moreover, while Hinduism (*Advaita Vedanta*) as he defined it best exemplified his position, he claimed that the genuine philosophical, theological and literary traditions in India and the West supported his position.

The 1930s and 1940s

He was knighted in 1931 and the same year he took up his administrative post as Vice Chancellor at the newly founded, though scarcely constructed, Andhra University at Waltair. *Sir Radhakrishanan* served there for five years as Vice Chancellor, when, in 1936, not only did the university in Calcutta affirm his position in perpetuity but Oxford University appointed him to the H.N. Spalding Chair of Eastern Religions and Ethics. In 1939, he took up his second Vice Chancellorship at Benares Hindus University (BHU), and served there during the course of the second world war until mid-January 1948.

Shortly after his resignation from BHU, he was named chairman of the University Education Commission. The Commission's 1949 Report assessed the state of university education and made recommendations for its improvement in the newly independent India. Though co-authored by others, his contribution could be appreciated on the aims of university education, producing intellectual adventurers and religious education.

During these years, the *question* of nationalism occupied his attention. The growing communalism he had witnessed in the 1920s was further intensified with the ideological flowering of the Hindu Mahasabha under the leadership of *Bhai Parmanand* and his heir *V.D. Savarkar*. Likewise, *Muhammad Iqbal*'s 1930 poetic vision and call for Muslim self-assertion furnished *Muhammad Jinnah* with an ideological template in which to lay claim to an independent Pakistan.

The issues of education and nationalism come together for *Radhakrishnan* in that, a university education which quickened the development of the whole individual was the only responsible and practical means to the creation of Indian solidarity and clarity of national vision. Throughout the 1930s and 1940s, he expressed his vision of an autonomous India. He envisioned an India built and guided by those who were truly educated, by those who had a personal vision of and commitment to raising Indian self-consciousness.

Post-Independence: Vice-presidency and Presidency

The years following Indian independence mark *Radhakrishnan*'s increasing involvement in Indian political as well as international affairs. The closing years of the 1940s were busy ones. He had been actively involved in the newly incorporated UNESCO (United Nations Educational, Scientific, and Cultural Organization), serving on its Executive Board as well as leading the Indian delegation from 1946-1951. He also served for the two years immediately following India's independence as a member of the Indian Constituent Assembly. his time and energy to UNESCO and the Constituent Assembly had also to be shared by the demands of the University Commission and his continuing obligations as *Spalding* Professor at Oxford.

Radhakrishnan was appointed by Prime Minister *Jawaharlal Nehru* as Indian Ambassador to Moscow, a post he held until 1952. The opportunity for him to put into practice his own philosophical political ideals came with his election to the Raja Sabha, in which he served as India's Vice-President (1952-1962) and later as President (1962-1967)

Radhakrishnan saw during his terms in office an increasing need for world unity and universal fellowship. The urgency of this need was pressed home to him by what he saw as the unfolding crises throughout the world. At the time of his taking up the office of Vice-President, the Korean was already in full swing. Political tensions with China in the early 1960s followed by the hostilities between India and Pakistan dominated his presidency. Moreover, the Cold War divided East and West, leaving each side suspicious of the other and on the defensive.

He challenged what he saw as the divisive potential and dominating character of self-professed international organizations. Instead, he called for the promotion of a creative internationalism on the spiritual foundations of integral experience. Only then could understanding and tolerance between people and between nations be promoted.

He retired from public life in 1967 and spent the last eight years of his life at the home he built in Mylapore, Madaras. He died on April 17, 1975.

Philosophy of Sarvepalli Radhakrishnan

(i) Metaphysics

Radhakrishnan located his metaphysics within the *Advaita* (non-dual) *Vedanta* tradition (*sampradaya*). And like other *Vedantis* before him, he wrote commentaries on the *Prasthanatraya* (that is, main primary texts of *Vedanta*): *the Bhagavadgita* (1948) the *Upanisads* (1953), and *Brahma Sutra* (1959).

As an *Advaitin*, he embraced a metaphysical idealism. But his idealism was such that it recognized the reality and diversity of the world of experience (*prakrti*) while at the same time preserving the notion of a wholly transcendent Absolute (*Brahman*), an Absolute that is identical to the self (*Atman*). While the world of experience and of everyday things were certainly not ultimate reality as these were subject to change and were characterized by finitude and multiplicity, they nonetheless had their origin and support in the Absolute (*Brahman*) which was free from all limits, diversity, and distinctions (*nirguna*). *Brahman* was the source of the world and its manifestations, but these modes did not affect the integrity of *Brahman*.

In this vein, Radhakrishnan did not merely reiterate the metaphysics of *Sankara* (8the century A.D.), arguably *Advaita Vedanta*'s most prominent and enduring figure, but sought to reinterpret *Advaita* for present needs. In particular, *Radhakrishnan* reinterpreted what he saw as *Sankara*'s understanding of *maya* strictly as illusion. For *Radhakrishnan*, *maya* was not to be understood to imply a strict objective idealism, one in which the world was taken to be inherently disconnected from *Brahman* but rather *maya* indicated, among other things, a subjective misperception of the world as ultimately real.

(ii) Epistemology:Intuition and the Varieties of Experience

(a) Intuition: Radhakrishnan associate a vast constellation of terms with intuition. At its best, intuition is an "integral experience". He used the term "integral" in at least three ways. First, intuition was integral in the sense that it coordinated and synthesized all other experiences. It integrated all other experiences into a more unified whole. Second, intuition was integral as it formed the basis of all other experiences. In other words, he held that all experiences were at bottom intuition. Third,

intuition was integral in the sense that the results of the experience were integrated into the life of the individual. For him, intuition found expression in the world of action and social relations.

At times, he preferred to emphasize the "mystical" and "spiritual" quality of intuition as attested to by the expressions "religious consciousness", "mystical experience", "spiritual idealism", "self-existent spiritual experience", "prophetic indications" and "the real ground in man's deepest being", "spiritual apprehension", "moments of vision", "revelation", "supreme light" and even "faith". But it is the creative potency of intuition, designated by his reference to the "creative centre" of the individual, "creative intuition", "creative spirit" and "creative energy" that was the lynchpin for his understanding of intuition. As he understood it, all progress was the result of the creative potency of intuition.

For him, intuition was a distinct form of experience. Intuition was of a self-certifying character (*svatassiddha*). It was sufficient and complete. It was self established (*svatasiddha*), self-evidencing (svasamveaya), and self-luminous (svayam-prakasa). Intuition entails pure comprehension, entire significance, complete validity. It is both truth-filled and truth-bearing. Intuition is its own cause and its own explanation. It is sovereign. Intuition is a positive feeling of calm and confidence, joy and strength. Intuition is profoundly satisfying. It is peace, power and joy. Intuition is the ultimate form of experience for him.

(b) Varieties of Experience: Radhakrishnan recognized three categories of cognitive experience: sense experience, discursive reasoning, and intuitive apprehension. For him, all of these experience contribute, in varying degrees, to a knowledge of the real (*Brahman*), and as such had their basis in intuition.

• Sense Experience

Of the cognitive forms of knowledge, *Radhakrishnan* suggested that sensory knowledge was in one respect closest to intuition, for it was in the act of sensing that one was in "direct contact" with the object. Sense experience "*helps us to know the outer characters of the external world. By means of it we acquired an acquaintance with the sensible qualities of the objects.*" "Intuitions", he believed, "*are convictions arising out of a fullness of life in a spontaneous way, more akin to sense than to imagination or intellect and more inevitable than either.*" In this sense, sense perception might be considered intuitive, though *Radhakrishnan* did not explicitly describe it as such.

• Discursive Reasoning

Discursive reasoning, and the logical knowledge it produced, was subsequent to sensory experience (perception). *"Logical knowledge is obtained by the processes of analysis and synthesis."* Unlike sense perception which he claimed to be closer to direct knowledge, logical knowledge "*is indirect and symbolic in its character. It helps us to handle and control the object and its working.*"

For him, discursive reasoning and the logical systems, they constructed, possessed an element of intuition.

• Intuitive Apprehension

He argued against what he saw as the prevalent (Western) temptation to reduce the intuitive to the logical. While logic dealt with facts already known, intuition went beyond logic to reveal previously unseen connections between facts. *"The art of discovery is confused with the logic of proof and an artificial simplification of the deeper movements of thought result. We forget that we invent by intuition though we prove by logic."* Intuition not only clarified the relations between facts and seemingly discordant systems, but lent itself to the discovery of new knowledge which then became an appropriate subject of philosophical inquiry and logical analysis.

• Psychic Experience

Perhaps the most understudied dimension of *Radhakrishnan*'s interpretations of experience was his recognition of "Supernormal" experiences. As early as his first volume of Indian Philosophy (1923), he affirmed the validity of what he identified as "psychic phenomena". He accounted for such experiences in terms of a highly developed sensitivity to intuition. "*The mind of man,*" he explained, "*has the three aspects of subconscious, the conscious, and the superconscious, and the 'abnormal' psychic phenomena, called by the different names of ecstasy, genius, inspiration, madness, are the workings of the superconscious mind.*" Such experiences were not "abnormal" according to him nor were they unscientific. Rather, they were the products of carefully controlled mental experiments.

As highly developed powers of apprehension, psychic experiences were a state of consciousness "*beyond the understanding of the normal, and the supernormal is traced to the supernatural.*"

• Aesthetic Experience

"*All art,*" *Radhakrishnan* declared, "*is the expression of experience in some medium.*" However, the artistic experience was not be confused with its expression. While the experience itself was ineffable, the challenge for the artist was to give the experience concrete expression. "*The success of art is measured by the extent to which it is able to render experiences of one dimension into terms of another.* For him art born out of a "*creative contemplation which is a process of travail of the spirit is an authentic crystallization of a life process*". At its ultimate and in its essence, the "*poetical character is derived from the creative intuition (that is, integral intuition) which holds sound, suggestion and sense in organic solution.*"

In his view, without the intuitive experience, art becomes mechanical and a rehearsal of old themes. Such "art" is an exercise was (re) production rather than a communication of the artist's intuitive encounter with reality. "*Technique without inspiration*," he declared, "*is barren intellectual powers, sense facts and imaginative fancies may result in clever verses, repetition of old themes, but they are only manufactured poetry*." It is not simply a difference of quality but a "*difference of kind in the source itself*." For him, true art was an expression of the whole personality, seized as it was with the creative impulse of the universe.

Art and Science

There was in *Radhakrishnan*'s mind a "scientific" temperament to genuine artistic expression. In what might be called the science of art, he believed that the "*experience or the vision is the artist's counterpart to the scientific discovery of a principle or law*."

Despite this synthetic impulse, *Radhakrishnan* was careful to explain that the two disciplines were not wholly the same. The difference turned on what he saw as the predominantly aesthetic and qualitative nature of artistic expression.

• *Ethical Experience*

Not surprisingly, intuition found a place in *Radhakrishnan*'s ethics. For him, ethical experiences were profoundly transformative. The experience resolved dilemmas and harmonized seemingly discordant paths of possible action. "*If the new harmony glimpsed in the moments of insight is to be achieved, the old order of habits must be renounced*." Moral intuitions resulted in "*a redemption of our loyalties and a remaking of our personalities*."

That he conceived of the ethical development of the individual as a form of conversion was noteworthy as it underscored his identification of ethics and religion. For him, an ethical transformation of the kind brought about by intuition was akin to religious growth and heightened realization. The force of this view was underscored by his willing acceptance of the interchangeability of the terms "intuition" and "religious experience."

Radhakrishnan willingly conceded that the vast majority of moral decisions were the result of conformity to well-established moral codes. However, it was in times of moral crisis that the creative force of ethical intuitions came to the fore.

He believed that ethical intuitions at their deepest transcended conventional and mechanically constructed ethical systems. Moral heroes exemplified his ethical ideal while at the same time provoking in those who accepted the ethical *status quo* to evaluate and to reconsider less than perfect moral codes. As the moral hero was "*fighting for the reshaping of his own society on sounder lines [his] behaviour might offend the sense of decorum of the cautious conventionalist*."

• ***Religious Experience***
At its most basic, religions, for him, represented the various interpretations of experience, while integral experience was the essence of all religions. "*If experience is the soul of religion, expression is the body through which it fulfills its destiny. We have the spiritual facts and their interpretations change.*"

For *Radhakrishnan*, the creeds and theological formulations of religion were but intellectual representations and symbols of experience. "*The Idea of God,*" he affirmed, "*is an interpretation of experience.*" It followed here that religious experiences were, for him, contexts relative and therefore, imperfect. They were informed by and experienced through specific cultural, historical, linguistic and religious lenses. Because of their contextuality and subsequent intellectualization, experiences in the religious sphere were limited.

To his mind, religious intuition was not only an autonomous form of experience, but also a form of experience which informed and validated all spheres of life and experience. Philosophical artistic, and ethical values of truth, beauty and goodness were not known through the senses or by reason. Rather, "*they are apprehended by intuition or faith...*" For him religious intuition informed, conjoined, and transcended an otherwise fragmentary consciousness.

Religious Pluralism
Radhakrishnan's hierarchy of religions was well-known. "Hinduism," he affirmed,

> "*accepts all religious notions as facts and arranges them in the order of their more or less intrinsic significance*": "*The worshippers of the Absolute are the highest in rank; second to them are the worshippers of the personal God; then come the worshipprs of the incarnations like Rama, Krsna, Buddha; below them are those who worship ancestors, deities and sages, and the lowest of all are the worshippers of the petty forces and spirits.*"

For *Radhakrishnan*, Hinduism at its *Vedantic* best is religion. Other religions, including what he understood as lower forms of Hinduism, were interpretations of *Advaita Vedanta*. Religion and religions were related in his mind as were experience and interpretation. The various religions are merely interpretations of his *Vedanta*.

For him, the intuitive, experiential immediacy of *Advaita Vedanta* was the genuine authority for all religions, and all religions as intellectually mediated interpretations derived from and were to ultimately defer to *Advaita Vedanta*.

Authority of Scripture and the Scientific Basis of Hinduism
Radhakrishnan argued that Hinduism, as he understood it, was a scientific

religion. According to him, "[*i*]*f philosophy of religions is to become scientific, it must become empirical and found itself on religious experience.*" True religion, argued he, remained open to experience and encouraged an experimental attitude with regard to its experiential data. Hinduism more than any other religion exemplified this scientific attitude. "*The Hindu philosophy of religion starts from and returns to an experimental basis.*" Unlike other religions, which set limits on the types of spiritual experience, the "*Hindu thinker readily admits of other points of view than his own and considers them to be just as worthy of attention.*" What set Hinduism apart from other religions was its unlimited appeal to and appreciation for all forms of experience. Experience and experimentation were the origin and end of Hinduism.

Criticism

There are numerous types of criticism that may be raised against *Radhakrishnan*'s philosophy. What follows is not an exhaustive list, but three of the most common criticism which may be levied against him.

(i) Epistemic Authority: The first is a criticism regarding the locus of epistemic authority. One might ask the question: Does the test for knowledge lie in scripture or in experience? *Radhakrishnan*'s view is that knowledge comes from intuitive experience (*anubhava*). He makes this claim on the basis of scripture, namely the *Upanisads. The Upanisads*, according to him, support a monistic ontology. He makes this claim on the basis that *the Upanisads* are the records of the personal experiences of the ancient sages. Thus, the validity of one's experience is determined by its proximity to that which is recorded in *the Upanishads*. Conversely, *the Upanisads* are authoritative because they are the records of monistic experiences. There is a circularity here. But this circularity is one with which he himself would likely not only acknowledge, but embrace. After all, he might argue, intuitive knowledge is non rational. An intuitive experience of Reality is not contrary to reason but beyond the constraints of logical analysis.

(ii) Cultural and Religious Construction: A second criticism of *Radhakrishnan*'s views surrounds his characterizations of the "East" and the "West". He characterizes the West, as well as Christianity, as inclined to dogmatism, the scientific method whose domain is limited to exploration of the outer natural world, and a reliance upon second-hand knowledge. The East, by contrast, is dominated by an openness to inner experience and spiritual experimentation. The West is rational and logical, while the East is predominantly religious and mystical. As pointed out by numerous scholars working in the areas of post-colonial studies and orientalism. *Radhakrishnan*'s constructions of "West" and "East" (these categories themselves being construction) accept and perpetuate orientalist and colonialist forms of knowledge constructed during the 18th and 19th centuries. Arguably, these characterizations are "imagined" in the sense that they reflect the philosophical and religious realities of neither "East" nor "West."

(iii) Selectivity of Evidence: A separate but related criticism that might be levied against *Radhakrishnan*'s views has to do with his theory of religious pluralism and his treatment of the religious traditions with which he deals.

First he minimizes the contributions of the monistic philosophers and religious mystics of the West. While he acknowledges the work of such thinkers as *Henri Bergon*, *Goethe*, and variety of Christian, Jewish, and Muslim mystics, he seems to imply that such approaches to religious and philosophical life in the West are exceptions rather than the rule. In fact, he goes so far as to suggest that such figures are imbued with the spirit of the East, and specifically Hinduism as he understands it.

Second, while he readily acknowledges the religious diversity within "Hinduism," his treatment of Western traditions is much less nuanced. In a sense, *Radhakrishnan* homonizes and generalizes Western traditions. In his hierarchy of religions, one or another form of Hinduism may be located within each of his religious categories (monistic, theistic, incarnational, ancestoral and natural). By contrast, he seems to imply that the theistic (second) and the incarnational (third) categories are the domains of Unitarian and Trintarian Christianity respectively.

Conclusion

Radhakrishnan's philosophical thoughts have influenced his views on education in that learning is the result of vaireties of experiences, and spiritual experience is an integral part of learning.

Summary

As an academic, philosopher, and statesman, Sarvepalli Radhakrishnan was one of the most recognized and influential Indian thinkers in academic circles in the 20th century. Throughout his life and extensive writing, career, he sought to define, defend, and promulgate his religion, a religion he variously identified as Hinduism *Vedanta*, and the religion of the Spirit. He sought to demonstrate that his Hinduism was both philosophically coherent and ethically viable. His concern for experience and his extensive knowledge of the Western philosophical and literary traditions has earned him the reputation of being a bridge-builder between India and the West. He often appears to feel at home in the Indian as well as the Western philosophical contexts, and draws from both Western and Indian sources throughout his writing. Because of this, Radhakrishnan has been held up in academic circles as a representative of Hinduism to the West. His lengthy writing career and his many published works have been influential in shaping the West's understanding of Hinduism, India, and the East.

28

How To Live Education

Sri Paramahansa Yogananda (1893-1952)

In the history of nations, sometimes are born quite a few geniuses in various fields of life but, sometimes, there has prevailed intellectual and spiritual barrenness. The greatness of India lies in its wealth of thinkers in some or the other field for many years. *Paramahansa Yogananda* comes in the category of the spiritual giants.

Life Sketch

Paramahansa Yogananda was born on January 5, 1893 in Gorakhpur, U.P. in 1915. He received a B.A. degree from Serampur College, an affiliate of Calcutta University. He had a deep desire for God-realisation and received training in the hermitage of his *Guru, Swami Yukteswar Giri,* for a decade. *Paramhansa* established a school for teaching seven boys in 1917 at Dihika in Bengal. Later, he established school in Ranchi, Bihar, with traditional high school curriculum and *Yoga.* In 1920, he left for the USA and began a series of lectures and classes in many cities. For over thirty years, he laid emphasis on the underlying unity of the scriptures of the east and west. He wrote many books and established self-realisation fellowship centres in many cities in the USA.

Yogoda Satsanga Society of India was established at Calcutta. He travelled to many countries in Europe, visited Palestine and India during 1935 and 1936. In India, he visited Wardha and spent time with *Gandhiji.* He left India in August 1936 for the USA. He entered *Mahasamadhi* in Los Angeles, California on March 7, 1952. *Yogada Satsanga Society* of India has been continuing his work. His work '*How to live education*' gives his views on education.

Scope

The implications of '*How to Live Education*' were:

(1) that a person was to receive formal education;
(2) he was to enrich himself with life experiences;
(3) he was to demonstrate the superiority of mind over body, and of soul over mind;

(4) he was to unite science and religion through realization of the unity of their underlying principles, and

(5) he was to establish *Yogoda Satsang* temples and individual temples to teach scientific techniques for attaining direct personal experience of God. Thus, education became life itself, and to live life was to live education.

Major Themes

To understand *How to Live Education*, it is important to highlight a few major themes in the philosophical positions of *Paramhansa*. The themes are:

(1) Firm faith in God
(2) Reincarnation
(3) Self-realisation
(4) *Kriya Yoga*

(1) Faith in God

- *Paramhansa*'s faith in God was not dogmatic. He offered reasons why the cause-effect views of the western world on universe being a "first idea" or a "cosmic plan" led to the realisation of Supreme Cause. The sages of India had gone a step forward in that for them, everything proceeded from and went back into its source: God.
- God revealed Himself to those who persisted in inner investigations to seek Him.
- Devotion and right activity attracted God's attention, and meditation was the highest form of activity.
- Man could find the Lord because of the gift of reason. Man was not to allow reason to be trampled by his ego and wrong habits.
- Nature of God was infinite and human beings had descended from infinite into finite. God's true nature was known only through intuition–the superconsciousness of the soul.
- We were expected to give God first place in our heart.
- If we lived in the joy of God, we would not know what death was.
- Prayer was a demand of the soul and God answered genuine prayers.
- God-realisation was attained only by great efforts on the part of the *yogi*. It required daily meditation.
- God in His infinite mercy gave us His joy, inspiration, true life, true wisdom, true happiness and true understanding through all the various experiences of our lives.

(2) Reincarnation

- If one believed in the existence of a just God, then a belief in reincarnation could follow very readily as the two concepts were really dependent on each other.

- The Hindu saints used scientific methods to discover the reality of spiritual law and hence of reincarnation and every other great cosmic truth. The spiritual laws were discovered by the *rishis* in their hermitages.
- The *Bhagavad Gita* said that the ego was continuously conscious of itself in childhood, youth and old age; the embodied soul attained another body after death; (in the long alternation between the physical and astral worlds).
- Reincarnation was the progress of a soul through many lives on the earth plane to perfection.
- How we lived this life determined what we were to be in the next life.
- Divine justice followed the law of reincarnation. Great souls would incarnate again. God gave them individuality and a divine role to play for Him.

(3) Self-realisation

- Self-realisation converted conviction into experience. One was to practise the truth, one heard and read about so that it was just not an idea, but a conviction form of experience. One was not to settle for intellectual satisfaction about truth, but convert truth into experience and one would know God through one's own self-realisation.
- If one wanted to have the spiritual experience, daily meditation was required. God was realised through meditation.
- The essential proof of self-realisation of God's consciousness in one was to be truly and unconditionally happy.
- In the world, if leaders were illumined by self-realisation and worked together, they could, within a few years, banish war and poverty from the earth.
- True religion satisfied the demands of one's soul by proof. One was to cling dogmatically only to wisdom and one would find God. Whatever religion one chose, one was to give it a good test. Without God communion, the life-blood of religion was missing.
- Realising God required long perseverence in the practice of those methods that led to self-realisation.
- Self-realisation converted conviction into experience.

***(4)* Kriya Yoga**

In a book entitled, *Man's Eternal Quest and Other Talks* by *Paramahansa*, *Kriya Yoga* was defined as:

A sacred spiritual science, originated millenniums ago in India. It includes certain techniques of meditation whose devoted practice leads to realisation of God. The Sanskrit root of *Kriya* is *kri*, which means to do, to act and react; the same root is found in the word *karma*, the natural principle of cause and effect. *Kriya Yoga* is, thus, union (yoga) with the Infinite through a certain action or rite (*kriya*). The cause and effect chain is broken by a *yogi* who follows the techniques of *kriya yoga*.

Kriya yoga's history was traced back to the *Gita* in which Lord *Krishna* talked of offering inhaling breath into the outgoing breath, and offering the outgoing breath into the inhaling breath. By this exercise, the *yogi* neutralized both these breaths. He, thus, released the life force from the front and brought it under his control. *Kriya Yoga* was also mentioned by the ancient sage, *Patanjali*–the exponent of *Yoga*. For him, *"liberation can be accomplished by that pranayama which is attained by disjoining in the course of inspiration and expiration"*. *Yukteswar*, the *guru* of *Yogananda*, explained that the secret of cosmic consciousness was intimately linked with breath master. The life force was to be freed for higher activities by a method of calming and stilling the ceaseless demands of the breath. *Kriya Yoga* required sustained effort on the part of a person under the guidance of a *guru* to be astrally transformed day-by-day into Infinity.

How to Live Education: An Analysis

(1) *Yogananda's* education was learner-centred as well as teacher-centred.

(2) It was "lived" in the formal institutions of learning and also informally: in fact, both ways.

(3) It was purposive.

(4) It was science as well as art.

(1) Learner-centred and Teacher-centred: *Paramhansa's* education was learner-centred in the sense that the devotee had a strong desire to master the art and science of concentration, *pranayam (*meditation) to become a *Kriya Yogi.*

The education was teacher-centred in the sense that the *guru* played a major role in teaching, correcting, improving and inspiring the devotee to disengage himself from physical and mental identification in favour of soul-individuality. *Paramhansa*'s parents were disciples of *Sri Sri Lahiri Mahasaya,* and who was the disciple of *Sri Sri Swami Yukteswar Giri. Yukteswar* had reminded his disciple that having renounced the life with a small family of relatives, he had to assume a greater responsibility to love and to serve as his own the large family of humanity.

Paramhansa was deeply interested in the education of the youth. As mentioned earlier, as a young man, he had established a school for seven boys in 1917 at Dihika, Bengal. In the following year, the Maharaja of Kasimbazar gave his palace and 25 acres of land in Ranchi, Bihar to serve as headquarters of the school, which was named *Yogoda Satsanga*

Vidyalaya. It was founded on the educational ideals of India's illumined *rishis*–sages whose forest *ashrams* were the ancient seats of learning. The curriculum included high school subjects as well as *yoga* concentration, meditation and the *Yogoda* system of physical development. *Mahatma Gandhi* and many other illustrious personages visited the unique high school. *Paramhansa* gave a series of lectures and conducted classes all over the USA and in some other countries in Europe and in India. In 1935, his class instructions were arranged into a series of studies and sent out from self-realisation headquarters in Los Angeles to students all over the world. His teachings were cyclostyled and sent from *Yogoda Satsang Sakha Math,* Ranchi in Bihar to students in India and surrounding territories. The *Yogoda Satsang Society* of India, Ranchi, had been disseminating the tenets of spiritual education. Thus, *Paramahansa's* education was learner-centred as well as teacher-centred.

(2) Formal and Informal Education: Generally speaking, formal education has pre-determined aims, specific place of learning, role expectations of pupils and teachers, curriculum and certification. *Paramhansa*'s concept of living education was formal in the sense that he taught young people at a school, following traditional subjects, and also spiritual ideas and ideals. Temples were also used as centres of learning. The curriculum consisted of standard high school subjects and *yoga.* In the *Brahmacharya Vidyalaya, Yogananda* played father-mother to the little children. The school conducted outdoor classes in grammar and high school subjects. Vocational training of some sort was given; sports and games were also encouraged and daily the boys undertook spiritual exercises. Self-discipline was practised. Perfection and endeavours for perfection, perhaps, culminated in something akin to certification. The system of correspondence lessons added an informal element to "*how to live education.*"

(3) Purposiveness of Education: Living education was also reflected by *Yogananda*'s assertion that the common institutes aimed at the development of the body and the intellect. Moral and spiritual values without whose appreciation no one could approach happiness was lacking in the formal curriculum. His education was purposive as it stood for all round development but all other aspects of development were merely the preparation for self-realisation. *Kriya Yogi* ultimately achieved victory over the last enemy-the death.

(4) Science and Art: Yoga was a system of scientific methods for uniting the soul with the spirit. In 1944 at California, *Yogananda* said that we came down from God and we had to reascend to Him. We have seemingly become separated from our Father, and we were to consciously reunite with Him. *Kriya Yoga* was an instrument through which human evolution could be quickened. The *Kriya Yogi* mentally directed his life energy to revolve upward and downward, around the six spiritual centres.

Kriya was accompanied by an accession of peace, and by soothing sensation of regenerative effect in the spine. The outgoing life force was not wasted and abused in the senses.

How to Live Education was also an art. It was an art as a good deal of imitation, supplementation and alterations were involved in the work of nature. The ten rules of happiness were basically the art of living. *Paramhansa* interpreted the Ten Commandments as follows:

- There was to be no other god in your life who meant more to you than God.
- True devotees did not allow their consciousness to dwell on the object but concentrated with deepest love and attention on the spirit behind of it.
- One was not to think of anything but the spirit when one was praying.
- The sabbath was to be a day of rest and cultivation of divine peace.
- One was to honour God in one's parents.
- One was not to kill for killing's sake.
- The highest use of sex was the sublimation of its power in order to manifest spiritual thought and ideals and wisdom.
- Happiness would come only by spiritual cooperation, when all men began to feel for other's necessities as for their own and to work for others as earnestly as for self.
- One was never carefully or maliciously to reveal information that could embarrass and hurt others.
- Covetousness was the source of discontent.

The Yogoda Satsanga Society of India, Ranchi

The society has the following aims and ideals:

- To disseminate among the nations knowledge of definite scientific techniques for attaining direct personal experience of God.
- To teach that the purpose of life was the evolution, through self-effort, of man's limited moral consciousness into God Consciousness; and to this end to establish *Yogoda Satsanga* temples for God-communion, and to encourage the establishment of individual temples of God in the homes and in the hearts of men.
- To reveal the complete harmony and basic oneness of original *Yoga* as taught by *Bhagwan Krishana* and original Christianity as taught by *Jesus Christ*; and to show that these principles of truth were the common scientific foundation of all true religions.
- To point out the one divine highway to which all paths of true religious beliefs eventually led: the highway of daily, scientific, devotional meditation on God.

- To liberate man from his threefold suffering: physical disease, mental inharmonies and spiritual ignorance.
- To encourage "plain living and high thinking", and to spread a spirit of brotherhood among all people by teaching the eternal basis of their unity: kinship with God.
- To demonstrate the superiority of mind over body, of soul over mind.
- To overcome evil by good, sorrow by joy, cruelty by kindness, ignorance by wisdom.
- To unite science and religion through realisation of the unity of their underlying principles.
- To advocate cultural and spiritual understanding between the East and the West, and the exchange of their finest distinctive features.
- To serve mankind as one's larger self.

Limitations

No human being is fallible–scientists, philosophers, spiritual leaders and statesmen have their strengths and weaknesses. It may be said that *Paramhansa*'s limitation lies in the field of over-emphasis on spiritual development and on individual aims of education.

Conclusion

Paramhansa's contribution to philosophical thought lay in his recapitulating the philosophical thoughts of our ancient scriptures, mastering them, experiencing them, introducing them to the western world, reminding our own countrymen to benefit from the spiritual past, generating literature, establishing societies and leaving behind messages which are relevant to our times. He *lived* education, and in a way, we are all living education–some completely, some partially–to reach those who, for various reasons, have not had the opportunities to "live education".

Summary

Paramahansa Yogananda was a spiritual giant. He preached in the USA, Europe and India, established *Satsang* Societies and wrote many books. He guided us about how to get educated and how to educate others in the ancient and modern knowledge and wisdom–eastern and western. He dealt with major themes like faith in God, reincarnation, self-realisation and *Kriya Yoga.* His views on education were learner as well as teacher-centred, these were formal and informal, these were science and art; and these were purposive. He emphasised spiritual aspects of education. The *Yogananda Satsang Society* of India is devoted to disseminating knowledge for the enlightenment of people.

29

Education for Creating New Values

Jiddu Krishnamurti (1895-1986)

Life-Sketch

Jiddu Krishnamurti was born into a Telgu Brahmin family on 11 May 1895 in Madanapalle in the state of Andhra Pradesh. He was one of the five children. After his retirement from public service Krishnamurti's father offered his services to the Theosophical Society in Chinnai (Madras) in exchange for accomodationa for his sons and himself. They eventually moved to Adyar, Chinnai in 1909.

According to *Meenakshi Thapar* in *Prospects: The Qurterly Review of Comparative Education,* in the early years of his youth, he and his brother, Niyananda, were adopted by *Dr. Annie Besant*, the President of the Theosophical Society, who saw certain spiritual qualities in nim that set him apart from others. This further resulted in Mrs. *Besant* and other theosophists proclaiming *Krishnamurti* as the vehicle for the World Teacher who was coming, in their words, to bring salvation to mankind. To prepare the world for the coming of this World Teacher, an organization called the Order of the Star in the East was formed in 1911 with *Krishnamurti* as its head. The role of World Teacher and spiritual leader was thrust upon him at a relatively young age and this daunting task influenced undoubtedly his own psychological development. This process did not, however, create the World Messiah, nor did it lead him to announce or proclaim his superiority over others. In fact, it had the contrary effect.

Although *Krishnamurti* underwent all the training and education befitting a budding World Teacher, he developed an independent perspective both about the nature of inquiry and about his own role in the pursuit of the good society. On 3 August 1929, in a historic and powerful speech, he dissolved the Order of the Star and said:

> *I maintain that Truth is a pathless land, and you can not approach it by any path whatsoever, by any religion, by any sect. Truth being limitless, unconditioned, unapproachable by any paty whatsoever, can not be organized; nor should any organization be formed to lead or coerce people along any particular part. My only concern is to set man absolutely, unconditionally free.*

By breaking away from the Theosophical Society and its organizational trappings, *Krishnamurti* asserted his independence, and his 'teachings': so to speak, unfolded over the remaining years of his life. He did not assert himself as a Teacher of Truth whose teachings had to be followed to attain *Nirvana* or self-understanding. He questioned whether such authority could actually initiate individual perception and change. The journey of understanding, therefore, was to be made by oneself, which meant that one had to discard every kind of authority: "*to be a light to ourselves we must be free of all tradition, all authority, including that of the speaker, so that our own minds can look and observe and learn.*"

He rejected the view that the 'teaching' was something that had to be first studied and then translated into action. On being asked what his teaching was, he said that it was a matter of partaking or sharing together rather than the giving or receiving of something. There was also an emphasis on the instantaneous nature of the transformation: it was "*not something that is accomplished gradually through striving, seeking and bringing one's life, one's conduct and thought by degrees more in conformity with some ideal.*" The state of 'becoming' or 'being' did not exist for *Krishnamurti*: it was more a state of timelessness, as it were.

His quest for self-knowledge or self-discovery did not take one very far from oneself. It was in the sense that, as he often said, "*the teachings are yourself*". There was also no culmination of this process of self-discovery: "*there is only the journey. There is no total knowing of oneself but rather an unending process of knowing oneself.*"

Krishnamurti constantly emphasized the right place of thought in daily life. But he also pointed out the dangers of thought when it became knowledge that acted as a calcified projection of the past. According to him, such action distorted our perception and full understanding of the world we lived in, and more specifically, the relationships that defined it. He saw knowledge as a necessary, but mechanical, function of the mind. The capacity of mind to record could present barriers, however. For example, hurtful words spoken in a relationship might become memories that influenced actions. Thus knowledge could present a division in a safety and security, and "*a sense of vitality.*" The recording created an image of oneself, of loved ones, politicians, priests, and of the ideal. If these images were fixed, one "*will always be getting hurt, always living in a pattern in which there is no freedom.*" But if one was able to "*listen to it completely without any reaction, then there is no centre which records.*" Fear and pleasure were life long themes in his public talks. He used the term "meditation" to mean something entirely different from the practice of any system or method to control the mind, or to consciously achieve a specific goal or state. He dealt with the subject of meditation in numerous public talks and discussions.

After World War II, many prominent personalities came to meet with *Krishnamurti*, including Prime Minister *Jawaharlal Nehru*. In his meetings with *Nehru*, when *Nehru* asked about relationships, "How does one start"? To that *Krishnamurti* repled, "*Begin where you are. Read every word, every phrase, every paragraph of the mind, as it operates through thought*".

Krishnamurti considered his message in meetings with *Indira Gandhi* as a possible influence in the lifting of certain emergency measures Gandhi had imposed during periods of political turmoil. In November 1985 Krishnamurti visited India for the last time, holding a number of what came to be known as "farewell" talks and discussions between then and in January 1986. These last talks included the fundamental questions he had been asking throught the years, as well as newer concerns related to then recent advances in science and technology, and their effect on humankind. He had commented to friends that he did not wish to invite death, but was not sure how long his body would last (he had already lost considerable weight), and once he could no longer talk, he would have "*no further purpose*" In his final talk, on January 4, 1986, in Chennai (Madras) he again invited the audience to examine with him the nature of inquiry, the effect of technology, the nature of life and meditation, and the nature of creation. He was also concerned about his legacy, about being unwittingly turned into some person whose teachings had been handed down to special individuals, rather than the world at large. He did not want anybody to pose as an interpreter of the teaching. He warned his associates on several occasions that they were not to present themselves as spoilsmen on his behalf, or as his successors after his death. A few days before his death, in a final statement, he dictated that nobody among either his associates or the general public had understood what had happened to him (as the conduit of the teaching), nor had they understood the teaching itself. He added that the "immense energy" operating in his lifetime would be gone with his death, again implying the impossibility of successors. However, he offered hope by stating that people could approach that energy and gain a measure of understanding "*...if they live the teachings*". He died in 1986 at the age of 90. His remains were cremated and scattered by friends and former associates in the three countries where he had spent most of his life: India, England, and the United States of America.

Views on Education

Education was not only learning from books, memorizing some facts, but also learning to look, how to listen to what the books were saying, whether they were saying something true or false. All that was part of education. Education was not just to pass examinations, take a degree and a job, get married and settle down, but also to be able to listen to the birds, to see the sky, to see the extraordinary beauty of a tree, and the shape of the hills, and to feel with them, to be reality, directly in touch with them. As you grew older, that sense of listening, seeing, unfortunately disappeared because you had children. You became jealous, ambitious, greedy, envious; so you lost the sense of the beauty of the earth. You knew what was happening in the world.

He continued to say:

You must be studying current events. There are wars, revolts, nation divided against nation. In this country too there is division, separation, more and more people being born, poverty, squalor and complete callousness. Man does not care what happens to another so long as he is perfectly safe. And you are being educated to fit into all this. Do you know the world is mad, that all this is madness—this fighting, quarrelling, tearing at each other? And you will grow up to fit into this. Is this right, is this what education is meant for, that you should willingly or unwillingly fit into this mad structure called society? And do you know what is happening to religions throughout the world? Here also man in disintegrating, nobody believes in anything any more; man has no faith and religions are merely the result or a vast propaganda.

Krishnamurti asked:

I am going to ask you something. Why are you being educated? Do you understand my question? Your parents send you to school. You attend classes, you learn mathematics, you learn geography, you learn history. Why? Have you ever asked why you want to be educated, what is the point of being educated? What is the point of your passing examinations and getting degrees? Is it to get married, get a job and settle down in life as millions and millions of people do? Is that what you are going to do, is that the meaning of education? Do you understand what I am talking about? This is really a very serious question. The whole world is questioning the basis of education. We see that education has been used for. Human beings throughout the world—whether in Russia or in China or in America or in Europe or in this country—are being educated to conform, to fit into society and into their culture, to fit into the stream of social and economic activity, to be sucked into that vast stream that has been flowing for thousands of years. Is that education, or is education something entirely different? Can education see to it that the human mind is not drawn into that vast stream and so destroyed; see that the mind is never sucked into that stream; so that, with such a mind, you can be an entirely different human being with a different quality of life? Are you going to be educated that way? Real education means that a human mind, your mind, not only is capable of being excellent in mathematics, geography and history, but also can never, under any circumstances, be drawn into the stream of society. Because that stream which we call living, is very corrupt, is immoral, is violent, is greedy. That stream is our culture. So, the question is how to bring about the right kind of education so that the mind can withstand all temptations, all influences, the bestiality of this civilization and this culture. We have come to a point in history where we have to create a new culture, a totally different kind of existence, not based on consumerism and industrialization, but a culture based upon a real quality of religion. Now how does one bring about, through education, a mind that is entirely different, a mind that is not greedy, not envious? How does one create a mind that is not ambitious, that is extraordinarily active, efficient; that has a real perception of what is true in daily life which is after all religion.

Now, let us find out what is the real meaning and intention of education. Can your mind, which has been conditioned to society, the culture in which you have lived, be transformed through education so that you will never under any circumstances enter the stream of society? Is it possible to educate you differently? 'Educate' in the real sense of that word; not to transmit from the teachers to the students some information about mathematics or history or geography, but in the very instruction of these subjects to bring about a change in your mind. Which means that you have to be extraordinarily critical. You have to learn never to accept anything which you yourself do not see clearly, never to repeat what another has said.

I think you should put these questions to yourself, not occasionally, but every day. Listen to everything, to the birds, to that cow calling. Learn about everything in yourself, because if you learn from yourself about yourself, then you will not be a secondhand human being. So you should, If I may suggest, from now on, find out how to live entirely differently and that is going to be difficult, for I am afraid, most of us like to find an easy way of living. We like to repeat and what other people say, what other people do, because it is the easiest way to live - to conform to the old pattern or to a new pattern. We have to find out what it means never to conform and what it means to live without fear. This is your life, and nobody is going to teach you, no book, no guru. You have to earn from yourself, not from books. There is a great deal to learn about yourself. It is an endless thing, it is a fascinating thing, and when you learn about yourself from yourself, out of that learning wisdom comes. Then you can live a most extraordinary, happy, beautiful life. Right? Now, will you ask me questions?

Education for Different Mind

About education for different mind, *Krishnamurty* asked:

Now, what is knowledge? Is knowledge related to intelligence? Intelligence uses knowledge, intelligence being the capacity to think clearly, objectively, sanely, healthily. Intelligence is a state in which there is no personal emotion involved, no personal opinion, prejudice or inclination. Intelligence is the capacity for direct understanding. I'm afraid this is rather difficult, but it is important, it is good for you to exercise your brain. So there is knowledge, which is the past continually being added to, and there is intelligence. Intelligence is the quality of the mind that is very sensitive, very alert, very aware. Intelligence does not hold on to any particular judgement or evaluation, but is capable of thinking very clearly, objectively. Intelligence has no involvement. Are you following? Now, how is this intelligence to be cultivated? What is the capacity of this intelligence? You are living here, being educated in all the various disciplines, in various branches of knowledge. Are you also being educated so that intelligence comes into being at the same time? Do you see the point? You may have a very good knowledge of mathematics or engineering. You may take a degree, enter a college and be a first class engineer. But at the same time, are you becoming sensitive, alert? Are you thinking objectively, clearly, with intelligence, understanding? Is there a harmony between knowledge and intelligence, a balance between the two? You can not think clearly if you are prejudiced, if you have opinions. You can not think clearly if you are not sensitive; sensitive to nature, sensitive to all the things that are happening around you, sensitive not only to what is happening outside you but also inside you. If you are not sensitive, if you are not aware, you can not think clearly. Intelligence implies that you see the beauty of the earth, the beauty of the trees, the beauty of the skies, the lovely sunset, the stars, the beauty of subtlety.

Now, is this intelligence being gathered by you here in this school? Are you gathering it or only gathering knowledge through books? If you have no intelligence, no sensitivity, then knowledge can become very dangerous. It can be used for destructive purposes. This is what the whole world is doing. Have you the intelligence that questions, tries to find out? What are the teachers and you doing to bring about this quality of intelligence, which sees the beauty of the land, the dirt, the squalor, and is also aware of the inner happenings, how one thinks, how one observes the subtley of thought? Are you doing all this? If not, what is the point of your being educated?

Role of Teachers

On the role of teachers, *Krishnamurty* started by asking:

Now what is the function of an educator? Is it merely to give you information, knowledge, or is it to bring about this intelligence in you? If I were a teacher here, do you know what I would do? First of all, I would want you to question me about everything—not about knowledge, that is very simple, but to question me about how to look, how to look at these hills, to look at that tamarind tree, how to listen to a bird, how to follow a stream. I would help you to look at the marvellous earth and nature, the beauty of the land, the redness of the soil. Then I would say, look at the peasants, the villagers. Look at them, do not criticize, just look at their squalor, their poverty, not the way you look at them at present, with utter indifference. There are those huts there, have you been there? Have the teachers been down there and looked at those huts, and if they all have, what have they done? So I will make you look, which is to make you sensitive, and you can not be sensitive if you are careless, indifferent to everything that is happening around you. Then I would say, "To be intelligent, you must know what you are doing, the way you walk, the way you talk, the way you eat." You understand? I would talk to you about your food. I would say, "Look, discuss, do not be afraid to ask any questions, find out, learn", and in your classes I would discuss a subject with you, how to read, how to learn, what it means to pay attention. If you say you want to look out of the window, I would say look out of the window, see everything that you want to see out of the window, and after you have seen it, look at your book with equal interest and pleasure. Then I would say, "Through books, through discussions I have helped you to be intelligent; let me help you to find out how to live in this world sanely, healthily, not half asleep." That is the function of a teacher, of an educator, not just to give you a lot of data, knowledge, but to show you the whole expanse of life, the beauty of it, the ugliness of it, the delight, the joy, the fear, the agony. So that when you leave this place, you are a tremendous human being who can use your intelligence in life, not just a thoughtless, destructive, callous human being.

Knowledge and Intelligence

On knowledge and intelligence, *Krishnamurty* set out to ask:

Why do you think we are conditioned? It is very simple. You have asked the question. Now, exercise your brain. Find out why you are conditioned. You are born in this country, you live in an environment, in a culture, you grow into a young child, and then what takes place? Watch the babies around you. Watch the mothers, the fathers, if they are Hindus or Muslims or communists or capitalists; they say to the child, "Do this, do that". The child sees the grandmother going to a temple, performing rituals, and the child gradually accepts all that. Or the parents may say "I don't believe in rituals" and the child also accepts that. The simple fact is that the mind, the brain of the child is like putty or clay and on that putty, impressions are made, like the grooves in a record. Everything is registered. So in a child everything is registered consciously or unconsciously, until gradually he becomes a Hindu, Muslim, Catholic or a non-believer. He makes divisions—as my belief, your belief, my god, your god, my country, your country. You have been conditioned to make tremendous effort; to fall into the trap of another conditioning, is that it? First of all, do you know that you are conditioned? How do you know? Is it only because somebody has told you that you are conditioned that you know? Do you see the difference? That is, somebody tells you that you are hungry, that is one thing, and to know for yourself that you are hungry is altogether different. These two statements are different, aren't they? In the same way, do you know for yourself without somebody telling you that you are conditioned, as a Hindu, a Muslim? Do you know it for yourself?

Now I will ask you a question and see whether there is a gap before you qnswer it. Right? Now observe, think very clearly, unemotional, without any prejudice. My question is, are you aware that you are conditioned without being told? Are you aware? It is not so very difficult.

Do you know what it means to be aware? When there is a pain in the thumb, you are aware there is pain, nobody tells you there is pain. You know it. Now, in the same way do you know that you are conditioned, conditioned into thinking that you are a Hindu, that you believe in this, that you do not believe in that, that you must go to a temple, that you must not go to a temple? Are you aware of it? To this, the obedient says yes.

Krishnamurti askes the student: You are? Now that you are aware that you are conditioned, what next?

The student replies: I will then see whether I want to be unconditioned.

Krishnamurti: You are conditioned and you become aware, then what takes place? Then I ask, what is wrong with being conditioned? Now I am conditioned as a Muslim and you are conditioned as a Hindu, right? What takes place? We may live in the same street, but because of my conditioning, my belief, my dogma, and you with your belief, with your dogma, thought we may meet in the same street, we are separate, aren't we? So where there is separation, there must be conflict. Where there are political, economic, social, nationalistic divisions, there must be conflict. So conditioning is the factor of division. Therefore, in order to live peacefully in this world, let us be free of conditioning, cease that one is conditioned, then seeing the effect of that conditioning in the world, the divisions, nationalistic, linguistic and so on, and seeing that where there is division there is conflict. You have to make an effort to study, to pass an examination, you have to make an effort to be good.

So, the question is how is the mind, which is conditioned, to unravel itself, to get out of conditioning? How do you propose to get out of it? Now exercise your intelligence to find out. Do not follow somebody who says, "Do this and you will get unconditioned; find out how you will decondition yourself.

Conditioning

Students ask a question to Krishnamurty: *Why are we 'conditioned' and how to uncondition? He answered in the following words:*

When you say, "how", what do you mean by that word? How am I to get up from this place? All that I have to do is to get up. I never ask how I am to get up? Use your intelligence. Do not be prejudiced. First be aware that you are prejudiced. Do not be told by others that your are prejudiced. They are prejudiced, so do not bother what other people say about your prejudices. First be aware that you are prejudiced. You see what prejudice does - it divides people. Therefore, you see that there must be intelligent action, which is that the mind must be capable of being free from prejudice, not ask "how" which means a system, a method. Find out whether your mind can be free from prejudice. See what is involved in it. Why are you prejudiced? Because part of your conditioning is to be prejudiced, and in prejudice there is a great deal of comfort, a great deal of pleasure. So first become aware, become aware of the beauty of the land, become aware of the trees, the colour, the shades, the depth of light, and the beauty of the moving trees, and watch the birds, be aware of all that is around you; then gradually move in, find out, be aware of yourself, be aware how you react in your relationships with your friends - all that brings intelligence. Is that enough for this morning? Then we will do something else.

First of all sit completely quiet, comfortably, sit very quietly, relax, I will show you. Now, look at the trees, at the hills, the shape of the hills, look at them, look at the quality of their colour, watch them. Do not listen to me. Watch and see those trees, the yellowing trees, the tamarind, and then look at the bougainvillaea. Look not with your mind but with your eyes. After having looked at all the colours, the shape of the land, of the hills, the rocks, the shadow, then go from the outside to the inside and close your eyes, close your eyes completely. You have finished looking at the things outside, and now with your eyes closed, you can look at what is happening inside. Watch what is happening inside you, do not think, but just watch, do not move your eyeballs, just keep them very, very quiet, because there is nothing to see now, you have seen all the things around you, now your are seeing what is happening inside your mind, and to see what is happening inside your mind, you have to be very quiet inside. And when you do this, do you know what happens to you? You become very sensitive, you become very alert to things outside and inside. Then you find out that the outside is the inside, then you find out that the observer is the observed.

Right Education

Education formed a central core of *Krishnamurti*'s world view. In fact, he spent his entire life talking about education as being the agent not only of inner renewal but also of social change. Education was therefore, the foundation on which the good society would build itself. He always asserted the individual's responsibility to the social order: '*You are the world*'. One individual's action therefore affected another, since '*to be is to be related*' and in this sense, there was no individual consciousness but only a collective human consciousness, which implied that the world was not separate from the individual. Krishnamurti pointed to the harmonious development of the inner and outer worlds of an individual: "*what one is inwardly will eventually bring about a good society or the gradual deterioration of human relationship.*" This harmony, however, "*can not possibly come about if our eyes are fixed only on the outer.*" The inner world was the "*source and continuation of the disorder*", and for him education was to be concerned with changing the source which was the individual, since it was "*human beings who create society, not some gods in heaven.*"

Krishnamurti asserted that the schools functioning under the auspices of the *Krishnamurti* Foundation India (KFI), some of which were established in his life time, did not exist as organizations for the indoctrination of children, but rather as places "*where students and teachers can flower, and where a future generation can be prepared because schools are meant for that.*" That notion of 'flowering' here implied an unfolding of the consciousness of individuals in relationship to one another in educational praxis. The psychological development of individuals was, therefore, as important as acquiring academic knowledge and skills. The intention of the KFI schools was that they "*are not only to be excellent academically but are to be concerned with the cultivation of the total human being.*" These schools 'fundamentally existed to help both the students and the teacher to flower in gayness. This demanded excellence in behaviour, in action and in relationship. This was our intent and why these schools had come into being; not to turn out mere crayonists but to bring about *"the excellence of spirit."*

At his talks given to teachers and students at the two KFI schools in India where he annual visited–Rishi Valley School in Andhra Pradesh and Rajghat Education Centre at Varanasi—*Krishnamurti* often asked the students questions about the meaning of education, the quality of education they received, the teacher' roles and attitudes, and their own contribution to the learning process. He discussed with them the purpose of education–not merely to pass examinations after learning a few facts and acquiring some skills, but to understand the complexity of life. He urged the students to appreciate their role in the creation of a 'new' world without fear, conflict or contradiction. This could only be done if there was 'right education' in an atmosphere of freedom, without fear or authority, where intelligence and goodness could be nutrured.

Talking to students, Krishnamurti reiterated that what education normally did was prepare students to fit into a "*particular frame or pattern, that was, the movement in a predetermined groove*" and this is what society called "*entering life*". With such an education, the student met life, which was "*like a little river meeting the vast sea*". However, such an education did not necessarily prepare the student to meet the psychological challenges and physical vicissitudes of life.

It was important that education was in fact to "*awaken intelligence*" and not simply reproduce a programmed machine or trained monkey, as he put it. Education therefore could not be only about reading from books but about the whole of life, and was to prepare students to meet the challenges of living in a complex social world. His views on how to do this, however, were rather extraordinary in their very simplicity. For example, in response to a student's question about how to live happily in a competitive world, he observed, "*You can live happily in this competitive world only if you yourself are not competitive.*" It was possible that such a response might be contentious to the extent that it might be perceived as being unrealistic in terms of the complex nature of society, where a non-competitive member could at best only survive, not really exist. But his argument was that "*competition is the very essence of violence. Our whole social structure is based on competition and we accept it as inevitable.*"

Evaluation

Meeenakshi Tondon commented on Krishnamurti's vision of right education as follows:

> *Discipline is regimentation. It compells the student to do what he does not love to do. It adapts the student by force to the so called ideals and ideas conceived by the educators. Discipline is an external conditioning and controlling of the student who is inwardly disintegrated and indisciplined. It involves suppression, resistance and opposition. It is a barrier to the understanding of the fact of inner indiscipline and disorder. Imposition of an outward order over the student can not bring about order and integration 'within'. The outward order of discipline is artificial and superficial. It is put together by thought which can never grasp true order. The order of thought is not creative and complete but destructive and incomplete. Allowed beyond the biological realm, thought goes berserk. All its ideals and ideas, including religion and God, invented as the sources of order are disorderly. They are, in fact, the source of confusion and chaos. That is why the student is disorderly and is indisciplined inspite of the patterns of discipline. Right education has to enable the students to observe disorder 'within'. It should not invent the patterns of order without understanding and ending inner disorder. Outer disorder is the extension of inner disorder. Disorder 'within' ceases to be when it is observed without choice. Ending of inner disorder is the*

beginning of true order which is love. The students in whom love is created, never do anything wrong. They love what they do and do what they love. They do what is right, irrespective of the authority of external discipline. They do not become licentious in the absence of external control. They do not do do whatever they like.

Krishnamurti admits of discipline in its true sense of constant learning about oneself without prejudice, opinions and conclusions. Discipline in this sense is not subjugation but diligence of actively watching or observing oneself without sinking into second-hand and imitative existence. A truly disciplined mind is never negligent but ever vigilant. It feels responsibility to all its actions and the environment around. "The word discipline comes from the word disciple—to learn, not conform, not rebel, but to learn about your down reactions, your down background, their limitation, and to go beyond them".

Discipline is Regimentation

G. Vedaparayana in *"Indian Philosophical Quarterly* xxix 4 Oct 2002" wrote on *Krishnamurti*'s philosophy of education about 'discipline' in the following words:

> *Krishnamurti holds that right education should accomplish in the student an intelligent mind which has two movements - the scientific and the religious. The scientific movement is factual. It is bases on thought and knowledge. It explores the world of matter through instrumental and experimental reason. Betterment of our biological survival is its concern, whereas the religious movement is the movement of truth. It is beyond thought and knowledge. It is a mind which is empty and realistic. The religious mind is not orthodox. It does not belong to any organised religion. It has nothing to do with belief and dogma. To be truly religious is to live truth in actuality. Religious life is the operation of truth in the world of reality. It is the working of the emptiness- the freedom of the mind - in daily living. Left to itself, the scientific movement creates havoc in life. Thought and knowledge are incomplete. That which is incomplete is bound to create problems. Thought and knowledge can not decisively solve the problems they bring about. It is therefore imperative that the scientific movement is rooted in the regigius movement. The religious spirit of the intelligent mind reveals the limitations of thought and knowledge. It does not allow them to enter the realm which is beyond their purview. It confines them strictly to the physical realm. It prevents them from cluttering the mind with beliefs, prejudices, opinions, conclusions in the name of religion or spirituality. True spirituality, as it is already mentioned, implies the sacredness of keeping the mind totally empty of all content except the factual knowledge, essential for biological living. To be spiritual is to have a mind which is absolutely and unconditionally free. In freedom, truth and love guide thought and*

knowledge and not vice versa. Truth and love as invented by thought and knowledge are pseudo and not real.

The present system of education is destroying the natural intelligence of the body, the physical organism. The intelligence of the body is the energy without division and dissipation. It is the functioning of the senses together in harmony. But the intelligence gets distorted when thought dominates over the body. Thought with its images, sensations, hopes, habits, remembrances, desires and pleasures, narrows down the energy by stimulating one sense as against the other senses. It fragments the harmonious functioning of the sense, the organism as a whole. It manipulates the energy towards a desired end. It directs the energy into the groove called the 'self'. Thus, thought is dominant over the body, may find delight in hearing great music and yet be insensitive to delicate colour, subtle smell or touch. Right education has to awaken in the student the intelligence of the body. It should enable the students to release their total energy. It should make them to function, respond with all the senses and with the same intensity of energy. The teacher has to point out the student the mischief of thought's interference in the harmonious functioning of the sense, the organism. In fact, there is no division as senses, sensation and the body. They form a single organism or movement. The division is brought about by thought. The total awareness of the fragmentation of thought release the total energy which is the intelligence of the body. Krishnamurti calls the release of total energy the flowering of goodness. The intelligence of the body is a part of an intelligent mind which is aware of the finites of thought. Only an intelligent mind has an intelligent body.

Conclusion

The following words of *Vedaparayana* present a fitting clusion to the brief account of *Krishnamurti*'s views on education.

The teachers as well as the parents have a great role and responsibility in educating the children and bringing about a new generation of human beings. The parents have to really love their children. They should not try to fulfil their desires and ambitions through them. The children are not the psychological extension of the parents. They are independent and unique beings. They should be allowed to grow and flower in real freedom, happiness and goodness. As Khali Gibran puts it, "Your children are not your children; they are the sons and daughters of life's longing for itself; they came through you and not from you. You give them your love but not your thoughts". The teachers have to transform themselves before transforming the students. It is not enough if the teachers impart knowledge to the students. They should understand the truth and help the student to understand it. They should live as human beings without images. They should be 'alone' without any identification. To be alone means to be undivided. To be undivided is to be one with all. Unless the teachers are philosophers, education can not accomplish the task of changing man and society radically and fundamentally. Educating the educators is the primary and the urgent need of the hour.

Summary

Jiddu Krishnamurti was born in a Brahmin family in Madanapalli of Chinnai in Andhra Pradesh. Mrs. Annie Besant the president of Theosophical Society took care of *Krishnamurti.*

According to him, true education can not be based on the established system of things: the real purpose of true education lies in helping people from mundane boundage guiding people to love each other and feeling pride in others and to become what they want to become for realising their real "selves" in various individual capacities. The danger lies in encouraging governments and religious bodies to control education.

Education worth its name is not possible where learners are motivated on the basis of any reward or punishment.

The right type of education gives freedom and emancipation and removes obstacles on the way of acquiring excellecne in life. Education is expected to create new values.

30

Not Education But Educare

Satya Sai Baba (1926-2011)

Satya Sai Baba was born on 23rd November, 1926. In his childhood itself, he gave indications of his spiritual interests. He was an educator and a spiritual leader and lived in Puttaparthy near Bangalore. He set up many schools, colleges, universities and hospitals throughout India and schools in other countries also. He died on 24th Nov. 2011.

Philosophy

Satya Sai baba believed in *Advaita*, the non-dual philosophy. The philosophy considered body, mind and intelligence as distinct and additional to one's own *Chitra* and *Antahkarana* or the inner heart. He was one of the greatest exponents of Indian culture. He gave importance to coordinating the *Atma* itself with the highest notion of *Paramàtma*, recognizing the oneness, though in the ultimate analysis. Divinity was not some incomprehensible figure or entity. Divinity was most easily experienced. Divinity incarnated in human form. It was in all the three paths of *Krma* (action), *Jnana* (spiritual knowledge) and *Upasna* (extolling) that man undertakes to achieve realization. He offered several forages to God and extoled divinity in several ways.

Philosophy of Education

Satya Sai Baba's philosophy of education was to deemphasize education and advance *educare*. In education, mind was shaped by external forces, in *educare*, mind was shaped by the divine source within. In the case of *educare*, action was influenced and determined solely by the external word; if *educare* is the foundation, the internal force generated by *Sathya, Dharma* and *Prema* determined the actions, performed in the external world. Education was survival philosophy (destroy opposition, bend the competition etc), *educare* was divine philosophy (love all, serve all) Education was for the head but *educare* was for the heart. Source for education was the world and for *educare*, source was the heart. The attitude in education was greed and aggression, but in *educare* it was love and compassion. Education manifested in selfish grabbing but manifestation of *educare* was in selfless service.

1. The Aims

In the western schools of philosophy, idealism was close to the aims of *Sai Baba*: idealism made spiritualism as an important component of education. *Sai baba's* message to educationists was that they were not to be content when students acquire knowledge and skills that could prepare them only for earning a living. They were to be equally concerned that education helped students to realize their full human potential–the realization of one's inherent divinity. It was through this awakening of human consciousness that students became educated and refined. Culture and refinement took them beyond the concerns for personal welfare to the welfare of all members of the society. Such individuals, who had recognized the prevailing unity within diversity, would then he guided by their sense of right and wrong, good and bad, and by what was helpful rather than harmful to others.

For *Sai Baba, "Educare has two aspects–the worldly and the spiritual. Wordlly education brought out the latent knowledge pertaining to the physical world, spiritual education brought out the inherent divinity in man. So, both worldly and spiritual education were essential values, without which the human life has no value".*

He believed that in the sphere of education, many revolutionary changes were needed. Secular and spiritual education were to be merged with a philosophy and pedagogy of education to serve the society. His system entailed lifelong process of transformation, strengthening the sacred connections between the individual, the family, the society and all creation–through all forms of educational activity and every level of educational advancement.

The principles of the term '*educare*' were: (a) divinity was love, and it was the undercurrent of all human values; (b) the inherent human values were translated into action in daily life; (c) the purpose of education was for living a fully human and spiritual life; and (d) the end of education was character which manifested itself as the unity of thought, word and deed.

Sai Baba said that *"Good education is that which teaches the method of achieving world peace; that which destroys narrow-mindedness and promotes unity, equality and peaceful existence among human beings".*

The Institutions of Learning

From its early beginnings with the *Bal Vikas* propgramme in India in the late 1960s, *Sathya Sai* Education had grown with a comprehensive education system, practised in all parts of the world and covered a wide range of formal, non-formal and informal education. Formal education was delivered by *Sathya Sai* Schools which included state government-funded and private schools, institutes, colleges and universities. Non-formal education was delivered by *Bal Vikas*, in community for adolescents and young adults, and in parenting programmes. Informal (continuing) education was provided by discoverers, *Sanathana Sarathi, Vahini series,* conferences and study circles.

In *Sai Baba's* words, a school was not to be considered to be just a commonplace arrangement, designed for teaching and learning. It was the purified place where the seeds of discipline, duty and devotion were planted and fostered into fruition.The goals of *Sathya Sai* schools are:

(a) to create an environment of culture and ethos in which the five human values are actively practised;
(b) the realization in students of the full potential of human excellence; and
(c) to provide a model of educational excellence for other schools to emulate.

In pursuit of these goals, schools promote:

(a) the teacher as examples;
(b) the spiritual transformation of students and teachers;
(c) academic excellence;
(d) identification with and respect for one's culture and nation;
(e) appreciation of the unity of the different faiths; and
(f) an active social conscience and an inclination to render selfless service to others.

Institutes of *Sathya Sai Baba* Education are established to:

(a) present educational models of excellence for *Satya Sai* education in the form of programmes in the community, state and private schools, and in partnership with universities, ministries of education and an international organization like the united nations.
(b) develop and implement the *Sai* Education Programmes.
(c) Improve the standards and quality of *Satya Sai* Schools and programmes in state and private schools; and
(d) carry out research and development relating to such education programmes.

In order to realize these goals, the institute carries out the following functions:

- It establishes, manages and supervises *Sathya Sai* Schools.
- Monitors and evaluates standards and the performance of *Sai* Schools.
- Plans and establishes professional links with non-*Sathya Sai* Schools, universities, ministries of education and international organizations and teacher training colleges.
- Develops teacher manuals, training modules, and curriculums,

conducts new and on-going self-evaluation of programmes, training and standards for effectiveness;

- Provides training for teachers, schools, ministries of education, international organizations and other venues of professional development, such as medicine, healthcare, social service professions and business in the form of professional development workshops and conferences, and diploma courses; provides supports in the form of training and materials for the teachers of *Sai* spiritual education when requested by the *Sai* organization;
- Provides education in human values for parents and young adults.
- *Satya Sai* University it based in Prasanthi Nilayam in Ahdhra Pradesh. There are three affiliated colleges—one for girls and two for boys. *Sathya Sai Baba* was the Chanceller. Schooling is for academic, human and environmental excellence–all establish a tradition in the school.

(iii) The Learners

In the view of *Sai Baba,* children were close to divinity. They had the spontaneity, creativity and innovative power. Children were the first national research for elders to interact in order to transform them. An attempt at transformation in society was normally to begin in a school ambience.

Sai Baba's advice to young students was to eat s*attwic* (vegetarion) food, cultivate *sattwic* thought and do *sattwic karmas,* move in the company of *sattwic* friends. *Sai baba* attached too much importance to s*attwic* food so that *Sattma gunas* were developed.

He also expected the students to practise the sanctity of teacher-taught relationship as it had existed in our ancient educational system.

An importance aspect of *Sai* education was that education was a lifelong process. Thus, his learners were children, adolescents, grown-up adults, middle-aged persons and even old people. At various stages of their life, they were exhorted to merge spiritual and secular education: spiritual education was from within, secular education was from without.

(iv) The Teachers

In the western world, the idealists assigned maximum responsibilities to the teachers; other philosophies like naturalism and pragmatism de-emphasid the role of the teacher. Realism balanced the importance of teacher and pupil in the learning process: very few philosophers of education had put so many responsibilities on the teacher as was done by *Sai Baba.*

At the heart of the system of *Sathya Sai Baba* was the teacher. The teachers at all levels of education were to teach through love. It was through love that transformation ultimately took place. When the process of the educator was uppermost in a teachers' mind, teaching and learning became experimental and joyful. The pedagogy of *Sathya Sai Baba* education enabled the teacher to merge the purely secular with the spiritual. The five teaching techniques, focused on human values when integrated with contemporary strategies to merge the body, mind and spirit of the learner. In this manner, any setting where *Sathya Sai* Education was taking place became a value-based learning environment.

According to *Sai Baba*, there were three kinds of teachers: those who informed, those who explained and those who inspired. The teacher moulded the rising generation into self-confident, self-reliant, *Atma*-conscious persons. He was the architect of happy homes, prosperous communities and peaceful nations.

(v) The Curriculum

As *Sathya Sai* Education was formal, non-formal and informal, the curriculum was comprehensive. Formal education provided an opportunity to apply the principles at the primary, secondary and tertiary levels–such education, when delivered within a regulated institutional environment, helped children to become responsible, attentive, respectful and disciplined.

The indispensable component of *Sathya Sai* Education was education in human values—truth, right conduct, peace, love and non-violence. Children were taught to respect people of all faiths as well as the importance of exercising control over their desires and rendering selfless service to others strengthened by citizenship and civic education. The Institutes of *Sathya Sai Baba* Education also provided education in human values for parents and adults.

Sathya Sai Baba inspired the establishment of schools that offered traditional academic curriculum as well as provided spiritual education and promote character development. Schools were based on the philosophy of integral education. Education was available to all, irrespective of their economic background

The formal schools operated within the legal, cultural an l educational farmework of their respective countries of location and followed the official curriculum of local or national educational curricula.

The *Sathya Sai Baba* University and its affiliated colleges combined secular with spiritual education. Spiritual education inculcated *tyaga* (sacrifice) and spiritual discipline.

The curriculum of non-formal education comprised spiritual education, education in human values to the community, young adults and parents, and informal education through discourses, magazines, *Vahin's* conferences, study centres and radio.

Sai Baba suggested five techniques of teaching. There were: story telling, prayers or quotation, silent sitting or tuning in, group singing and group activities. Story telling captured the imagination, engaging the heart and the intellect in a dynamic process of making meaning and relevance in one's life, while providing models of human behaviour. Silent sitting developed the capacity for concentration, creativity and quietitude. Group activities were assigned to integrate the experience of the human values in thought, word, and deed. The five teaching techniques could form the core of a complete lesson or a curriculum focused on human values combined with other compatible teaching strategies. These could easily he integrated with any academic curriculum.

Conclusion

Some western and Indian philosophers of education have advocated the merger of secular and spiritual education. *Sathya Sai Baba* also stood for such merger: in fact, integration of secular and spiritual elements, not only in theory but also in practice in India and other countries, by establishing institutions at all levels. However, some critics have not accepted his views on science, evolution of earth, God etc.

Summary

Sathya Sai Baba was born on 23rd November, 1926 and died on 24th Nov., 2011. His childhood gave indications about his spiritual greatness. He believed in *advaita*: Divinity incarnated in human form. His philosophy of education was *educare* which involved the spiritual development. But he stood for integral education by merging spiritual and secular education. He established institutions for the primary level, through secondary to university levels. He advocated value-based education—truth, right conduct, peace, love and non-violence. Some critics have not agreed with his opinions on science, evolution and God.

31

Views and Visions on Education: A Bird's Eye View

In chapter 31 are summarised some of the views and visions on education of:

Maulana Abul Kalam Azad
Dr. Zakir Hussain
Dr. B.R. Ambedkar
Narendra Damodardas Modi (Prime Minister of India)

MAULANA ABUL KALAM AZAD (1880-1958)

Mohd. Akhtar Siddiqui in "Education in India" (2011) presented Maulana Azad's 'educational vision and contribution' and made some noteworthy evaluation of his views and visions. Azad wanted to remove illiteracy through universalisation of elementary education up to the secondary standard and by means of a drive for women education, he stood for equalization of educational opportunities in the Indian society where exploitation on the basis of class and caste divisions were rampant; he was the advocate of the three language formulae where the state language and Hindi would be the medium of instruction, but English was to remain as an important second language, and to infuse quality in quantity, he wanted sound primary education throughout the country.

One of the main objectives of education of Maulana Azad was the making of man by imparting character building education which ensured truth, justice, enlightenment, cooperation and unity, courtesy and chivalry and humility. The second objective was 'education for democracy by means of linking adult education with social education,' emphasising impartation of literacy, inculcation of a lively sense of rights and duties of citizenship and creation of an educated mind in the masses which were deprived of literacy education. The third objective was to impart education for development by encouraging the growth of science and technology. The fourth objective was to provide 'education for national integration and secularism' by stressing the importance of text books and reading material, especially in history, civics, geography and literature. The fifth objective was to promote education for 'internationalization and global citizenship', by cooperating with UNESCO and changing the entire method of teaching of history and geography in schools.

Azad recommended alterations in and enrichment of the curriculum in that at the elementary level, the stress was to be on 'learning by doing', at the secondary stage, the curriculum was to train learners in diverse skills and aptitudes and prepare them for higher education and the curriculum at the university level was to be broadened and enriched. He suggested to pay more attention to adult and social education, women education, physical education, suitable text books, research and evaluation, reforms in the examination system and international cooperation in education.

He attached a great importance to teacher and teacher preparation by improving their salaries and by making them efficient, devoted and dedicated.

Azad faced the challenge of dual control of education by the states and centre by recognising the need for cooperation between the centre and the states.

A comment by the author, Azad's greatness lies in his humility in assigning credit to others for the success of any programme of education and accepting responsibility for its limitations.

DR. B.R. AMBEDKAR (1891-1956)

Padma Velaskar in SASE Journals, July 2012 vol 9 no. 2 in an article titled "Education for Liberation: Ambedkar's Thought and Dalit Women's Perspective," the abstract of which is presented below, had this to say:

> *Despite the phenomenal impact that it has had in transforming the lives of dalits and its continuing contemporary relevance, Ambedkar's social and educational thought remains surprisingly neglected in Indian educational discourse. Education was assigned a revolutionary role in Ambedkar's conception of social progress and in his vision of a just and equal society. It was identified as a key instrument of liberation from oppressive structures of Hindu caste-patriarchy as well as of reconstruction of a new social order. Women were integral to this visionary egalitarianism and were consciously mobilised as political actors in the dalit liberation movement led by Ambedkar in the early decades of the twentieth century. This article explores the interface between Ambedkar's ideologies of liberation and education, on the one hand, and dalit women's thoughts and perspectives, on the other hand. It seeks to incorporate gender in the understanding of the historical processes of social change. It argues that an emancipatory discourse on gender was an important component of Ambedkar's philosophy of social democratic liberalism and permitted women an authentic identification*

> *with its underlying principles with a view to achieving a full and enlightened citizenship. The article shows how the imbibing of Ambedkar's thought and participation in his movement constituted the bedrock of dalit women's political involvement and they played foundational roles as political educators and educational activists. Dalit women redefined ideals of both womanhood and educational purpose in terms of counter-hegemonic reconstructions of nation, society and community and articulated new subject positions grounded in them.*

Dr. Bhalchandra Munjekar, Vice Chancellor, University of Mumbai, in an article, titled: Education: The only key to Dalit Progress in *Worldwide* concluded the article as shown below:

What to be Done? Or the Task Before Dalit Organisations

Dr. Babasaheb Ambedkar correctly understood the importance of education as the most powerful instrument to free the Dalits from the century-old miseries, sufferings, insult and stigma inflicted on them by the caste system. It is in view of this that his life symbolised upheavals, and relentless activities. He established in 1945 the People's Education Society. The Society had played a pioneering role in spreading the higher education among all the deprived sections of the society including obviously the Dalit. The entire post-independence Dalit generation in Maharashtra is the creation of the People's Education Society.

But now the things are changing fast. The whole world as also India have set in the motion the forces of globalisation, liberalization and privatization. Market is fast replacing the 'Welfare State'. Competition has become the order of the day. The Reservation Policy of the State that did help the Dalit to secure socio-economic mobility and upliftment is fast eroding. Under such circumstances, what will be the future of Dalits in general and those in rural areas without access to land, capital, other types of skills etc. in particular? The task is indeed formidable. I therefore would take liberty to suggest a few things as a matter of agenda relating to the Dalit Education. This is because I am fully convinced that in the midst of all sorts of inequalities and changing scenario, it is only the higher education that would act as the surest and soundest key to the Dalit progress.

The suggestions are as follows:

(i) Educated Dalits must undertake a mass movement to encourage literacy among the Dalit communities.

(ii) All school and college going–Dalit boys and girls must devote some of their time to help their illiterate fraternity to become literate.

(iii) All Dalit voluntary organizations must make serious efforts to enhance the school attending rates and prevent high drop-out rates.

(iv) Even after 50 years of independence, the country could not achieve more than 52 percent literacy rate. All deprived sections and particularly Dalit men and women are the main victims of illiteracy. This makes imperative that all Dalits struggle and pressurize the Government for making free primary education to all.

(v) Dalit must come forward and establish secondary schools and colleges on co-operative basis.

(vi) They should undertake establishing other educational institutions which could conduct professional courses in finance, marketing management, information technology, journalism, mass media and so on. These vocational courses would enable Dalit boys and girls to acquire access to skills which are very much essential in the contemporary economy demanding skilled personnel.

(vii) The Dalit organization instutions and academicians must concentrate on establishing and running residential hostels in every taluka in the country. They must bring pressure on the Government to adopt such poor-friendly educational policy and spend more and meaningfully on the education of the poor and particularly the Dalits.

(viii) Such comprehensive, long-drawn and sustained campaign and programme will certainly usher new dawn in the midst of the present stalement, created by all sorts of unfavourable factors. Education is, thus, not only a means of livelihood but also an effective instrument for social transformation. It is only the access to better education that would enable the Dalit to exercise their human rights in more effective and meaningful manner.

(ix) This calls for co-operation of all international Dalit organizations. I would suggest the formation of the *International Dalit Organisation*, on par with ILO, to monitor and guide such national/international campaign. It should act as a catalyst(ic) agent for spreading of the revolutionary message which is an integral part of the comprehensive strategy of social transformation including the establishment and exercise of Dalit human rights.

A Comment by the Author: It has been observed that the educated and prosperous dalit community emerges in to an elite class by itself. Such a class does continue talking about the down trodden dalit, but their social interactions (marriages etc.) are well within the elite parameters. The elite dalit class also tries to hobnob with the other so-called forward classes, which, though pay a lip service to equality, may rather keep the social climbers, where they are. It is true that education is capable of doing a lot to the learners, but in certain situations, education may find it difficult to change the value orientation of all, particularly in relation to attitudes.

DR. ZAKIR HUSSAIN (1897-1967)

The Aims of Education

The aims of education of Zakir Hussain were:

1. All round development of personality
2. Creative development
3. Social orientation
4. Spiritual regeneration
5. Balancing material and spiritual values

1. *All Round Development of Personality:* The learner was to become physically strong, socially well adjusted, morally round spiritually enlightened and aesthetically refined.

2. *Creative Development:* In the activities of the school, the education was to be creative in co-circular and extra-co-circular activities.

3. *Social Orientation:* The learner was to be encouraged to be a member of the peer group, and societies, and join other children in team sports and games. At home, he was to have respect for the elders and love for his juniors. Some interaction with the neighbours and the community was essential to ensuring social development.

4. *Spiritual Regeneration*: By spiritual regeneration, Zakir Hussain meant education for character development, for imbibing cultural and ethical values and for having a positive attitude towards values which were ultimate.

5. *Balancing Spiritual and Material Values*: Spiritual values were required not merely as a preparation for the other worldliness, but these were also for good conduct in the present life. Material values like wealth, house, farm, factory etc., were worth possessing but not at the cost of spiritual values like truth, goodness and beauty.

He wanted to realise the aims by means of the curriculum: languages–mother tongue and one other with Indian or foreign languages; science and technology; social sciences; and art and music. He also recommended instructional principles like: learning by doing, social orientation and individual differences.

Four stages in Education

He identified four stages in any educative activity. These were:

1. The clear consciousness of the problem–i.e., what exactly was to be done?

2. The formation of a plan of work, choice of appropriate means, thinking about the steps required.
3. The execution of the plan.
4. Objectification in which evaluation or self criticism of the result of the work was carried out.

Characteristics of a Good School

For Zakir Hussain, a good school was to have six fold criteria:

- Individuality of the pupil was the first concerns.
- The school always kept in view the stage of development of the individuality.
- It directed its efforts to the development of the whole mental structure of its pupils.
- It provided purposeful activity of educationally productive work.
- It related individual accomplishment to social achievement.
- It initiated in its pupils the process of self-education.

An Ideal Teacher

For him an ideal teacher had the following characteristics in that he:

- guided, helped and directed the young so as to develop in them a sense of responsibility for their action.
- awakened in them the urge towards self-education.
- gave them the fullest measures of freedom and self determination.
- transmitted to them higher values through his personality through the goods of culture and got the values realized by them.
- did not dictate or dominate, but helped and served, undertook and shaped in Faith and Love and Reverence.
- recognized that the individual was not just a unit of calculation, an identity card or number but was to be helped to grow through work, knowledge and experience.

Freedom and Authority in Education

Dr. Zakir Hussain stood for self discipline in which freedom and authority were complimentary to each other. According to him, there was no authority in education, which did not recognise inner freedom. Similarly, there was no freedom without regulation and orderliness. Authority did not signify compulsion and freedom did not stand for license and arbitrariness. Without regulative principles, society would be a chaotic jumble. But reasonable authority was essential for correct guidance and helpful direction at the beginning and at the end. Guidance it was required because of the emergence of value, accepted for self-direction.

Dr. Zakir Hussain supported the Basic Education of Mahatma Gandhi, but differed with the Mahatma with some of the rough ideals. Dr Hussain developed Jamia Millia Islamia into a renowned centre of learning and provided a new orientation to education in India.

A Comment by the Author: The greatness of Zakir Hussain as an educational thinker lies in his academic achievements, administrative acumen, industriousness, frankness, litrary output, statesmanship and large humanity. He lived his exhortation: "*work, work and more work, silent and sincerely work–work for one's self and work for the society.*"

Select Bibliography

Adams, J. Herbartian, *Psychology Applied to Education*, London: Heath; 1907.

Adamson, J.W., *A Short History of Education*, New York: The Mecmillan Company; 1920.

Aggarwal, J.C., *Great Philosophers and Thinkers on Education*, Delhi, Shipra Publications, 2006.

Barker, Ernest, (Editor) *Social Contract: Essays* by Locke, Hume and Rousseau, London Oxford University Press, 1960.

Bornett, J., *Aristotle on Education*, Cambridge C.V.P.; 1926.

Boyd, W., *The History of Western Education*, London, Admsand Charles Black; 1964.

Bramold, Theodore, *Philosophies of Education in Cultural Perspective*. New York, The Dryden Press: 1955.

Brubacher John S., *Modern Philosophies of Education* (Second Edition), New York, Mcgraw Hill Book Company; 1950.

Butts, R. Freeman, *A Culture History of Education*, New York, McGraw Hill Book Company; 1950.

Cubberley, Ellwood T., *The History of Education*, Cambridge Masachusetts; Houghton Miffin Company; 1948.

Cole, I., *Education from Sacrates to Montessori*, New York, Rine-hart and Company, Ltd; 1950.

Cole, P.E. Herbart and Froebel, *An Attempt at Synthesis*, New York, Columbia, 1907.

Curtis, S.J. and Boultwood, M.E.A., *A Short History of Educational Ideas.* Foxion, Tutorial Press Ltd.

Dewey, John, *Democracy and Education*. New York, The Macmilan Company; 1916.

Fletcher, S.S. and Welton, J., *Froebel's Chief Writings on Education*. London, Longmans Green and Comopany; 1912.

Friere, Paulo, *Pedagogy of the Oppressed*, New York, Continuum, 1993.

Green, J.A. and Collie, E.A. Pestalozzi's Educational Writings, London, Arnold; 1912.

Keller, George F. (Ed.), Foundations of Education, New York, John Willey and Sons, Inc., 1963.

Lee, Desmond. (Transt), *Plato Republic*, London, Penguin Brothers, 1947.

Lodge, Rupert, *Philosophy of Education,* New York, Harper and Brothers, 1947.

Mayer, Fredrick, *A History of Educational Thought*, Columbus, Ohio, Charles E. Merrill Publishing Co; 1966.

Monroe, Paul, *Source Book of the History of Education*, New York, The Macmillan Company; 1923.

Pounds, Ralph, *The Development of Education in Western Culture*, New York, Merdith Corporation, 1968.

Power, Edward J., *Main Currents in the History of Education*, New York; Mcgraw-Hill Book Co; Inc; 1962.

Radhakrishnan, S. (ed), *History of Philosophy Eastern and Western*, Vols I & II. London, Geoge Allen and Unwin Ltd., 1953.

Rusk, R., *Doctrines of Great Educators*. London: Macmillan; 1979.

Sheed, F.J., *The Confessions of St. Augustine*, New York, Sheed and Ward, Inc; 1943.

Thakur, A.S., *The Philosophical and Sociological Foundations of Education,* New Delhi, National Publishing House, 2003.

Thakur, AS. And S. Berwal, *Education in Emerging Indian Society*, Noida, Mayur Paper Backs; 2007.

Thut, I.N., *The Story of Educational Thought*, New York, McGraw Hill Book Co; 1947.

Ulich, Robert, *History of Educational Thought*; New York American Book Co; 1945.

Walia, J.S., *Philosophical and Sociological Basis of Education*, Jalandhar City: Paul Publishers; 2002.